Formation Processes in
Archaeological Context

Contributors

Ofer Bar-Yosef
Department of Anthropology
Peabody Museum
Harvard University
Cambridge, Massachusetts, 02138, USA

C. Michael Barton
Department of Anthropology
Arizona State University
Tempe, Arizona, 85287, USA

Geoffrey A. Clark
Department of Anthropology
Arizona State University
Tempe, Arizona, 85287, USA

Marie-Agnès Courty
Centre National de la Recherche Scientifique
Laboratoire de Science des Sols et Hydrologie
Institut National Agronomique, Paris-Grignon
78850, Thiverval-Grignon, FRANCE

George M. Crothers
Department of Anthropology
Washington University
St. Louis, Missouri, 63130, USA

William R. Farrand
Department of Geological Sciences
University of Michigan
Ann Arbor, Michigan, 48109, USA

Thierry Gé
Centre National de la Recherche Scientifique
Laboratoire de Science des Sols et Hydrologie
Institut National Agronomique, Paris-Grignon
78850, Thiverval-Grignon, FRANCE

Paul Goldberg
Texas Archeological Research Laboratory
University of Texas, Austin
Austin, Texas, 78712, USA

Todd A. Koetje
Department of Anthropology
Indiana University of Pennsylvania
Indiana, Pennsylvania, 15705, USA

Wendy Matthews
Department of Archaeology
University of Cambridge
Cambridge CB3 9DA, ENGLAND

David T. Nash
Department of Anthropology
University of New Mexico
Albuquerque, New Mexico, 87131, USA

K. Paddayya
Department of Archaeology
Deccan College
411 006, Pune, INDIA

Michael D. Petraglia
Department of Anthropology
National Museum of Natural History
Smithsonian Institution
Washington, D.C., 20560, USA

Arlene Miller Rosen
Archaeological Division
Ben-Gurion University of the Negev
P.O. Box 653
84105 Beer-Sheva, ISRAEL

Lawrence G. Straus
Department of Anthropology
University of New Mexico
Albuquerque, New Mexico, 87131, USA

Patty Jo Watson
Department of Anthropology
Washington University
St. Louis, Missouri, 63130, USA

Julia Wattez
Centre National de la Recherche Scientifique
Laboratoire de Science des Sols et Hydrologie
Institut National Agronomique, Paris-Grignon
78850, Thiverval-Grignon, FRANCE

Ian Whitbread
Fitch Laboratory
British School at Athens
52 Odos Sovedias
GR 10676 Athens, GREECE

Formation Processes in Archaeological Context

Edited by

Paul Goldberg
David T. Nash
Michael D. Petraglia

Monographs in World Archaeology No. 17

PREHISTORY PRESS
Madison Wisconsin

Prehistory Press
2515 Frazier Ave.
Madison, Wisconsin 53713-1505
Order directly by mail or phone 608/221-5515 or fax 221-5510

James A. Knight, Publisher
Carol J. Bracewell, Production Manager

ISBN 1-881094-06-5
ISSN 1055-2316

Library of Congress Cataloging-in-Publication Data

Formation processes in archaeological context / edited by Paul Goldberg, David T. Nash, Michael D.
Petraglia.
     p.   cm. -- (Monographs in world archaeology; no. 17)
Includes bibliographical references.
ISBN 1-881094-06-5: $35.00
1. Excavations (Archaeology) 2. Caves.   I. Goldberg, Paul.
II. Nash, D. T. (David T.) III. Petraglia, M. D. (Michael D.) IV. Series.
CC75.F66   1993
930.1--dc20   93-37178
                                                                 CIP

Contents

v

Preface

The concept of archaeological site formation was formally recognized and treated in Michael Schiffer's pioneering article, "Archaeological context and systemic context" (1972) and later in his book, *Behavioral Archeology* (1976). Schiffer codified the concept during the 1980's with the publication of the article, "Toward the identification of formation processes" (1983) and in his major compendium, *Formation Processes of the Archaeological Record* (1987). Schiffer made the explicit distinction between the systemic context, the way artifacts participated in the past, and the archaeological context, the way in which we find cultural debris in the record. Schiffer discussed some of the best known cultural and natural formation processes, provided guidelines to identify these processes, and attempted to formalize general principles of site formation. By specifying the conditions known to operate in the past, empirical generalizations were developed to indicate the operation and prevalence of certain processes in particular contexts (see also Reid 1985). Although formation processes were recognized to be highly varied and their potential combinations seemingly infinite, regularities were considered to be important for sorting out the more and less likely probabilities. The site formation approach therefore provided a practical and viable way to examine the archaeological record, and to infer the meaning of archaeological patterning.

Paralleling the development of the site formation approach in archaeology, geoarchaeological research was growing and maturing in ways which had significant implications for the evaluation of the archaeological record. The contributions that geological research could make to archaeology was well summarized in Karl Butzer's, *Archaeology as Human Ecology* (1982). Geoarchaeologists emphasized the dynamic interactions between humans, the natural environment, and their depositional contexts.

Much recent archaeological research has stressed the value of designing and carrying out research on site formation processes. Indeed, the processes which form the archaeological record have become better understood because of the continued growth of various lines of inquiry, including geoarchaeology, ethnoarchaeology, taphonomy, and experimental approaches (e.g., Behrensmeyer and Hill 1980; Stein and Farrand 1985; Kent 1987; Nash and Petraglia 1987; Bonnichsen and Sorg 1989; Gamble and Boismier 1991; Waters 1992).

While most archaeologists appear to agree that we have to understand the multitude of cultural and natural sources which create the properties remaining in the archaeological record, the means of reliably inferring information about the past appears to vary dramatically, often as a result of differing approaches and paradigms. For instance, while Schiffer's attention to formation processes has been well received, his transformation approach, which concentrates on the "life history" of artifacts, or the way material elements operated in systemic context, has not been roundly accepted or routinely applied. Binford (1981) presented a major challenge to the transformation approach, criticizing the view that the archaeological record was a "distorted" manifestation of human behavior. In Binford's (1981, 1982) view, the archaeological record was a consequence of the organized systems in which material was used during complex cultural operations, some aspects of operations producing "fall out" and patterned residues. It is the linkages between actions, material, and its patterned residues that yield information about the organization of past systems. Binford thus argues that archaeologists must study patterned material consequences in order to examine aspects of the operation of a past cultural system, rather than the study of how material interacted with all actions of human behavior during its life cycle or its flow through the system.

Because of these differences in theoretical orientation, archaeologists have dealt with "deposits" and their inherent material patterning in very different ways. Given that there is no necessary relationship between depositional units and behavioral episodes (Binford 1982), the question becomes how to identify the appropriate units of measurement for documenting patterns of human behavior. Because Schiffer (1987) wishes to examine cultural actions and transformations, he argues that deposits should be identified on the basis of inferred cultural and natural formation processes. On the other hand, Stein (1987) points out that deposits should be classified and examined on the basis of descriptive attributes or observable units. Thus Stein makes the strong case that processes of transport, deposition, and post-depositional change can be delimited, and agents involved in the formation of the deposit can be made explicit on the basis of observations and tests.

The foregoing lines of reasoning and criticisms are extremely critical to any discussion of site formation, raising questions of the appropriate levels of archaeological inference. We would argue that it is unproductive, if not impossible, to account for all of the various processes, and combinations of processes, which account for archaeological patterning. Therefore, we would argue that the goal of archaeology should not be reconstructionist in nature, attempting to examine all detailed aspects of human action, or attempting to "read into" observed archaeological patterning. Rather, studies should be directed towards explaining the conditions which created observed material residues of the system, and measuring the organizational aspect to which this

residue relates. The challenge is to link specific processes and causes to observed responses and effects, whether short-term or long-term.

Rick (1989) has challenged the notion that most formation processes can ever lead to generalized principles, since there are so many context-sensitive qualifiers and that sophisticated analysis of formation processes will always be tailored to specific circumstances. While we certainly agree that each and every site will vary in terms of preservation conditions, patterning, and the behavioral resolution within archaeological deposits, this does not mean that the archaeological record consists of a mixture of random actions and idiosyncratic processes. Indeed, we would also argue that identification of the variability in formation processes does not lead away from general principles of site formation. Confusion on this matter seems mainly to exist on the basis of the scale at which formation processes are viewed and the level at which inferences are made.

Formation Processes in Archaeological Context pays attention to some of the foregoing controversies and arguments, illustrating some analytical and inferential problems, and how they may be examined and potentially resolved. The authors in this volume are united by a common goal, that of deciphering the underlying causes of site formation and defining contextual constraints on archaeological interpretations. This volume also attempts to fill a void in the literature, since, in spite of the recognized importance of formation processes, the number of studies explicitly designed to this end have remained relatively limited.

As the editors of this volume, we have attempted to assemble a number of papers that represent how research on formation processes is currently being investigated and applied to a number of archaeological contexts in different parts of the world. We have made a deliberate attempt to choose papers that are broad in scope, and written by both archaeologists and by those with training in the earth sciences. The chapters in this volume include studies of sites of varying age, ranging from the Lower Paleolithic to the present, and in different depositional contexts, from caves to open-air sites. We hope that by exposing the reader to a variety of research endeavors, and presenting the practical issues involved in such investigations, that he or she will be convinced of the necessity of focusing on formation processes. We believe that a focus on formation processes is necessary in order to comprehend and evaluate the significance of archaeological patterns.

Although researchers are aware that there is an accumulating body of knowledge about formation processes, theoretical principles and methods have not been routinely applied in solving archaeological problems. Schiffer (1987: xix) has pointed out this problem, noting that there is a clear disjunction between method and theory and the practice of archaeology. We believe that the chapters in this volume show that archaeologists are better able to identify the cultural and natural processes responsible for archaeological patterns and are now beginning to develop organizing concepts.

We have organized this volume into three main sections, the inter-site, the intra-site, and the microscopic scale, providing different perspectives for viewing archaeological data. We have organized this volume in this manner not for merely illustrative purposes, but because we believe that this changing analytical scale is central and most practical for developing archaeological concepts and theories of site formation. We are in total agreement with Schiffer (1987) that ranges of scale and contextual realm provides a body of knowledge that will allow for development of models of patterned and regular formation processes, ultimately relevant for theoretical growth.

Although new ways to investigate the archaeological record are emerging, we are aware that much work remains to be done on the appropriate use of these investigations in pursuing goals of scientific archaeology, as well as their integration to form an overall strategy of archaeological inquiry. As the chapters in this volume attest, we stand today at an important juncture in archaeology, learning more about the processes which form archaeological patterns, and building concepts which will ultimately be of use for general theories of culture. While we are still identifying many causes and effects, we look forward to a stimulating future for formation studies, with a growth in methodological and conceptual development.

Formation Processes in Archaeological Context was borne out of two separate but complementary symposia, "Cave and Rockshelter Formation Processes" (organized by David Nash and Michael Petraglia), and "Site Formation Processes — New Techniques and Cultural Implications" (organized by Ofer Bar-Yosef and Paul Goldberg), held at the 56th Annual Meeting of the Society for American Archaeology (SAA), in New Orleans, Louisiana. Selected presentations from these two symposia were assembled and invited papers were solicited.

The editors owe a special debt of gratitude to two individuals, Lawrence Straus and Ofer Bar-Yosef. Learning of the two complimentary symposia to be held at the SAA meetings, Lawrence strongly encouraged communication between the four organizers. Because of Lawrence's efforts, we all derived tremendous long-term benefits from our subsequent conversations. Recognizing the importance of the two complimentary symposia, Ofer was the first to suggest that the papers be combined and published into a broad ranging volume on formation processes. Ofer coordinated the consolidation of the volume, discussed the publication of the volume with Prehistory Press, and in a completely unselfish manner, he insisted that we take the credit for editorship.

We would like to thank all the contributors in this volume who improved and expanded their papers to reflect the importance of their work to a wider audience. Michael Schiffer of the University of Arizona formally reviewed this volume for Prehistory Press. We thank him for his insightful comments and suggestions on this volume, and for his intellectual stimulation, for without his pioneering efforts, this volume would not exist. We would also like to thank James Knight of Prehistory Press, for his decision to publish this volume and for his valuable advice during the editorial process. Finally, but importantly, we wish to thank Carol Bracewell for her editorial expertise.

Paul Goldberg
Austin, Texas

David T. Nash
Fort Collins, Colorado

Michael D. Petraglia
Washington, D.C.

References Cited

Behrensmeyer, A.K., and A.P. Hill (editors)
  1980 *Fossils in the Making.* Chicago University Press, Chicago.
Binford, L.R.
  1981 Behavioral Archaeology and the 'Pompeii Premise'. *Journal of Anthropological Research* 37:195-208.
  1982 The Archaeology of Place. *Journal of Anthropological Archaeology* 1:5-31.
Bonnichsen, R., and M.H. Sorg (editors)
  1989 *Bone Modification.* Center for the Study of Early Man, Orono.
Butzer, K.W.
  1982 *Archaeology as Human Ecology.* Cambridge University Press, Cambridge.
Gamble, C.S., and W.A. Boismier (editors)
  1991 *Ethnoarchaeological Approaches to Mobile Campsites.* International Monographs in Prehistory, Ann Arbor.
Kent, S. (editor)
  1987 *Method and Theory for Activity Area Research: An Ethnoarchaeological Approach.* Columbia University Press, New York.
Nash, D.T., and M.D. Petraglia (editors)
  1987 *Natural Formation Processes and the Archaeological Record.* BAR International Series, 352, Oxford.
Reid, J.J.
  1985 Formation Processes for the Practical Prehistorian: An Example from the Southeast. In *Structure and Process in Southeastern Archaeology,* edited by R.S. Dickens, Jr., and H.T. Ward, pp. 11-33. The University of Alabama Press, University, Alabama.
Rick, J.
  1989 Review of *Formation Processes of the Archaeological Record, American Antiquity* 54:656-657.
Schiffer, M.B.
  1972 Archaeological Context and Systemic Context. *American Antiquity* 37:156-165.
  1976 *Behavioral Archeology.* Academic Press, New York.
  1983 Toward the Identification of Formation Processes. *American Antiquity* 48:675-706.
  1987 *Formation Processes of the Archaeological Record.* University of New Mexico Press, Albuquerque.
Stein, J.K.
  1987 Deposits for Archaeologists. In *Advances in Archaeological Method and Theory,* vol. 11, edited by M.B. Schiffer, pp. 337-395. Academic Press, New York.
Stein, J.K., and W.R. Farrand (editors)
  1985 *Archaeological Sediments in Context.* Center for the Study of Early Man, Orono.
Waters, M.R.
  1992 *Principles of Geoarchaeology: A North American Perspective.* The University of Arizona Press, Tucson.

1

Hidden Assets and Liabilities:
Exploring Archaeology from the Earth

Lawrence Guy Straus
University of New Mexico

The archaeological record from repetitively occupied site types such as caves, rockshelters and tells is both very fertile in potential information and exquisitely complex in nature. Such sites may be both much more and much less than what they seem at first glance. It is in circumstances such as caves, rockshelters and tells that the archaeologist really earns his/her stripes as both detective and anatomist. The papers in this volume are excellent examples of how:

1.) we must try to understand and control for natural processes of formation, disturbance, alteration and destruction, including long-term variable rates and changing types of processes, before we can attempt behavioral reconstructions of activities and site use;

2.) natural and cultural conditions and processes (Schiffer's "N-and C-transforms") may interact in complicated webs of linkages that need to be fully understood and appreciated;

3.) the record can yield much more (and more subtle) information than generally imagined; but, on the contrary

4.) the record can be riddled with lacunae that, if not detected, can cause major misperceptions of human occupations and adaptive change;

5.) an understanding of the past inevitably (albeit perilously) relies on application of uniformitarian principles derived from observations of present phenomena.

This volume provides a nice mix of actualistic studies (experiments in and observations of the modern record) with archaeological cases, both at the intra- and inter-site levels. The fact that it is but one of several recent volumes (e.g., Butzer 1982; Schiffer 1987; Nash and Petraglia 1987) to address the complexity of the archaeological record and to sketch out examples of how to deal with specific problems therein, is evidence of a mature, rational, scientific response to the "cautionary tales" that began to appear in the literature in the 1970's and 1980's (e.g., Stockton 1973; Gifford and Behrensmeyer 1977; Villa 1977, 1982; Villa and Courtin 1983; Wood and Johnson 1978; Stein 1983; Bocek 1986). The profession is clearly responding with concerted new research and critical reanalysis of old results to the calls of the "middle-range" researchers, such as those just cited. This volume is an outgrowth of the approach adopted by Schiffer, as exemplified in his recent "manual" on the subject of formation processes (Schiffer 1987). His transformation theory requires us to systematically, rigorously try to control for as many factors as possible that may be involved in the creation of the archaeological record—depositional, erosional and alterational. It is an approach that argues for an objective, interpretive archaeological research, based on a realistic, critical, scientific appraisal of our sources of information on past human behavior/activities. Thus, while naysayers in some sectors of "Post-processualism" (e.g., Shanks and Tilley 1987) are decrying the entire enterprise, constructive scientists in both the Old World and the New, are diligently seeking to put interpretations about past ecology, social and economic systems in mainstream archae-ology on a firmer footing, by coming to grips with the nature of the very real, material record left behind by our ancestors.

Proponents of scientific archaeology would likely agree that there is an archaeological record, that the residues of past human activities and non-human processes or conditions can be interpreted in reliable, replicable and objective fashion. Although there are serious problems with *every* archaeological site (even Pompeii has been subjected to processes other than straightforward sealing), these are issues to be explored and deciphered. The task of archaeologists (together with geoarchaeologists, zooarchaeologists, micromorphologists and others) is to discern what has happened to create the specific record in its present state, to assess these processes along a scale that runs from "totally redeposited" to "nearly pristine" and then to provide interpretations that are reasonable and appropriate to the situation at hand. For instance, many areas of human activity that are far from "intact" or that have only a coarse degree of behav-ioral resolution (i.e., sites that are definitely not in the extraordinary category of Pincevent, a French Magdalenian camp, whose individual occupation residues were periodically sealed in Seine River silt [Leroi-Gourhan and Brézillon 1972]), can nonetheless provide valuable information on the timing, nature, distribution and relative frequency of human activi-ties on paleo-landsurfaces.

It is very clear that, even when sites have not been massively disturbed, archaeological layers are almost always and inevitably palimpsests. Much has been made in recent years of the compounded nature of levels defined by archaeologists and the interpretative problems this fact can cause (especially when researchers operate under the assumption of "moments in time") (cf., Bordes [1975], who severely criticized the notion of living floors, or Binford [1977a], who cogently critiqued the "direct" behav-ioral interpretation of artifact-bone "associations" on landsurfaces at Olorgesailie.) Fortunately, it is a commonsense truth that human activities, behaviors and responses to structured situations are often regular, repetitive and redundant (e.g., Straus 1979; Binford 1978, 1982). While individual episodes of human activity may often elude us, "averaged",

patterned residues of site use can be elicited, allowing us to understand "the big picture". This should not disturb us, unless our goal is to paint pictures of "some precise moments in the remote past" (Roe 1980). I would argue that such a goal is not only elusive, but ultimately, in and of itself, non-productive. I freely admit, however, that this is a processualist view, one that is concerned with the regularities of human behavior under specified environmental and demo-graphic conditions in the Stone Age.

The remainder of this chapter is devoted to a comparison of and commentary on the papers in this volume, and to add some relevant anecdotal examples from my own research. I wish to highlight the impor-tance of investigating site formation processes at different types of sites and at the intra- and inter-site levels of analysis.

Show and Tells

Three chapters in this volume (Gé et al., Goldberg and Whitbread, Rosen) deal specifically with the as-yet relatively little tapped potential of micromorphology and microartifacts. Coincidentally, these chapters all concentrate on Middle Eastern sites and all show how cryptic artifacts and sedimentary alterations can be informative about human activities and buried human occupation structures.

The Gé et al. article shows how micromorpholog-ical signals lead to specific interpretative conclusions. This relatively new method (derived from pedology) can yield linkages between microscopic observations on the structure and contents of indurated sediment thin sections and behavioral or natural processes (e.g., Courty and Fedoroff 1983). It is theoretically support-able by means of actualistic experiments linking observed processes to observed microscopic modifica-tions of sediment—a classic application of the principle of uniformitarianism.

Along those lines, Goldberg and Whitbread provide an excellent actualistic study of the hidden evidence of human activity in the dirt across a Bedouin campsite and tent. This paper clearly shows the interpretative potential for micromorphology anchored in a well-controlled use of the modern record to extrapolate back into the past. This is a good, concrete example of the practice of ethnoarchae-ology, *sensu* "behavioral archaeology" à la Schiffer (1976) *and sensu* "middle range theory" à la Binford (1977b). As Goldberg and Whitbread stress, more micromorphological studies in modern camps are needed to build a comparative basis for reasoned interpretations especially of complex sites (such as tells) with long formational histories characterized by many different human and natural processes, frequent episodes of disturbance and reuse, and deep stratigraphies.

Until fairly recently, archaeologists have tended to ignore (or not even collect) very small artifacts (mainly tiny sherds and lithic debitage, such as trimming flakes and shatter smaller than 1 cm). But, with the regular adoption of fine-screening and flotation techniques in both the Old and New Worlds, we have found a new source of valuable information both on aspects of technology (manufacturing practices) and on spatial activity organization within sites. The logic of this approach has recently been carried to the level of microdebitage smaller than 1 mm (e.g., Fladmark 1982; Backer and Guilbaud 1989).

Rosen's study of microartifacts is an important example of how much can be revealed about intra-site functional variability from the kinds of hidden traces so often and so easily ignored by standard archaeological methods. The analysis of microartifacts in a tell shows the utility of integrating paleobotanical and zooarchaeological methods and results, with those of archaeology *sensu stricto*.

Further back in time, in Paleolithic studies, it is also becoming clear how much more detail can be gained by collecting (or at least sampling) small and micro-debitage—both in terms of spatial/activity area studies and technological analyses of complete "operatory chains" (Geneste 1985). These classes of artifacts are becoming important sources of information on activity area patterning, precisely because they are likely to be dropped and to remain where they were produced. For example, at the Magdalenian site of the Abri Dufaure, France, and in our current excavations at the open-air Gravettian site of Huccorgne, Belgium, analysis of debitage smaller than 1 cm has been of great use to us in determining the loci of *in situ* flint knapping, especially when combined with core refitting work using large debitage core remnants (Straus n.d.; Straus et al. 1992a).

In addition to the chapters of this book that are focused exclusively on micromorphology or microdebitage, the chapter by Bar-Yosef can be mentioned in this regard. One of the principal themes running it is that archaeologists must increasingly rely on microscopic evidence to understand the nature and causal agencies of site deposits; this derives in particular from examination of microartifacts and micromorphology. However, Bar-Yosef also wisely stresses the role of common sense archaeological judgement and of such time-honored techniques as refitting studies.

Cryptic Cavities

A group of the chapters (Bar-Yosef, Farrand, Clark and Barton, Petraglia, Koetje, Crothers and Watson) deals with caves and rockshelters. These types of sites have special characteristics both as sediment containers and as loci of human occupation (e.g., Straus and Clark 1986; Straus 1979, 1990, n.d.). While there is no doubt that the worldwide prehistoric archaeological record is skewed in favor of the generally good living conditions and preservation conditions of these cavities, cave entrances and rock-shelters bring with them often incredibly complex histories of use, deposition and disturbance. Bar-Yosef clearly describes the complicated nature of cave deposition, disturbance and erosion processes—of causes both "natural" and anthropogenic, both autochthonous and allochthonous. On the other hand, the physical features of cave mouths and rock-shelters (the bedrock walls and overhang, roof-fall blocks, adjacent talus slope, etc.) serve to structure the spatial organization of human activities in redundant fashion. And as the physical aspects of the space change (e.g., as the overhang retreats, as the anthropogenic and naturally deposited materials accumulate), there can be major changes in how space within the cave mouth or rockshelter is used (or indeed how the whole cavity itself is used within a settlement system) (see, for example, Thomas 1983). While we tend to think of caves and rockshelters as sediment traps, there are clearly times when few or no sediments are being accumulated (due to factors at the scale of the cavity itself, or at a local, regional or continental scale) and others when erosion outweighs deposition. The latter is generally caused by flowing water, due either to karstic rejuvenation (in the case of true caves) or to raised water level in a stream, river or ocean adjacent to the cavity. Either because of interruptions in sedimentation or because of erosion, major hiati can occur in cave stratigraphies, although often not obvious at first sight to archaeologists. This is the point graphically made by Farrand in his analysis of the Franchthi Cave sequence on the Argolid Peninsula of Greece. Radiocarbon dating has often had the effect of revealing occult hiati, as in the cases of Grotte XVI (Dordogne) (Stafford et al. 1991) or La Riera (Asturias) (Laville 1986; Leroi-Gourhan 1986; Straus 1986). Difficulties in correlating strata between one area of a cave/rockshelter excavation and another (sometimes with "horizontally" conflicting radio-carbon dates, as between the Front and Rear sectors of the Abri Pataud [Movius 1977]) can often be explained by the physical impossibility of tracing real strati-graphic continuity across huge rockfall blocks. The archaeological "impression" of continuity along both the vertical and horizontal axes within cave/rock-shelter deposits may often turn out to be chimeric, requiring the geomorphologist's expertise to decipher the cryptic tale. Even catastrophic events such as debris flows (solifluction) within caves (as well as on talus slopes) may be hidden and require careful geomorphological analysis to be revealed (e.g., Colcutt 1986).

The import of several of the observations by Clark and Barton follows along the lines of much of what I have said above.

I would add that, beside the problems they suggest in the interpretation of TL/ESR dates from caves, are the possibilities of mixture due to intensive human use of favored sites and of changes in groundwater conditions (Grün and Stringer 1991:191) (thereby potentially affecting uranium equilibria systems in dated samples).

Archaeologists need to come to grips with millennia of sediment homogenization or churning. Bar-Yosef's chapter, because of his long, varied field research experience, provides lucid anecdotal evidence for this and many of the other salient points concerning cave sites. Along those lines, I would like to add a few examples from my recent research in Portugal and Belgium.

In Vidigal Cave (Alentejo) it quickly became clear that there were few old deposits free of intrusive pits—some with "fresh" human bones. In fact, such caves were recently (or still are) in use by landless people (Straus 1991; LeGall et al. n.d.). Worse still, the narrow vestibule of Mulher Morta Cave (Algarve) had been *completely* dug and refilled, probably by several generations of pothunters who homogenized its Chalcolithic, Bronze Age and Muslim contents. This complete churning had been utterly invisible to us in our initial inspection of this cave (with a cave geologist) and only was revealed during excavation.

Besides what the late François Bordes called "two-legged badgers", the genuine article can have an extraordinary effect on deposits within their favored cave habitats. Sometimes we are lucky: in Toxugueira and Igrejinha dos Soidos caves (Algarve) badger burrows were filled with ash (Straus et al. 1992b). This is because people hunt these large, prodigiously burrowing mustelids by putting burning brush into their holes, incidentally making them show up beautifully in profiles. In le Trou Magrite (Belgium) we found an intact badger skeleton with bones far lighter that the rest of the bones in an Early Upper Paleolithic level (Straus et al. 1992a). Without this find, we could have been misled to think the deposit "intact", since the sediments of the stratum were all of much the same color and texture. We need to imagine millennia of deposit churning and homogenization by man and beast in caves and rockshelters.

Following along the lines of cryptic (or nearly cryptic) lines of evidence or of disturbance taken in this volume, it would be well to note the significance of raptorial birds (especially owls) in caves/rockshelters (see Brain 1981; Andrews 1990). Regurgitation pellets rich in microfaunal remains are valuable sources of sensitive, local-scale ecological information and they may give clues to the episodic, ephemeral nature of *human* occupations, since presumably owls would vacate their roosts during times of significant human habitation. In two caves that I have recently excavated (Goldra in the Algarve, Portugal, and le Trou Magrite in Namur Province, Belgium), there have been lenses of nearly solid rodent and insectivore bones, at the former in a bed following the Middle Neolithic occupation (Straus et al. 1992b; Crispim et al. n.d.) and at the latter in the midst of an ephemeral Mousterian occupation (Straus et al. 1992a). The abundance and diversity of large and medium-size carnivore remains in the same Trou Magrite stratum is added indication of the relative insignificance of human use of this cave at the time (see Brain 1981; Straus 1982; Gamble 1983).

During excavations at the Abri Dufaure, it became evident that formation and disturbance processes at this rockshelter/talus site had to be dissected before developing behavioral interpretations of human activity during the Magdalenian and Azilian periods (15,000-9000 BP). As discussed in Petraglia's paper, the excavations revealed areas of the site that appeared relatively intact, others that seemed partially disturbed (possibly by running water), others that had been totally stripped of Paleolithic deposits, and still others where jumbled, redeposited materials seem to have accumulated. To deal with the complexity of the situation we dug a continuous stratigraphic trench connecting the upper and lower slope areas, and recorded weights, orientations and inclinations (as well as 3-dimensional coordinates) on many artifacts, manuports and faunal remains. In collaboration with H. Laville and myself, Petraglia combined analysis of many of these data with refitting trials to work out the details of the complex depositional/disturbance history of the Abri Dufaure. Part of his research, summarized here, involved the discovery (by computer-assisted mapping) of occult yet intact burning areas—classic "latent structures" *sensu* André Leroi-Gourhan and Brézillon (1972). The cryptic evidence substantially supported our preliminary conclusions on the intactness of the paved central upper slope area. In addition to the observations made by Petraglia here, it is worth noting that this area (totally unlike the footslope) contained fragile faunal parts, with some cases of elements in anatomical connection. It also had fragile antler artifacts, with several cases of fragment refits found within short distances—despite the steepness of the slope and density of cobbles. Thus, within one relatively small site there were a wide variety of states of intactness, depending on accidents of location and of geomorphological processes (e.g., shelter form or exposure to solifluction events). Some aspects of this were apparent during excavation, but others had to be revealed through painstaking laboratory and computer analyses.

Finally, although Petraglia himself obtained some preliminary results concerning the human uses of the site area, his site formation work prepared the way for exhaustive, detailed activity area analyses by K.Akoshima (Straus et al. 1988; Akoshima 1993). Combining visual inspection of our accurate scaled plans and computer spatial analyses with lithic microwear analyses, Akoshima has been able to discern distinct patterns in the use of the terrace, upper slope and middle slope areas. And he has been able to show that the patterns of site use changed on several occasions during the span of time that people used Dufaure. Dufaure as a human dwelling place on the Tardiglacial landscape seems to have changed from pattern to pattern. But within discernible time ranges, patterns of the use of the site space seem to have remained fairly stable and redundant. Thus, while the strata are palimpsests, they do bear evidence of redundant behavioral activity. It is the task of the archaeologist to reveal those fundamental regularities in the human organization of activities in the available space. The lessons of the Dufaure research and, specifically, Petraglia's paper are that:

1.) site formation/disturbance factors need to be controlled for before developing definitive on-site behavioral/activity interpretations;

2.) preservation conditions can vary widely even within the area of a small site due to subtle microtopographic factors;

3.) hidden data are often the key to working out both natural and cultural aspects of formation;

4.) palimpsests can yield valuable behavioral information, since humans structure their repeated occupations of sites in redundant ways based on trans-occupational similarities in activities and on fundamental physical features of site lay-out.

Koetje's chapter in this volume similarly explores the changing Magdalenian activities at the Flageolet II rockshelter site (see Rigaud 1979). He shows through both simple and more elaborate statistical analyses— and good common sense—that although the basic role of the site may have remained similar through a long series of occupations, humans were obliged to arrange the site habitat, probably because of increasing local moisture. The role of pavements in providing dry,

stable working and living surfaces in the face of humid climate is precisely the explanation set forth for the extensive pavements of Duruthy and Dufaure (Arambourou 1978; Straus n.d.), and might work as well for the penecontemporaneous Isle Valley sites (Gaussen 1980). The paper by Crothers and Watson takes us into a truly hidden world, that of deep caves. The interior parts of complex karstic systems are less (or not at all) subject to both deposition and erosion from the exterior. Many contain fossilized living floors on the present cave surface, along with often extraordinarily well preserved traces of human presence, including inorganic and organic artifacts and manuports, works of art, faunal remains and sometimes the human prehistoric spelunkers themselves. Crothers and Watson remind us of the often ignored archaeological wealth of the deep caverns of the Eastern Woodlands of the U.S. Watson's (1969, 1974), investigations in Salts and Mammoth Caves represent a development of the study of "paleospeleology" parallel to those of the Old World, notably in SW France.

In both cases, deep cave interiors often preserve evidence of functionally and temporally discrete episodes of human behavior, relatively uncomplicated by the vast palimpsests resulting from more or less continuous human and non-human processes in cave entrances. One of the best bodies of data with which to compare the Crothers/Watson material is the detailed evidence of extensive underground activities in the vast caves of the Pyrenees some 15-11,000 years ago (e.g., Bégouën and Clottes 1981; Clottes 1985; Clottes and Simonnet 1990; Garcia et al. 1990; Rouzaud 1978; Bégouën et al. 1989). Both the American and French researches clearly indicate how careful modern day spelunkers must be when first penetrating chambers that could have remained untouched since their last human visits in remote prehistory. For here we may really come close to true "Pompeiis"! Fairly recent discoveries of pristine Upper Paleolithic living floors in association with rupestral art in the sealed caves of Tito Bustillo (Asturias), Fuente del Salín (Cantabria), Erberua (Pyrénées-Atlantiques), Fontanet (Ariège) and Cosquer (Bouches-du-Rhône) reveal to us in the late 20th century, rare glimpses of extinct activity laid out on the surface, ready to be mapped. One final comparison that the Crothers and Watson paper brings to mind is the fabulous, still-unfolding discovery of disarticulated skeletal elements from large numbers of individuals of *Homo heidelbergensis* at the base of a deep karstic shaft at Atapuerca (Burgos, Spain)(Arsuaga et al. 1990). These massed human remains in a non-occupational setting are provisionally dated to greater than 300,000 years ago

(J.M. Bischoff, personal communication). Sepulchral caves may go back much farther than we had thought—well beyond the European Neolithic and Eastern North America's Jaguar Cave—back to the Middle Pleistocene.

Acheulean Awash?

The chapter by Paddayya and Petraglia has an interesting origin. The senior author, one of India's foremost specialists in Paleolithic prehistory and in archaeological theory, had published a monograph on his surface finds and excavations of Acheulean sites in the Hunsgi Valley of Karnataka (Paddayya 1982). In a review this work (Straus 1983), I had suggested that some of Paddayya's activity reconstructions might be compromised by fluvial/colluvial disturbance processes, particularly because of the surficial nature of the sites on granitic bedrock on seriously eroded landsurfaces. Paddayya responded as a true scientist. He took the criticism to heart and, together with Petraglia, sought to deal constructively with the possibility of significant disturbance (much as the late Glyn Isaac and his students had dealt with Lewis Binford's criticisms of the Acheulean site of Olorgesailie [1977a] by their meticulous excavation and analyses of FxJj50 [Bunn et al. 1980]). Distinguishing relatively intact Acheulean sites from those that have been "re-worked" by running water is a major issue in paleoanthropological research (e.g., Gifford and Behrensmeyer 1977), as testified to by the recent restudies of Torralba and Ambrona in comparison to Aridos, all in central Spain (e.g., Klein 1987; Villa 1990).

In this context Paddayya's and Petraglia's research shows that the Mysore sites run the gamut from totally redeposited to relatively intact, and thus can be used for different, appropriate levels of interpretation and reconstruction (from the mere placing of findspots on the map of Acheulean settlement distribution to discussion of more-or-less *in situ* activities) (cf. Mishra 1992). The fact is that each archaeological occurrence anywhere in the world lies somewhere along a *continuum* between the "pristine" and the totally redeposited. This is the point made by Bar-Yosef in his four-class typology of site intactness. The Paddayya/Petraglia chapter adds to the growing literature on the many seemingly cryptic reasons why ancient stone tools may come to be physically associated with one another, and sometimes with bones, in places we call sites—reasons of humans and of nature. In his far-reaching chapter, Bar-Yosef also deals with open-air contexts. In many respects, this paper sums up the working archaeologist's pragmatic search for understanding the formation of the physical record upon which he/she must ultimately base explana-

tions of past hominid history, behavior and adaptations, whether from the culture-historical or processual perspective.

Cavernous Cracked Rocks

In the chapter by Nash, he correctly shows the importance of examining lithic fracture mechanics in order to distinguish anthropogenic from "natural" flaking. The latter can include flaking by animal trampling, by rolling in stream bed-loads, by solifluction, by cryoturbation, and—as in this case—by rockfall in caves (and in shelters and at cliff bases). Archaeologists have been debating this issue since the eolith controversies of the early part of this century (see Breuil and Lantier 1959, Ch.4; Grayson 1986) and continue to argue over what are genuine human-made stone artifacts, especially in the controversies over the dating of the initial hominid occupations of Europe and of the Americas, as Nash rightly points out in his chapter. His experiments go a long way in showing how (as with site taphonomy) lithics may lie along a continuum between unequivocally "artifactual" and unequivocally "naturefactual". Archaeologists need to pay more and closer attention to the development of criteria for distinguishing lithics along this continuum—beyond the usual criterion of raw material. Sometimes artifacts are not hidden—they are simply subtle and overlooked within the sedimentary matrix of our cave sites, having been "mined" from the walls and roof and then deliberately worked, however expediently.

One point that I would add to Nash's *exposé* is the fact that even limestones can be and indeed were used to make tools. This has been recognized (albeit not consistently) at least since the 1910-14 excavation of El Castillo cave in Cantabrian Spain (Breuil 1952). Recent excavations in Trou Magrite cave have revealed surprising quantities of hard limestone artifacts (mainly large flakes and blades with minimal or no retouching, but also including a few formal Upper Paleolithic tool types) (Straus et al. 1992a).

Experiments such as those of Nash, designed to try to decipher the record in a particular setting (Haystack Cave, Colorado), must be multiplied in order to build a generalizable corpus of data on natural agencies of formation and alteration useful widely in world archaeology.

Conclusions

In general we must have more appropriate ethnoarchaeological studies to construct valid uniformitarian principles on the relationship of human action to the archaeological record and its residues.

And although there are many studies of ongoing geomorphological and diagenetic processes, their number, detail and specific archaeological focus could be augmented. The interrelatedness of human and non-human factors in the formation, disturbance and destruction of archaeological sites is in need of serious exploration.

This volume clearly contributes to this on-going search for solid bases upon which to build our understanding of the past. It continues the worldwide, interdisciplinary dialogue on the reality and complexity of the archaeological data base. That the record is complex and imperfect, is not to say that valid, objective (in the sense of falsifiable, "scientific") interpretations of past human activity and behavior cannot be extracted from it.

The authors, coming from different disciplines, from different research traditions and from different backgrounds of fieldwork experience, nonetheless present a coherently optimistic view of what can be learned of the past, once the means are devised to decipher the often cryptic residues of our ancestors' lives. It is an approach fundamentally rooted in the principle of uniformitarianism. Some things can justifiably be held constant.

References Cited

Akoshima, K.

n.d. Analyse des structures d'habitat de la Couche 4, In *Les Derniers Chasseurs du Renne le Long des Pyrénées: L'Abri Dufaure, Un Gisement Tardiglaciaire en Gascogne*, edited by L. Straus, Mémoires de la Société Préhistorique Française, Paris, in press.

1993 A Compartive Study of Final Paleolithic Site Structure, Spatial Patterning, and the Organization of Lithic Technology. Unpublished Ph.D. dissertation, University of New Mexico.

Andrews, P.

1990 *Owls, Caves and Fossils*. University of Chicago Press, Chicago.

Arambourou, R.

1978 *Le Gisement Préhistorique de Duruthy*. Mémoires de la Société Préhistorique Française 13, Paris.

Arsuaga, J., J. Carreterro, A. Garcia, and I. Martínez

1990 Taphonomical Analysis of the Human Sample from the Sima de los Huesos Middle Pleistocene Site. *Human Evolution* 5:505-513.

Backer, A., and M. Guilbaud

1989 Spatial Distributions, Debitage and Microdebitage in Aurignacian and Castelperronian levels of Saint-Césaire, Charente-Maritime. Paper presented at the 54th Annual Meeting of the Society for American Archaeology, Atlanta.

Bégouën, R., and J. Clottes

1981 Apports mobiliers dans les cavernes du Volp. In *Altamira Symposium*, pp. 157-187. Ministerio de Cultura, Madrid.

Bégouën, R., J. Clottes, J. Giraud, and F. Rouzaud

1989 Les foyers de la caverne d'Enlène. In *Nature et Fonction des Foyers Préhistoriques*, edited by M. Olive and Y. Taborin, pp. 165-186. Mémoires du Musée de Préhistoire d'Ile de France 2, Nemours.

Binford, L.

1977a *Olorgesailie* Deserves More than the Usual Book Review. *Journal of Anthropological Research* 33:493-502.

1977b General Introduction. In *For Theory Building in Archaeology*, edited by L. Binford, pp. 1-13. Academic Press, New York.

1978 Dimensional Analysis of Behavior and Site Structure: Learning from an Eskimo Hunting Stand. *American Antiquity* 43:330-361.

1982 The Archaeology of Place. *Journal of Anthropological Archaeology* 1:5-31.

Bocek, B.

1986 Rodent Ecology and Burrowing Behavior: Predicted Effects on Archaeological Site Formation. *American Archaeology* 51:589-603.

Bordes, F.

1975 Sur la notion de sol d'habitat en préhistoire paléolithique. *Bulletin de la Société Préhistorique Française* 72:139-144.

Brain C.
1981 *The Hunters or the Hunted?* University of Chicago Press, Chicago.

Breuil, H.
1952 Note sur l'outillage en calcaire taillé du Magdalénien du Castillo, Santander. *Bulletin de la Société Préhistorique Française* 49:23-25.

Breuil, H., and R. Lantier
1959 *Les Hommes de la Pierre Ancienne.* Payot, Paris.

Bunn, H., J. Harris, G. Isaac, Z. Kaufulu, E. Kroll, K. Schick, N. Toth, and A. Behrensmeyer
1990 FxJj50: an Early Pleistocene Site in Northern Kenya. *World Archaeology* 12:109-136.

Butzer, K.
1982 *Archaeology as Human Ecology.* Cambridge University Press, Cambridge.

Clottes, J.
1985 Conservation des traces et des empreintes. *Histoire et Archéologie* 90:40-49.

Clottes, J., and R. Simonnet
1990 Retour au Réseau Clastres. *Bulletin de la Société Préhistorique Ariège-Pyrénées* 45:51-139.

Colcutt, S.
1986 Contextual Archaeology: the Example of Debris Flows in Caves. In *The Palaeolithic of Britain and its Nearest Neighbors,* edited by S. Colcutt, pp. 57-58. University of Sheffield, Sheffield.

Courty, M.A., and N. Fedoroff
1983 Micromorphology of a Holocene dwelling. PACT 7(2):257-277.

Crispim, J.A., L. Póvoas, and L. Straus
n.d. Further Studies of Algarão de Goldra and Igrejinha dós
dos Soidos
n.d. Archeological Cave Sites in the Algarve. ALGAR: Bóletim da Sociedade Portuguesa de Espeleología, in press.

Fladmark, K.
1982 Microdebitage Analysis: Initial Considerations. *Journal of Archaeological Science* 9:205-220.

Gamble, C.
1983 Caves and Faunas from Last Glacial Europe. In *Animals and Archaeology,* edited by J. Clutton-Brock and C. Grigson, vol.1, pp. 163-172. BAR, S163, Oxford.

Garcia, M., H. Duday, and P. Courtaud
1990 Les empreintes humaines du Réseau Clastres. *Bulletin de la Société Préhistorique Ariège-Pyrénées* 45:167-174.

Gaussen, J.
1980 *Le Paléolithique Supérieur de Plein Air en Périgord.* CNRS, Paris.

Geneste, J.M.
1985 Analyse lithique d'Industries moustériennes du Périgord: Une Approche technologiques du Comportement des Groupes humains au Paléolithique moyen. Unpublished doctoral dissertation, Institut du Quaternaire, Université de Bordeaux I.

Gifford, D., and A. Behrensmeyer
1977 Observed Formation and Burial of a Recent Human Occupation Site in Kenya. *Quaternary Research* 8:245-266.

Grayson, D.
1986 Eoliths, archaeological ambiguity, and the generation of "middle-range" research. In *American Archaeology Past and Future,* edited by D. Meltzer, D. Fowler, and J. Sabloff, pp. 77-134. Smithsonian Institution Press, Washington, D.C.

Grün, R., and C. Stringer
1991 Electron Spin Resonance Dating and the Evolution of Modern Humans. *Archaeometry* 33:153-199.

Klein, R.
1987 Reconstructing how Early People Exploited Animals: Problems and Prospects. In *The Evolution of Human Hunting,* edited by M. Nitecki and D. Nitecki, pp. 11-45. Plenum, New York.

Laville, H.
1986 Stratigraphy, Sedimentology and Chronology of the La Riera Cave Deposits. In *La Riera Cave,* edited by L. Straus and G. Clark, pp. 25-56. Anthropological Research Papers 36, Tempe.

LeGall, O., J. Altuna, and L. Straus
   n.d. Les faunes mésolithique et néolithique de Vidigal. *Archaeozoologia,* in press.
Leroi-Gourhan, A., and M. Brézillon
   1972 *Fouilles de Pincevent.* CNRS, Paris.
Leroi-Gourhan, Arl.
   1986 The Palynology of La Riera Cave. In *La Riera Cave,* edited by L. Straus and G. Clark, pp. 59-64.
      Anthropological Research Papers 36, Tempe.
Mishra, S.
   1992 The Age of the Acheulian in India: New Evidence. *Current Anthropology* 33:325-328.
Movius, H.
   1977 *Excavation of the Abri Pataud: Stratigraphy.* American School of Prehistoric Research Bulletin 31,
      Cambridge, MA.
Nash, D., and M. Petraglia
   1987 *Natural Formation Processes and the Archaeological Record.* BAR, S-352, Oxford.
Paddayya, K.
   1982 *The Acheulian Culture of the Hunsgi Valley (Peninsular India): A Settlement System Perspective.*
      Deccan College, Poona.
Rigaud, J.
   1979. A propos des industries magdaléniennes du Flageolet. In *La Fin des Temps Glaiaires en Europe,*
      edited by D. de Sonneville-Bordes, pp. 467-469. CNRS, Paris.
Roe, D.
   1980 Introduction: Precise Moments in Remote Time. *World Archaeology* 12:107-108.
Rouzaud, F.
   1978. *La Paléospéléologie.* Archives d'Ecologie Préhistorique 3, Toulouse.
Schiffer, M.
   1976 *Behavioral Archeology.* Academic Press, New York.
   1987 *Formation Processes of the Archaeological Record.* University of New Mexico Press, Albuquerque.
Shanks, M., and C. Tilley
   1987 *Reconstructing Archaeology: Theory and Practice.* Cambridge University Press, Cambridge.
Stafford, T., P. Hare, L. Currie, A. Jull, and D. Donahue
   1991 Accelerator Radiocarbon Dating at the Molecular Level. *Journal of Archaeological Science* 18:35-
      72.
Stein, J.
   1983 Earthworm Activity: a Source of Potential Disturbance of Archaeological Sediments. *American
      Antiquity* 48:277-289.
Stockton, E.
   1973 Shaw's Creek Shelter: Human Displacement of Artifacts and its Significance. *Mankind* 9:112-
      117.
Straus, L. G.
   1979 Caves: a Palaeoanthropological Resource. *World Archaeology* 10:331-339.
   1982 Carnivores and Cave Sites in Cantabrian Spain. *Journal of Anthropological Research* 38:755-96.
   1983 Review of *The Acheulian Culture of the Hunsgi Valley* by K. Paddayya. *Journal of Anthropological
      Research* 39:447-449.
   1986 An Overview of the La Riera Chronology. In *La Riera Cave,* edited by L. Straus and G. Clark,
      pp. 19-24. Anthropological Research Papers 36, Tempe.
   1990 Underground Archaeology: Perspectives on Caves and Rockshelters. In *Archaeological Method
      and Theory,* edited by M. Schiffer, vol. 2, pp. 255-304. University of Arizona Press, Tucson.
   1991 The "Mesolithic-Neolithic transition" in Portugal: a View from Vidigal. *Antiquity* 65:899-903.
   n.d. *Les Derniers Chasseurs du Renne le Long des Pyrénées: L'Abri Dufaure, Un Gisement Tardiglaciaire en
      Gascogne.* Mémoires de la Société Préhistorique Française, Paris, in press.
Straus, L., and G. Clark
   1986 *La Riera Cave.* Anthropological Research Papers 36, Tempe.
Straus, L., K. Akoshima, M. Petraglia, and M. Séronie-Vivien
   1988 Terminal Pleistocene adaptations in Pyrenean France: the nature and role of the Abri Dufaure
      site. *World Archaeology* 19:328-348.

Straus, L., M. Otte, J. Léotard, A. Gautier, and P. Haesaerts
   1992a Middle and Early Upper Paleolithic excavations in southern Belgium: a preliminary report. *Old World Archaeology Newsletter* 15(2):10-18.
Straus, L, J. Altuna, D. Ford, L. Marambat, J. Rhine, H. Schwarcz, and J. Vernet
   1992b Early Farming in the Algarve: a Preliminary View from Two Cave Excavations near Faro. *Trabalhos de Antropología e Etnología* 32:141-172.
Thomas, D.H.
   1983 *The Archaeology of Monitor Valley: Gatecliff Shelter.* Anthropological Papers of the American Museum of Natural History 59(1), New York.
Villa, P.
   1977 Sols et niveaux d'habitat du Paléolithique inférieur en Europe et au Proche Orient. *Quaternaria* 19:107-134.
   1982 Conjoinable Pieces and Site Formation Processes. *American Antiquity* 47:276-290.
   1990 Torralba and Aridos: Elephant Exploitation in Middle Pleistocene Spain. *Journal of Human Evolution* 19:299-309.
Villa, P., and J. Courtin
   1983 The Interpretation of Stratified Sites: a View from Underground. *Journal of Archaeological Science* 10:267-281.
Watson, P.
   1969 *The Prehistory of Salts Cave, Kentucky.* Reports of Investigations 11, Illinois State Museum, Springfield.
   1974 *Archaeology of the Mammoth Cave Area.* Academic Press, New York.
Wood, W.R., and D. Johnson
   1978 A Survey of Disturbance Processes in Archaeological Site Formation. *Advances in Archaeological Method and Theory*, edited by M. Schiffer, vol. 1, pp. 315-381. Academic Press, New York.

Section I

The Inter-Site Scale

The inter-site scale provides an appropriate starting point from which to examine cultural and natural formation processes. An inter-site perspective provides the archaeologist with an opportunity to search for similarities between sites or types of sites. Comparison of two or more sites provides the archaeologist with a basis to evaluate common expressions and variability in depositional integrity, the behavioral resolution of material patterns, and the influence of natural processes. In other words, the greater the variability in the types of sites studied, the greater are our chances to begin to see repetition in process.

In the first chapter of this section, Ofer Bar-Yosef draws on his broad experience in the Levant, and effectively shows that while there is tremendous variability in the archaeological record, cultural and natural processes are often not random or idiosyncratic residues specific to a particular time and place. Rather, Bar-Yosef demonstrates that by analyzing a variety of sites, whether open-air, caves, or tells, we can observe that there are certain regularities in site formation, and that these processes may be patterned and decipherable.

Two chapters in this section specifically examine cave contexts. The chapter by C. Michael Barton and Geoffrey Clark examines caves and rockshelters from different regions in the Mediterranean. The authors make the important point that while these contexts share certain common depositional characteristics, which are critical for accurately assessing cultural and natural formation, some degree of caution in interpretation is warranted since these contexts may in fact be quite variable and they may thus preserve particular nuances in site formation. These nuances need to be carefully assessed in order to avoid the pitfall of oversimplifying observed patterning. The chapter by George Crothers and Patty Jo Watson examines a particular type of cave, that of deep chambers found in the midwestern United States. The chapter presents unique examples of the processes encountered in deep caves, also demonstrating that circumstances of preservation and use of each of the sites vary considerably.

The final chapter in this section, by K. Paddayya and Michael Petraglia, examines the variability in preservation of open-air localities distributed throughout two valleys in India. The investigators studied a variety of depositional contexts and analyzed a number of variables in order to rank the sites in terms of the degree to which they have been affected by natural processes. Assessments of the degree of preservation are used to determine the level at which behavioral information can be extracted from these early man sites.

The chapters in this section are examples of how site formation research can be performed at an inter-site level. Sites within common depositional contexts, or groups of sites in a variety of settings, may be analyzed to examine similarities and differences in cultural and natural formation processes. This variability is a useful starting point to the study of formation processes, providing a means to gauge the appropriate level of inferences that may be made.

2

Site Formation Processes from a Levantine Viewpoint

Ofer Bar-Yosef
Harvard University

Archaeological research is motivated by the wish to learn more about past lifeways of humans and the history and evolution of social entities. Whether one uses the historical-cultural, the processual or post-processual approaches, it seems that basic goals, especially concerning field work, remain the same. The differences are generally expressed at the level of expectations and satisfactions from the results of the investigations. Some scholars wish to understand the processes that lie behind the formation of stone tools or pottery assemblages while others wish to reconstruct the history of social groups in space and time. Most would like to know the reasons for the observable changes in material culture, and a few are interested in reconstructing the spiritual world of past societies. Although we employ the results of previous excavations and surveys in order to study a particular process or a situation, no one will conclude today that we should stop surveying and digging. This is especially true in a world where rapid development with heavy machinery, or the flooding of river valleys, causes the ultimate destruction of the archaeological record. The suggestion made two decades ago, that the available information in site reports, museum collections and especially the backlogs of so many archaeologists if published, would be sufficient for testing rival hypotheses, is today untenable. New questions are being asked and new analytical techniques are being developed. In many instances the questions cannot be answered by re-scrutinizing the available data (including unpublished information), and new techniques cannot be employed, especially when a certain portion of each assemblage, or certain types of samples, are missing. A few examples are probably in order.

Consider, for example, the detailed analysis of animal bones, including all fragments, that is needed today in order to evaluate whether the assemblage resulted from the activities of humans as hunters and/or scavengers or of animal predators and scavengers (e.g., Cruze-Uribe 1991; Stiner 1991). If the excavator of the site did not keep the small fragments or the so-called "unidentifiable pieces," such an analysis cannot be accomplished. Similar queries are raised concerning lithic assemblages where all the debitage, once called "waste," was not conserved, or in cases where sherds were selected according to certain body parts and decorations while those of the locally-made pots were not curated. In addition, in many instances the field observations are missing or are too brief to enable a re-analysis of the collections. For example, only meager information is available concerning the exact stratigraphic position of the skeletal remains from Skhul cave (Mount Carmel), where most human fossils are considered to be early modern humans. We cannot test the hypothesis that these were interred over a relatively long period of time.

In trying to comprehend the archaeological past, archaeological investigations went through various phases. Two hundred years ago it was important to establish that artifacts and animal bones were incorporated in the same geological layer. Later, uncovering the stratification and the subdivision of the long prehistoric sequences were the main goals. The intuitive notion concerning the relationship between environmental fluctuations and human survival made the reconstruction of paleo-climatic sequences a research goal that was based on the study of the deposits in prehistoric sites. Human behavior and mind were seen as reflected in stone, bone and antler artifacts as well as in art objects. Features such as burials, hearths, houses and so on were implicitly viewed as representing behavior and environmental adaptation. From the writings of earlier scholars it is clear that they aimed to achieve a general picture, in which ethnography and archaeological remains were seen as part of the same continuum. This trend is clearly expressed in the pre-1950 general summaries (e.g., Sollas 1915; MacCurdy 1924). We often forget that the early generations of prehistorians were not just archaeologists but were well-versed in Quaternary geology, geography and ethnography. Many of their intuitive interpretations were directly based on ethnographic analogies. In addition, in their time, they were not so numerous as we are today and therefore they did not feel the need to state explicitly how the sites were excavated or how their proposed interpretations were reached.

Once the cultural sequences were established, the time was ripe for additional questions. The assumption that humans were hunters from their early stage (which for most archaeologists, until the discoveries of Louis Leakey in Africa, meant the early Acheulean in Europe), received further attention (e.g., Brain 1981; Binford 1981a). The chronological prolongation of the prehistoric past of "Man the Tool Maker" since 2.5 Ma forced many to reconsider the concepts embedded in the previous historico-cultural approach. And, as happened many times in the post-1950 years, American scholars were among the pioneers in expressing their doubts and suggesting new hypotheses concerning the causes for typological variability among Middle Paleolithic industries, the behavioral interpretation of sites or the causes for the accumulation of bones in prehistoric deposits (e.g., Binford and Binford 1966; Schiffer 1976; Binford 1981a). The impetus to find out if sites were the results of human activities, or, alternatively, what kind of geological and biogenic agencies were responsible for

their formation and for the observable alterations in both accumulating sediments and archaeological assemblages (e.g., Isaac 1967), led to the formulation of geoarchaeology as an independent subject and profession (e.g., Hassan 1979; Butzer 1982).

The study of site formation processes is part of geoarchaeology. When new techniques for providing a detailed geological understanding were proposed, it was rather easy to implement them (e.g., Laville et al. 1980). For example, one can easily visit Paleolithic caves and rockshelters where excavations were carried out in the past and initiate a detailed geoarchaeological study of the stratigraphy. In these sites one often obtains a two-dimensional view including the width and depth of the outcrop (e.g., Laville et al. 1980, e.g., Fig.4.1). What is missed is the third dimension, which provides the spatial variability. This dimension is important if we would like to find out how humans used the space and what the depositional traces that reflect their activities are.

The situation is different in Holocene mounds (i.e., tells) or shell middens. In these, only portions of the site had often been removed by early excavators. In fact, there are many Near Eastern tells that were never excavated and where modern excavation and recovery techniques can be practiced. However, tells contain the remains of later prehistoric and historic cultures sometime since the Natufian (ca. 12,800-10,300 B.P.) and more often from the Neolithic through the Byzantine and early Arabic periods (3rd to the 15th centuries A.D.). This means that by digging Holocene mounds, where exposures may amount to a hectare or more, geoarchaeologists are able to improve our options for learning about the past.

Finally, in this general list of options, the extreme case of well-preserved sites should be mentioned. Suddenly covered by volcanic ashes, the excavations of Pompeii became the ultimate example for the conservation of "moments of the past". Pompeii or the Minoan Acrotiri on the island of Santorini in the Mediterranean, represent rare discoveries, similar to the recently found frozen Bronze Age man in the Alps (Evolutionary Anthropology). The "Pompeii premise" (Binford 1981b) in the general sense means superb preservation of prehistoric floor levels, dwelling structures, domestic objects made of organic substances, spatial distribution that reflects the "real" array of activities, and so on. Such conditions often characterize water-logged situations or very dry caves and rockshelters. The wider the array of preserved materials, the larger the body of information that is commonly missing from the ordinary Paleolithic and Neolithic sites. Well-researched "Pompeii premises" should enable geoarchaeologists to calibrate their interpretational tools and to test the quality of their assertions concerning the primary conditions. Together with actualistic studies, such sites provide a base line on which the effects of time can be estimated.

An additional aspect of Paleolithic archaeology is the study of the landscape as conceived by G. Isaac (1984) and currently practiced by R. Potts at Olorgesailie (Potts 1988). Again, such investigation is more easily done in Holocene archaeology. Landscape archaeology combines both the detailed study of a site with a broad areal scope that tries to encompass all human activities in their immediate environment.

There are various ways in which we can examine what we know and what we would like to know about site formation processes. We may begin with either the definition of an archaeological site according to whether it is an isolated feature such as a monolith or storage facility, or the classification of sites by nature (open-air versus caves or rockshelters). We may review the already known natural processes and human activities that were responsible for the formation of sites from the Lower Paleolithic to modern garbage dumps. Already, previous generations, while building the sequence of "ages," "phases," "cultures," and "industries," were intrigued by the nature of the depositional context of artifacts and bones. In particular, they have indicated their concern as to whether the earliest stone artifacts were left behind by prehistoric artisans or were the random production of nature (e.g., Sollas 1915). Their conclusions hold today.

The general rule is that if the artifacts are as fresh as the day they were made, it could demonstrate the in situ or primary nature of the archaeological context. If the animal bones were abraded or rolled, but the artifacts were in mint condition, or alternately, abraded, it meant and it still means that their association is the result of secondary or tertiary redeposition. Thus, reports on the physical condition of the the finds served as a primary clue concerning site formation processes.

Studies of Lower Paleolithic sites, which cover most of the time span of human evolution, are still concerned with basic uncertainties. Claims for the presence of hominids earlier than 1.0 Ma in Eurasia, on the basis of the occurrence of stone artifacts, are constantly scrutinized, and the first question asked is whether these artifacts are effectively in situ (e.g., Villa 1991).

In view of the difficulties with the interpretation of site deposition, geology and pedology became an inseparable part of Quaternary archaeology during the nineteenth century. It is from these fields that many of the needed methods for the deciphering of site stratigraphies were borrowed (e.g., Laville et al. 1980; Courty et al. 1989). Moreover, as a rule, in the last fifty years Paleolithic archaeologists often worked together with a geologist. In addition, in many cave sites and rockshelters that were excavated during the nineteenth and early twentieth centuries, geological observations were made where deep cuts were already exposed and a large bulk of the sediments was removed. Therefore, in these locations only limited information concerning site formation process is available. Today, the daily involvement of a geologist during the course of the excavation season often enables a three-dimensional study and an elaborate reconstruction of the dynamic processes that led to the observable accumulation (e.g., Laville and Goldberg 1989; Goldberg and Laville 1991). As mentioned above, open-air sites with large exposures provide somewhat better opportunities for three-dimensional reconstruction which can be later expressed in block diagrams (e.g., Bar-Yosef and Tchernov 1972).

Finally, there is a point to be made concerning the practice of archaeology by scholars who were trained in different schools but who do their field work in the same region. In this respect, the Near East is unique. The history of archaeology of the last 150 years demonstrates that the Near East is the only region of the world where the largest number of schools of archaeology have been involved in field work. There is no other region where different schools of various nationalities, represented by established institutions or by individuals whose work is done under the auspices of universities or museums, have carried out excavations in sites of the same age. Even a cursory examination of conference proceedings on Near Eastern prehistory or later archaeology will elucidate this observation. The meaning of this phenomenon is that there is no one dominant viewpoint that dictates the nature, strategies and procedures of field techniques. There is no one prevailing model that is employed to interpret Paleolithic or Neolithic sites. In addition, the interaction among the various schools has had an impact on the quality and strategies of excavations. However, the cumulative Near Eastern experiences were hardly used by those who write about theoretical issues. Archaeologists trained in European or American schools learned, while working in the Near East often only during the summer, that observations based on their personal experiences in their home countries are not necessarily applicable to that region. Such approaches, when used uncritically, lead to erroneous conclusions concerning the nature of the sites, their paleoclimatic interpretation, or the interpretation of assemblage variability. It would, on the other hand, be interesting to see how Near Eastern-trained archaeologists operate in Europe or the Americas.

In the following pages I deal only with the aspects of site formation processes of Paleolithic and Neolithic sites in the Near East where I have spent most of my career as a field archaeologist (Bar-Yosef 1991). For the sake of brevity and clarity, the interesting aspects of the immediate environments of the sites and "off-site archaeology" are not discussed in this paper. In the first part I will summarize the categories of site formation processes. This will be followed by the "old" and "new" ways of looking at the aspects of preservation. Formation processes in the Levantine cave and open-air sites will form the second part of the paper. The concluding remarks will bear the stamp of practical suggestions.

Categories of Site Formation Processes

The following is a generalized classification of site formation processes and the difficulties created by them which often hamper our understanding of the observable accumulations:

Anthropogenic Processes

These processes result from regular or unique human activities (c-transforms; Schiffer 1976). They include the modifications of the locale such as levelling, digging pits and graves, building dwellings, installations and hearths, the production, use and discard of artifacts, bringing in raw materials, food, and rare commodities, and dumping residues of food processing and consumption (e.g., bones, plant remains), perishable tools, and clothing. In addition to the domestic, ritual activities were responsible for certain, not always easily identifiable, relics. Based on systematic recovery of physical, organic and inorganic remains, we would like to reconstruct the duration of occupations, the size of the social unit, labor division, and information concerning food acquisition techniques as well as methods of artifact manufacture and use. The desire to find out whether the site was single component or re-occupied over a long period of time is of crucial importance for interpreting the intra- and inter-settlement pattern. While hunter-gatherers are considered mobile, most farming communities are viewed as sedentary. However, the ethnographic records provide a more complex view with various ranges of mobility and degrees of sedentism. Complex behavior is recorded where environmental variability dominates over relatively short distances, as in the Levant. In addition, climatic fluctuations complicate the situation, and the deciphering of the archaeological accumulations becomes a complex task. On-site anthropogenic effects should take into account the

potential of human activities within such a given region and the potential changes through time.

Non-Human Biological Processes

These processes often include the use of sites by carnivores such as hyenas, cave dwellers such as bats and barn owls, or immediately next-door occupants such as the eagle owls who nest in trees just above the cave entrance (e.g., Tchernov 1968; Brain 1981; Andrews 1990). Porcupines are capable of boring deep tunnels into the sediments; beetles, earthworms and bacteria also play a role. While we understand the effects of hyenas and smaller carnivores, as well as of barn owls, we are also far from recognizing and correctly identifying many of the effects that are due to the activities of apparently smaller biological agencies (e.g., earthworms, burrowing bees, ants, beetles).

Geomorphic Processes

Due to over one hundred years of the experience of Quaternary geologists, geomorphologists and sedimentologists, large-scale natural processes are more easily identified than the impact of human activities. The list of accumulating deposits include rock-fall, windblown sands, desertic loess, washed in colluvial or alluvial clasts and all these are often coeval with the human occupations and become more evident as their duration increases (e.g., Butzer 1982; Petraglia and Nash 1987). On the whole, the effects of erosion, subsidence, aggradation and deflation are discernable, but identifying the results of the interplay among the geogenic, biogenic and anthropogenic agencies is more complicated.

Postdepositional processes are viewed as an important factor which determines the preservation of the archaeological remains. For example, if a prehistoric site had not been occupied for 10,000 years or more, the impact of these processes could be devastating. If one part of the site had been left intact, covered by finer sediments (clay, sand, etc.), the rest was perhaps removed by erosion and transported stone artifacts were redeposited downward in a channel or left on the slope. Diagenic processes caused the disappearance of the bones both in the in situ remains as well as the removed assemblage. Describing and discussing what had happened to the site after its abandonment is essential, and such discussions are often well-presented in many site reports.

The set of postdepositional effects that in my view are the more important and less understood are those that can be regarded as essentially penecontemporaneous in prehistoric cave sites and rockshelters as well as in mounds. In Paleolithic sites the archaeological and/or geological layers, as defined by the observers, represent time units of often unknown duration. The thickness of these layers vary and therefore the 'post-depositional processes' that are of a destructive nature take part in an interplay of various processes. For example, a layer is formed when a cave site is occupied by a group of people for several seasons, say a few consecutive summers. However, in their absence, atmospheric changes, proliferation of bacteria, burrowing bees, barn owls, dripping water in certain corners, etc., cause varied effects on the abandoned materials (stone artifacts, broken animal bones, pieces of cloths, remains of firewood and sleeping grounds, etc.). In addition, during a temporary abandonment for several years the cave may become a carnivore den or lair causing trampling, the gnawing of bones and the introduction of "new" bones (for a fuller list of activities see Cruze-Uribe 1991). The excavated assemblage from this particular layer is therefore the sum result of all these penecontemporaneous processes. In addition, stratified rockshelters and caves provide examples for disturbances caused by later occupants. For example, the Natufians at Hayonim cave dug graves into the Aurignacian and Mousterian layers (Bar-Yosef and Goren 1973; Belfer-Cohen and Bar-Yosef 1981). Chemical weathering also played an important role. Its effects, known as diagenic processes, are now being studied in Levantine cave-sites (e.g., Goldberg 1979; Bar-Yosef et al. 1992; Weiner et al. in press).

The need to better understand, calibrate, and scale both human and natural processes as involved in site formation led to the appearance of data collection either passively under the categories known as ethnoarchaeology, ethnozoology, ethnobotany or actively through experimental studies (e.g., Kramer 1982; Watson 1979; Seedan 1982; Seedan and Wilson 1988; Binford 1981a; Brain 1981). From ethnoarchaeology we derive the principles that govern the relationships between the behavior of the people and the residues of their activities, whether domestic or ritualistic. Observations from actualistic studies in zooarchaeology are considered the best way to understand past processes responsible for bone accumulations with the understanding that they suffer from biases caused by the effects of modernization (Cruze-Uribe 1991). Ethnobotany records the ways in which the plant world is exploited by humans and the various processes through which plant remains become incorporated in the archaeological record. Experimental studies explore the variable methods employed in raw material procurement, knapping, tool making and utilization, pottery production and destruction, or how dwelling structures were built and collapsed. All these fields

contribute to what was already observed by past archaeologists and enable us to use additional analytical techniques.

Micromorphology is a new and powerful technique for identifying past processes that were involved in site formation (Courty et al. 1989). The correct deciphering of the thin sections depends on the achievements of soil scientists and the results obtained by experimental or actualistic studies. But if we are to succeed in integrating data from archaeology, bioarchaeology and geoarchaeology in order to achieve a truly "contextual archaeology" (Butzer 1982), we need to review some of the basic questions concerning our field observations. Two such field observations, which relate to one another and to the question of the degree of preservation, are notions expressed in the terms "in situ" and "living floors".

Aspects of Preservation

Attributes of site and/or assemblage preservation are of extreme importance. It is perhaps obvious that observations concerning the degree of preservation of what were the original "living floor", "activity area", and "hut foundations" are what determine the ensuing interpretation. However, it is also in this respect that, due to the lack of accepted standards, field archaeologists differ from one another. Among the attributes that enable us to determine or define the degree of preservation are: the position of artifacts (lying on dorsal or ventral faces, stuck on an edge, etc.), their physical condition (fresh, coated with incrustations, slightly abraded or eolianized, rolled, etc.) and their relationships to the matrix in, or on, which they are found. Similar observations are made concerning bones. The search for cut marks and the identification of gnaw marks led to the recognition that the surface of the bones also conserve damage created by rolling, washing and trampling (e.g., Gifford-Gonzales 1989). In addition, even bones considered by the paleontologists as well preserved can be chemically deprived through diagenic processes (Weiner and Bar-Yosef 1990). Similar observations can be made in mounds. Plotting broken pots, refitting, and careful sieving (e.g., Miller Rosen 1989) provide valuable information concerning human activities and penecontemporaneous biogenic and geogenic processes.

Most references concerning preservation in prehistoric sites are related to the state of artifacts and bones. But there are other essential elements that, when preserved, provide solid foundations for the reconstruction of past lifeways. Such, for example, are hearths, identifiable distributions of lithics and bones, the presence of human and animal coproliths, microvertebrates, land snails, and plant remains. Until now most evaluations were based on personal experience using the naked eye. In addition, the contributions of the other substances, if preserved, were reported in the specialists' reports, often with minimal evaluation of how these data can be integrated or affect the behavioral interpretation.

New techniques, such as micromorphology (Courty et al. 1989) and Infra Red Spectroscopy (Weiner and Goldberg 1990), enable us today to gain better insights by verifying whether plant remains, coproliths and bones were present in the excavated layers while their macro elements had already disappeared. In the lack of an accepted scale for evaluating the degree of preservation, only the two ends of the spectrum are generally reported as naked-eye observations. Sites and assemblages are either "well-preserved" or "poorly-preserved". The extreme categories may be classified and subdivided as follows:

Type A1. In situ sites which were buried immediately or shortly (within weeks or months but less than a year) after their abandonment and remained buried until exposed by archaeologists. For example, the degree of patination on lithics is limited or nil in such sites. Patination results from a combination of light and the nature of the bedrock; the process can be measured in a few weeks or months (personal observations). Preservation of plant remains and bones depends on the nature of the sediments. For example, Upper Paleolithic sites in sandy deposits in northern Sinai contained charcoal but no bones (Bar-Yosef and Belfer 1977), while in sites of the same period, buried in the marls in Wadi Feiran, southern Sinai, both were preserved (Phillips 1988).

Type A2. In situ sites exposed by deflation or sheet wash erosion and the overlain sediments (generally sand or silt) removed without considerably disturbing the original (post-abandonment) array of the artifacts. The degree of preservation can be tested in those cases where lithic knapping and/or secondary retouching, occurred in place. Careful sieving will recover the small chips which accompany all core-reduction techniques or micro flakes resulting from retouch. For example finding microburins, either the regular ones or those known as Krukowski microburins will indicate the exact technique employed by the knapper to shape the microliths from already obtained blade

blanks. Absence of small and light pieces is the first indication of disturbance caused by water or wind action (e.g., Bar-Yosef and Goren 1980).

Type B1. Reworked sites that include diagnostic artifacts or a scattering of artifacts which have been redeposited a few meters away from their original location. Such artifacts were buried in deposits which might be generally of the "same age" as their time of manufacture (during the same century or millennium) and will enable their definition as "in situ geologically". This phenomenon is known in both open-air and cave sites. In such cases microscopic or macroscopic damage can be observed on the edges of the lithics; also scratches caused by moving sand and gravel on the bones. For example, this is the case in most of the 'Ubeidiya levels (Bar-Yosef 1989; Bar-Yosef and Goren-Inbar 1993), all of the Acheulean find spots in the terraces of Nahr el Kebir in northern Syria (Sanlaville 1979), layers 12-14 in Qafzeh cave (Vandermeersch 1981; Bar-Yosef and Vandermeersch 1981) and layer C in Shukbah (Garrod and Bate 1942).

Type B2. Reworked surface sites as isolated pieces or a scattering of artifacts found on the surface; it is often impossible to ascertain distance of movement from their original location. Such artifacts can be in almost mint condition, but their original context remains unknown (e.g., the Upper Acheulean site of Ma'ayan Barukh; Stekelis and Gilead 1966; Ronen et al. 1980).

Only rarely do archaeologists find that type A1 sites, which were episodes of time, preserved due to special circumstances (Binford 1981b). Sites such as Pincevent (Leroi-Gourhan and Brézillon 1966, 1972), Pompeii or the "Burned House" in Jerusalem dated to August 70 A.D. (Avigad 1981), come to mind immediately. But even in these places one may wonder how much "last minute changes" are recorded.

Archaeologists often designated the exposed well-preserved levels as "living floors." An important measure of preservation directly related to these "living floors" is the tedious refitting of lithics and pottery. As a standard procedure, it first began years ago in the excavations of Magdalenian sites in the Paris basin (Leroi-Gourhan and Brézillon 1966, 1972), and has since gained considerable support through work done at a number of Lower, Middle and Upper Paleolithic assemblages (e.g., Marks 1983; Gilead and Grigson 1984; Goring-Morris 1987 and papers in

Cziesla et al. 1990). However, the meaning of many pieces being refitted to cores, or of the rejuvenation of various tools, in terms of human activities, is still subject to debate. A few examples are in place. Cahen and Moeyersons demonstrated that artifacts from a stratified site in Africa, with two different 14C dates, conjoined over a depth of 1.5 m (Cahen and Moeyersons 1977). In the Lower Paleolithic site of Terra Amata, refitted pieces from different levels led to rejection of the claimed superimposed living floors (Villa 1983). Sometimes the original explanation (such as at Meer II in Belgium) that has indicated the presence of a few people for a short time (Cahen et al. 1979) was re-interpreted to fall in line with other similar Late Paleolithic (Magdalenian) remains in the lowlands of western Europe (Cahen 1984). In another example, conjoined pieces from several deflated scatterings at the marginal Saharan landscape (attributed to the Capsian of Neolithic tradition) enabled the reconstruction of on-site activities, including re-tooling, that were spread over a large area (Tixier et al. 1976).

Although most authorities agree that the conjoined pieces indicate the contemporaneity of the artifacts, two aspects remain debatable: the length of time involved in the accumulation and the paleoanthropological interpretation. Most scholars view conjoined pieces as indicating short-term occupation (a few hours, days, or at most some weeks) and therefore all the residues are attributed to the activities of a single social unit (a few people or a few families). Others accept the notion of contemporaneity but leave the question of time length open and view the possibility that the total assemblages of artifacts resulted from the activities of various social units, which may have been even foreign to each other (e.g., Bordes 1980). Additional insight into how quickly the site was buried is gained through high and low power magnification studies of edge damage. Under immediate burial, artifacts preserve the signs of use; slow deposition, redeposition and movement of artifacts cause a natural microscopic damage that impedes the use of both techniques.

Equipped with these generalizations, let us now examine a few Levantine caves and open-air sites.

The Levantine Caves

Caves and rockshelters in the Levant have been the subjects for excavations and geological studies since 1925. Caves are still sought to answer new research questions because past experience of archaeologists demonstrates their potential in providing long sequences of stratified assemblages. But rarely were the agents responsible for these thick accumulations studied thoroughly. The prevailing convention that

cave deposits resulted from both natural (indoor and outdoor agencies) as well human and other biological contributions was taken for granted and the search for details is still in its incipient phase (Goldberg 1979, 1980; Laville and Goldberg 1989; Courty et al. 1989; Goldberg and Laville 1991).

Most of the known Levantine caves are limestone cavities formed under phreatic conditions, often along vertical and horizontal joints. In certain cases they have chimneys in their ceilings and series of domes (chimneys in formation) and a sinkhole (or several sinkholes) in their lower part. These make the cave floors an irregular shape, which means that since the onset of the accumulation, the earlier deposits were hardly horizontal. Moreover, the renewal of karstic activities, even on a minor scale, caused the evacuation of the sinkhole and the following collapse of sediments into it (Farrand 1979; Roe 1983; Goldberg and Laville 1991; Laville and Goldberg 1989).

The direct natural processes which caused sedimentation in karstic caves are generally known from the completed reports on several sites such as Douara cave (Endo 1978), Yabrud I, Qafzeh, Tabun, and Hayonim (Farrand 1979; Goldberg 1979). More often "outdoor" agencies were responsible for the "indoor" accumulations. Such are the blown-in sand and silts and the washed-in colluvium and alluvium. Rarely does one find the typical *éboulis* which resulted from frost-shattering in colder zones (e.g., Laville et al. 1980) in the Levantine caves. In most cases this *éboulis* is related to the friable state of the cave wall (e.g., Amud cave and Qafzeh cave).

Indoor activities are generally expressed by dripping water, either from the ceiling on the soft deposits, or on the walls. Formation of stalactites, stalagmites, and carbonate crusts are often well-recorded phenomena (e.g., Zuttiyeh, Hayonim caves). The consolidation of sediments into what is known in the archaeological literature as "brecciated deposits" or just "breccia" is one result of water activity which obliterates considerably the details of past events. Percolating water sometimes creates tunnels through the deposits and is seen as spring activity or just as evidence for the renewal of the karstic regime. Examples are Tabun, Qafzeh, Shukbah and Kebara (e.g., Farrand 1979; Bar-Yosef et al. 1992).

Animal activities in cave-sites are of various kinds. Carnivores such as hyenas bring in bones, trample over them, defecate, and dig some shallow basins. Only one striped hyena den in the Negev has been studied in Israel (Skinner et al. 1980). Striped hyenas were common during the Levantine Upper Pleistocene and affected the bone accumulations. As shown in the example of the Upper Paleolithic and Mousterian assemblages at Kebara cave, their main contribution was the removal of bones from the cave (Speth in Bar-Yosef et al. 1992).

Most common among the birds of prey is the Barn Owl which spits its pellets. These contain the remains of rodents, reptiles and occasionally small birds. The analysis of recent pellets was used by Tchernov to measure and evaluate the microvertebrate assemblages collected carefully in a number of prehistoric excavations (see Tchernov 1968, 1984, 1988 with references). In his studies, the sampling of the Barn Owl as averaged through time (each unit is based on the archaeologist's definition of a layer), is taken as representing the immediate environments of the site. Bats, and today especially fruit bats, inhabit many Near Eastern caves. Their guano is considered an important factor in post-occupational chemical alterations (Farrand in Jelinek et al. 1973; Farrand 1979).

Finally, the role of porcupines, who burrow quite long and wide tunnels through cave deposits, should be mentioned. In Kunji cave, in the Zagros mountains, the activities of porcupines were considered the cause for the total mixing of the Mousterian levels in the site (Speth in Bar-Yosef et al. 1992). From an episodal experience at Hayonim cave, it seems to me that porcupines burrow when a small "cliff" is available. In this case, it was the exposed vertical face of a couple of squares near the cave entrance that attracted this large rodent; its tunnels spread inward from one hole.

Even with such a list, the role played by the cave fauna is not yet fully known. Moreover, the interaction between the vegetation which grows in caves and the living creatures is hardly studied. This vegetation exploits the wetness of these karstic caves. But as most caves went through dry periods, the cave vegetation disappeared. In situations where the cave and the slope in front of it formed one unit the growth of herbaceous vegetation resulted in bush fires and the accumulation of ashy layers as interpreted by Jelinek (1973) in the Mousterian layer C at Tabun cave. Finally, lichens which were thoroughly studied in open air sites (Danin 1985) also inhabit caves and affect the weathering processes of the walls and ceiling.

As mentioned above, viewing the Paleolithic cave deposits as the result of mainly natural activities (roof weathering, in-blown sand, washed-in colluvium, in situ pedogenesis, etc.) led to the use of the geological techniques designed to recognize these processes. Grain-size analysis (granulometry), calcimetry, measures of sphericity, clay analysis, etc. were used daily to detect the sequence of climatic changes (e.g., Farrand 1979). While in the rockshelters of temperate Europe sterile deposits quite often separate "cultural layers," this does not seem to be the case in the Levant. Instead, there are identifiable nonconformities. One way of explaining the lack of observable

sterile layers in Levantine caves is that in most cases the natural rate of sedimentation was very slow. When a cave was re-occupied by humans several millennia later, the new occupation resulted in a layer with a mixture of old and new artifacts and bones (e.g., Olami 1962). Continued occupation, depending on how often the cave was inhabited (e.g., annual basis or decade), resulted in a thin or thick archaeological layer. This is true for the Upper Acheulean through the Natufian. For example, in Kebara cave the Mousterian sequence is 3.5-4.0 meters thick and accumulated during 12 kyr TL years (Valladas et al. 1987; Bar-Yosef et al. 1992). In Hayonim cave major gaps but no sterile sediments were observed between the Mousterian and the Aurignacian (at least 15 kyr are missing), and between the Aurignacian and the Natufian (ca. 14 kyr are missing) (Bar-Yosef 1991).

Human activities in cave sites are often seen in the introduction of inorganic materials. Lithics were brought in, in the form of cobbles, partially worked, or fully shaped artifacts. In some cases blocks of limestone were carried in to serve as work tables or grinding stones; in the Natufian they served as building materials (e.g., Bar-Yosef 1991). Less is known about the frequency of introduction of animal tissues by humans, although scavenging and hunting are seen as food acquisition techniques since at least the Acheulo-Yabrudian, some 400/300 kyr ago. Bone accumulations inside caves, therefore, resulted from both human and carnivore activities.

Little is known about the introduction by humans of wood, branches, reeds and leaves for tool making, fires, bed spreads, and food. Preliminary analyses carried out at Kebara cave indicate that vetch pods were gathered and oak wood and grasses were used as combustibles (Bar-Yosef et al. 1992; Lev 1992). The micromorphological study enables the recognition of microscopic carbonized plant remains which are not easily retrievable in even the most careful flotation technique.

One can keep adding to the list of aspects that must and can be studied but, above all, we should put forward the crucial questions: how were all these processes intermingled to create what is defined as "layers" or "beds" and how can we, after recognizing and understanding the processes, interpret past human activities?

While it is not easy to answer this question, one may suggest ways in which to go about resolving several of the aforementioned problems. For example, the excavation of a site with good preservation, where hearths, bones, charcoal and lithics are retrievable, may provide spatial information or insights into ancient technologies which employed organic remains other than bones. This would enable us to recognize where certain activities took place and derive a few conclusions concerning the behavioral aspects. In such a site we have the opportunity to break away from the study of lithics that, despite the understanding of the operational sequence *(chaîne opératoire)* and the information about motions and materials as reflected in micro-wear and edge damage, is still only one aspect of the prehistoric behavior. It seems to me that too often, and especially lately, in the course of the debate concerning the origin of modern humans, the discussion centers on lithics and human fossils alone. In practice, many colleagues exploit these two data sets as the only sources for learning about past patterns of behavior. While human bones inform us of past activities, especially when rough work was involved, or of dietary trends, stone tools were basically employed for similar purposes over many periods. The need for cutting, scraping, butchering, whittling and so on was part of the daily activity of humans during the last million years or more. When one compares the published reports of micro-wear and edge-damage analysts, across sites and periods, the general motions and materials are similar.

Taking into account the above observations and comments, the following is a brief presentation of several examples where obtaining a better understanding of site formation processes may lead to some interesting conclusions.

Tabun cave is a case where understanding the effects of diagenic processes indicates the need for a re-interpretation of the chronology. The parts of the site excavated by D. Garrod, especially in the deeper deposits of layers E (Acheulo-Yabrudian) and D (early Mousterian), contained animal bones (Garrod and Bate 1937) with fewer bones in layer F (Upper Acheulean). In the later excavations (Jelinek et al. 1973; Farrand 1979) the absence of bones from these layers was found to be the result of diagenic processes. It seems that the bones in layers F-D at the back of the cave, an area that lies directly under the chimney, were destroyed. In addition, high densities of lithics per cubic meter characterize layer F and especially layer E, resembling deflated open-air sites. Thus, together with the destruction of the bones and the disappearance of the hearths (evidenced by the presence of burnt flints), certain fractions of the deposits are undoubtedly missing. The processes of "concentration" resulted in the reduction of the original volume of the deposits. This, in my view, led to the erroneous chronological conclusions proposed after the excavations (e.g., Jelinek 1981, 1982; Farrand 1979). The recently published ESR dates (Grün et al. 1991) indicate a previously unsuspected longer period of human occupation of Tabun cave. The time length

represented in Tabun cave, given the various erosional events, may reach several hundred thousand years, and is much longer than previously perceived, even by those who did not accept the chronology of Tabun as proposed by Farrand (1979; Bar-Yosef 1989).

In the upper part of the sequence, a change in the depositional processes resulted from the opening of the chimney and terra rossa soil was washed in from the plateau above the cave. This clayey sediment enabled the conservation of bones in layers C, B and the chimney fill that is attributed today to the period of 150/130 to 50 ka (Bar-Yosef 1992).

Another example is Qafzeh cave where a change in the set of operating processes resulted in the subdivision of the entire Mousterian sequence into two parts. The lower layers differ considerably from the upper ones. Both are present in the so-called "terrace" that is actually the entrance area to the cave. There, in the lower layers (XVII-XXIV) that are about 2 m in thickness (Vandermeersch 1981, Figs. 4-6), the hominid burials were uncovered. These deposits, are relatively poor in artifacts, provided rare large or medium size mammalian bones and partially preserved small hearths. In addition these layers contain extremely rich assemblages of micro-mammal bones testifying to long periods of abandonment when birds of prey nested in the cave or on trees above the entrance. The proliferation of the African rat *(Mastomys batei)* in the rodent assemblages was interpreted by Tchernov (1984) as indicating abundant refuse typical to human habitations. It seems that this intensive human occupation did not take place in the cave, as birds of prey and humans do not cohabit in such a small space. It is possible that there was another site nearby, perhaps on a wadi terrace below the cave (100 - 200 m away) or at the edge of the plain into which the Wadi el Haj descends (400 m away and about 100 m topographically lower than the cave).

This situation is in contrast to the upper Mousterian layers in Qafzeh (upper XV-V), which are rich in broken animal bones, abundant in lithics, have no micro-mammals (especially rodents), no human burials and no distinct features such as hearths. It seems that the nature of the occupation entirely changed and with it the character of the deposits. The absence of hearths, if we may judge on the basis of the experience from digging in Kebara cave (Bar-Yosef et al. 1992), is due to the leaching of the deposits by water. This process is evidenced in the breccification of the upper layers and is possibly responsible for the higher concentrations of bones and artifacts. This interpretation is supported by micromorphological observations as yet unpublished (Goldberg, personal communication, 1992).

Kebara cave is an example of a site where the preservation of charcoal, carbonized plant remains, hearths, and animal bones provided along with the distribution of the lithics, information concerning the spatial behavior of humans (Bar-Yosef et al. 1992). To mention one point, the separation between the ashy accumulations of hearths with some lithics from the masses of lithics (including the small debris) and the bones was shown to be a prehistoric "reality" and not the results of diagenic processes (Weiner et al. in press). Such a distribution pattern indicates that Middle Paleolithic hunter-gatherers were probably responsible for a spatial organization that resembles that of Upper Paleolithic humans (Bar-Yosef et al. 1992).

Upper Paleolithic cave occupations are not numerous in the Levant except for the impressive sequence of Ksar Akil which, with the gaps, amounts to ca. 18 meters (Ohnuma 1988; Bergman 1987). In this site, which resembles a rockshelter, colluvial-alluvial deposits played an important role. The constant mixing of biogenic residues with the terra rossa soil facilitated the preservation of the bones (e.g., Hooijer 1961; Kersten 1991), although hearths are not reported.

In closed caves such as Hayonim, the Aurignacian inhabitants occupied a shallow basin created by the subsidence of the top of the Mousterian layers. In these and the other caves where Upper Paleolithic remains were uncovered, human modification of the living floors seemed to have been minimal. Even if the entire picture is yet unknown, it stands in contrast to the Natufian cave occupations.

The excavations at Hayonim cave demonstrated that the Natufians were builders (Bar-Yosef and Goren 1973; Bar-Yosef 1991) and imported considerable amounts of undressed stones from outside into the cave. These were used in order to build rooms that divided the interior frontal space. The special use of some of these rooms is discussed elsewhere (e.g., Bar-Yosef 1991; Belfer-Cohen 1988). Undoubtedly, similar structures were built inside El-Wad cave, as shown in unpublished archival photos (kept in the Rockefeller Museum; personal observations), but which were missed as the rocks were removed without recording them (Garrod and Bate 1937).

Open-Air Sites

Most prehistoric sites fall into the category of open-air sites, although the nineteenth century discoveries in caves and rockshelters created a false image of prehistoric people as "cave men." The excavations of open-air sites in the various continents of the Old World furnished a wealth of information about varied situations. In the topographic variability of the

Levant the most common locations are flatish spaces (silty, sandy or basaltic), close to water courses or springs. Numerous terraces along wadi beds served as chosen locales for prehistoric campsites (e.g., Goldberg 1986).

The type of in situ occurrence that conveys "precise moments in the past" is rare. The common situations are those listed above as Types A1 and A2, but none of these is free from difficulties in their interpretations. Questions are now being asked which put in doubt many of our cherished cultural or paleoanthropological interpretations. The naive acceptance of a uni-cultural or thinly deposited archaeological horizon as representing a single short-term occupation has been constantly challenged in recent years. However, refitting as discussed above is often considered the best test for the integrity of the assemblage (e.g., Boker Tachtit, see Marks 1983).

More substantial is the criticism addressed toward some of the early Lower Paleolithic sites (Binford 1981a, 1987) and the misunderstanding of the factors that were responsible for the formation of clusters of artifacts and bones (Isaac 1984). Most of this criticism concerns the various layers at the site of 'Ubeidiya, which, as far as we know, is one of the oldest manifestations of *Homo erectus* occupation outside Africa (Bar-Yosef 1987). Following the general suggestions of Isaac (1984), assemblages of bones and artifacts could have been the results of (1) hydraulic jumbles; (2) common amenities used independently by carnivores and hominids (such as shade trees); (3) carnivore accumulations used by hominids; (4) scavenging opportunities where dead animals or hunted animals were butchered by humans; and (5) a place of central foraging where hominids met to share the obtained animal tissues within the group or the family or both. Testing each of these configurations is of great importance not only for the East African record but also for Levantine sites. Figuring out what were the technical capacities and social behavior of *Homo erectus* while moving from the subtropical belt into the temperate zone is of extreme importance for evaluating the fragmentary Lower Paleolithic records of Eurasia.

The clear advantage of studying the various natural aspects which in Africa, under every circumstance, need to include predators' activities, is that the natural parks of this continent provide the possibilities for conducting controlled actualistic studies (e.g., Toth 1987; Schick 1991; Sept 1992; Tappan 1992; Blumenschine 1987, 1988, 1989). Once the assemblages which were affected by water abrasion or by predation and the sites where most carnivores dispersed their bones have been recognized, we are left with fewer interpretative possibilities. Sites where the artifacts are in mint condition indicate that hominids were directly involved. Cut marks on bones would add to the human intervention in the formation of the cluster. What will remain unclear is the degree of transportation. The cut marks on bones are the best evidence for hominid activities, but whether they were scavengers (as most probably was the case until late in the Middle Pleistocene) or hunters should be determined by examining the frequency of body parts and fragmentation indices. More information from the early African sites can be gained by micromorphology. The microscopic view of these early Paleolithic sites is of extreme importance. Where preservation was fairly good, there are opportunities to identify human feces, plant remains and phytoliths.

In comparison to the richness in animal and human bones of the East African early hominid sites, the Levantine Lower Paleolithic record is rather poor. The richest and best documented site is 'Ubeidiya (e.g., Bar-Yosef and Tchernov 1972; Bar-Yosef and Goren-Inbar 1993; Tchernov 1986); although most of the bones have not yet been systematically examined for the identification of human activities, they reveal some cut marks, breakage impact, gnaw marks and trampling and striation caused by water transport (personal observations).

Traditionally the techno-typological determinations used in Lower Paleolithic studies have been derived from the type-lists used for the study of Middle and Upper Paleolithic assemblages. By giving the same names to Lower Paleolithic "tool-types" we assume what we actually have yet to demonstrate— namely, that early hominids had the same cognitive abilities as the later ones (Wynn 1981; Wynn and McGrew 1989). The debate concerning this issue is well known (Isaac 1986), but if we follow Leakey's (1971) type-list which includes categories such as "choppers," "heavy duty scrapers," "notches," "awls," "burins," etc., while ignoring the results of geomorphic processes, we add another bias into our interpretations. At 'Ubeidiya, and probably in other Lower Paleolithic sites in the Near East, there is a possible relationship between increased frequencies of retouched flakes and depositional environments. Trampling, water abrasion and rolling may produce a variety of "retouched pieces" (e.g., Flenniken and Haggarty 1979).

The archaeological reports on the 'Ubeidiya lithics noted that each assemblage contains abraded and slightly abraded pieces besides those in fresh condition (Stekelis et al. 1969; Bar-Yosef and Goren-Inbar 1993). The abrasion was not considered to have any implications for the gross typology, which at the time was mainly directed toward the recognition of morphological patterns, based on the larger pieces. Similar observations were recorded in Olduvai Gorge (Leakey 1971) and at Latamne, where one-third of the assemblage was not fresh (Clark 1967, 1969).

At 'Ubeidiya the frequency of retouched pieces is generally correlated with the depositional environment. This is demonstrated by the following percentages: in clayey, swampy deposits retouched flakes are 8% - 16%, in clayey layers that laterally grade into gravelly beaches, 29% - 36%, in stony beaches, 21% - 47%, and in wadi gravels, 39% - 67% (Bar-Yosef and Goren-Inbar 1993). These frequencies, however, do not exclude the possibility that early hominids were responsible for the modification of some of the retouch, either intentionally or as a by-product of their use.

The generalized conclusion is that employing a Middle-Upper Paleolithic type-list for describing the typological variability of flaked pieces from Lower Paleolithic assemblages should be done with great caution. The superficial resemblance of Middle or even Upper Paleolithic artifacts to earlier items can be simply the results of site formation processes.

Processes of deposition and/or erosion in these topographic/sedimentary situations are often studied by geoarchaeologists (e.g., Goldberg and Bar-Yosef 1990 with references). In most cases the archaeological remains, lithics and bones, are seen as incorporated in the matrix. Human active interference in the course of the deposition or in its nature, besides leaving behind artifacts and bones, was never observed in Lower Paleolithic sites such as 'Ubeidiya or Evron-Quarry (Ronen 1991). Instead, ample evidence is accumulating in a few Middle Paleolithic sites where spatial distribution of artifacts is related to human activities such as in Rosh Ein Mor (Stevens and Hietala 1977), Farah II (Gilead 1988) and Quneitra (Goren-Inbar 1990).

The better preserved evidence for active human participation in the process of site formation is clearer in Upper and Epi-Paleolithic contexts. Beginning at the earliest by 19 kyr B.P., the digging of shallow basins that serve as foundations for huts and the constructing of hearths are well documented (Nadel and Hershkovitz 1991; Nadel 1991). In addition, modifications, such as leveling and digging shallow basins for hearths, are known from the arid zone sites (Goring-Morris 1988; Phillips 1988). However, sleeping grounds, either open or under a small brush shelter, were not yet identified.

In Upper and Epi-Paleolithic sites with a thickness over 10-20 cm the viable option of refitting, as mentioned above, in order to study the core reduction strategies and degrees of curation, is often available. In addition, artifact densities serve as proxy evidence for human activities and natural modifications as indicated by the various numbers in Table 1.

In spite of noting the type of sediment in each site, we do not know whether there is a tendency to get denser lithics (due to leaching, deflation and erosion) in a certain sediment type or in sites where building activities were practiced. One clue concerning sandy deposits is provided by our previous work in Northern Sinai (Bar-Yosef and Phillips 1977). Upper and Epi-Paleolithic sites were both surface collected and excavated from sandy formations (Table 2).

The relative densities, although calculated per retouched pieces, seem to indicate the amount of deflation. In most lithic assemblages the ratios of tools per debitage products are quite similar and range from 3-7%. Therefore, the small number of retouched pieces per m² are the results of the natural dispersal of the artifacts once the occupational horizons were abandoned or exposed. Site Mushbi I is an exception due to its topographic situation, on a flatish surface in the wadi course, and possibly having been recently exposed.

In sites within the Mediterranean phytogeographical belt, such as those in Table 1, the simplest interpretation is to view artifact densities as resulting from repeated occupations followed by deflation or some sort of sheet erosion and colluviation. On the other hand, continuous accumulation, demonstrated by the thickness of the layers in some sites, testify to a more complex process, including the intervention of humans, the growth of certain vegetation, and the effects of burrowing bees, ants, rodents and bacteria. Unfortunately, no detailed observations, such as required by a continuous series of thin sections, are available; therefore our understanding of thick accumulations (>20 cm) is rather patchy.

Table 1. Deposits and Tools per m^3 in Some Levantine Sites (from Bar-Yosef 1983).

Entity and Site	Nature of the Deposit	Tools per m^3
Natufian		
Erq-el-Ahmar Rock Shelter *	Silt	50
Hayonim Cave	Silt and building cobbles	94–167
Salibya I	Clay and Silt	476
Hayonim Terrace	Clay and colluvium	1,067
Rosh Horesha	Silt and colluvium	1,040
Eynan Ib	Clay and colluvium	2.055
Eynan IVa (floor)	Clay, some colluvium	1,342
Fazael IV	Clay and colluvium	2,022
Mushabian		
Mushabi XIV-1	Sand	97
Mushabi V	Sand	165
Geometric Kebaran		
Mushabi XIV-2	Sand	211
Lagama North VIII	Sand	180
Kebaran		
Fazael III-4	Clay	1,150
Fazael III-6	Clay	427
Fazael VII	Clay and fine gravel	390
Late Upper Paleolithic		
Fazael IX	Clay and colluvium	760
Fazael X	Clay and colluvium	867

* This site was not sieved as carefully as all the other samples. The tools often represent 2–6% of the total assemblage and, in spite of the effects of curation, are taken to indicate the average densities per site.

The danger in interpreting such sites is that the arbitrary levels of the excavations, either horizontal or slanted with what could have been the original dip (5 or 10 cm thick), become the equivalent of "floors."

Floors of packed earth can be recognized in thin sections when not observable by the naked eye. Calculating a table of densities per volume of units (such as the arbitrary 5 cm thick of each 1/4 square

Table 2. Tool Densities at Selected Sites in Gebel Maghara (from Bar-Yosef and Goren 1980).

Industry	Site	Tools per m^2		area m^2
		Excavated Sampled	Surface-collected	
	Lagama VII	31.76		26
	Lagama VI		3.85	20
	Lagama XV	17.21		7.5
	Lagama XV		2.68	61.5
Lagaman	Lagama XVI	13.9		5.75
(Upper	Lagama V		3.05	106
Paleolithic)	Lagama VI		1.00	16
	Lagama XI		2.91	36
	Lagama XII		2.31	66
	Lagama XIII		0.85	60
Other Upper	Lagama X		11.75	56
Paleolithic	Lagama III D		4.00	117
	Mushabi XIV:2	28.7		7
	Mushabi XVIII	20.0		1.5
Geometric	Lagama No. VIII	15.8		80
Kebaran	Mushabi XVII	15.9		3
	Lagama I F		4.1	24
	Lagama No. IV		3.1	19
	Lagama I C		1.3	100
	Mushabi V	23.8		36.5
	Mushabi V		4.7	30
Mushabian	Mushabi I		17.8	170
	Mushabi XIV:1	9.7		28
	Mushabi XIV		2.6	96
	Mushabi XIX		3.0	214
	Mushabi XX		3.6	128
Harifian	Mushabi III		2.4	158
	Lagama IV		2.1	100
	Mushabi XV		1.8	84

meter) can be illuminating. Higher densities would possibly mark the position of already obliterated floors. But without some refitting experiments such a proposition should be kept as a working hypothesis and not as established observation. The situation is sometimes facilitated, even if the site does not contain the remains of dwelling structures, by the presence of built fireplaces, post holes and dug-out graves.

Everyone who has experienced digging in a site embedded in terra rossa knows fairly well how difficult it is to identify prehistoric floors. In these situations as well, the preservation of plant remains is rather poor and carbonized material moves up and down, as exemplified by the dates of the seeds from Nahal Oren (Legge 1986) or the Terrace of Hayonim (Hedges et al. 1992). One may wonder to what extent other artifacts, especially microliths, penetrate into lower levels. Therefore, when poorly preserved, most Upper Paleolithic and Epi-Paleolithic sites exhibit minimal modifications by humans.

Sandy and silty deposits sometimes provide better preservation. One example is the dug-out shallow hut foundations at the Kebaran sites of Ein Gev I and III, on the east side of Lake Kinneret (e.g., Arensburg and Bar-Yosef 1973; Martin and Bar-Yosef 1978). The observations made in the 1970's are currently supported by Ohalo II, a newly uncovered 19,000 year-old water-logged site, in the receding Lake Kinneret (Nadel and Hershkovitz 1991). In the Ein Gev sites, which are buried in reworked calcareous Miocene sand, the combination of deflation and low energy erosion, coupled with seasonal abandonment, created a series of "floors" and layers with varying densities of artifacts intercalated with semi-sterile layers. We proposed to see the Ein Gev I and III as huts, where the walls of the dwelling from the subterranean shallow oval pit, 5-7 meters in diameter, were erected with branches and hides. In the site of Ohalo II, straight brushes and bundles of reeds were identified in the lower part of the semi-subterranean foundations (Nadel 1991), indicating that the proposed reconstruction was not far from reality.

Complicated situations of digging, building, refilling, erosion, and colluviation were encountered in Natufian and Early Neolithic sites. The most intriguing examples are the terrace sites (e.g., Nahal Oren, El-Khiam) and others on more moderate slopes such as Eynan (Ain Mallaha). The high densities of lithics in the Natufian sites differ from the later Early Neolithic mounds (Jericho, Netiv Hagdud, Gilgal). These were the results of different human contributions bringing in different building materials. The Natufians built with undressed stones, employed some type of a "plaster," perhaps mud mixed with burned and pounded limestone (Kingery et al. 1988;

Bar-Yosef 1991). The superstructure was probably made of organic materials such as brushes, reeds, straw and perhaps even hides. The Early Neolithic farming communities, whose remains are buried in mounds, used mud as building substance either by shaping bricks (such as the famous plano-convex bricks in Jericho) or by building in the wattle and daub method. In addition, these communities did a lot of roasting, which left behind large amounts of fire-cracked rocks. The combination of such rocks and the deteriorated mud walls created a volume of sediments which resulted in low densities of chipped stone industry (Table 1). Fire-cracked rocks are also found in Natufian sites, but, without the large volume of mud (or mudbricks), they hardly influence the relative lithic densities.

On the whole, Early Neolithic sites exhibit almost the same variety of site formation processes as historical mounds (Miller Rosen 1986; Courty et al. 1989). Large volumes of each site were created by the stones brought in for building walls and fireplaces, clays for mud-brick manufacture, and wood and brush for building, cooking, wood working and basketry. The obvious result is the decrease in lithic densities per cubic meter. Important phenomena are the use and re-use of wood and dead wood (often expressed in aberrant ^{14}C dates), the mixing of the lithics on-site and the mixing with brought-in lithics (included in the clays), the dumping of organic residues in open spaces or as filling of pits, etc.

Final Remarks

In sum, in order to achieve a better understanding of prehistoric contexts that eventually will lead to improved behavioral interpretations, we need to invest considerably more effort toward deciphering the intricacies of taphonomic processes. It would be more insightful if we dedicated extensive energy to the excavation of well-preserved sites even if they were rare, far apart, and difficult to find. Well-conserved hearths, distributions of charcoal and carbonized plant remains, preserved animal bones, lithics in mint condition and hopefully other features such as pits and burials, will provide information concerning many aspects of human behavior. In addition, buildings with floors and collapsed roofs, wooden structures and wooden objects will facilitate the interpretation of early village sites. Such operations cannot be achieved without the constant cooperation of researchers with various interests such as geoarchaeologists, faunal analysts, and paleoethnobotanists, during field work. Daily group discussions in the course of the excavation, while mineralogical and micromorphological research is routinely done will enable rapid exchange of information and the immediate testing of partial interpretations of field observations.

It is very clear to anyone who is interested in the subject that there is no recipe book that will give all the answers concerning site formation processes. The more we are aware of the intricacies of these processes, the better the methods for deciphering them will be. The process of learning can often be agonizing. We sometimes have to abandon cherished notions and observations made by esteemed colleagues or mentors, and accept interpretations offered by past generations of archaeologists solely on the basis of common sense. It seems, today, that macro-natural processes are generally better understood than in the past. However, the results of human activities and the interplay between humans and the micro-size biological agents as well as diagenic processes are far from being well known. Unfortunately, the set of techniques such as micromorphology, mineralogical analysis, phytolith analysis and others are not yet adopted in every field project. Undoubtedly this is due to limited funds and the number of investigators who are full-time practitioners of these techniques. Archaeologists are therefore required to make operational decisions while being aware that missing sets of information will hamper the behavioral interpretations of the excavated sites.

Acknowledgments

This paper is based on my cumulative experience as a field archaeologist since 1959. The text has benefited from comments on earlier drafts by P. Goldberg, M. Petraglia, D. Nash, and J. D. Speth. Through the years, I had the pleasure of working with numerous specialists, but my long-standing cooperation with Baruch Arensburg (Sackler School of Medicine, Tel Aviv University), Paul Goldberg (Austin, Texas), Henri Laville (CNRS-University of Bordeaux I) and Eitan Tchernov (Institute of Life Sciences, Hebrew University) was most influential. I am grateful to Stephen Weiner (Department of Structural Biology, Weizmann Institute of Science), who met the challenge of unanswered questions concerning site formation processes in Kebara cave, and who, by joining us, added an important technique which enabled us to test certain hypotheses. However, I am solely responsible for the way in which observations and ideas are expressed in this paper.

References Cited

Andrews, P.
  1990 *Owls, Caves and Fossils*. Natural History Museum Publications: London.
Arensburg, G., and O. Bar-Yosef
  1973 Human Remains from Ein Gev I, Jordan Valley, Israel. *Paléorient* 1:201-206.
Avigad, N.
  1981 Jerusalem - "The City Full of People". In *Recent Archaeology in the Land of Israel*, edited by H. Shenks and B. Mazar, pp.129-140. Biblical Archaeological Society: Washington and Israel Exploration Society: Jerusalem.
Bar-Yosef, O.
  1983 The Natufian of the Southern Levant. In *The Hilly Flanks and Beyond: Essays on the Prehistory of Southwestern Asia*, edited by C. T. Young, P. E. L. Smith and P. Mortensen, pp. 11-42. University of Chicago Press, Chicago.
  1987 Pleistocene Connections Between Africa and Southwest Asia: An Archaeological Perspective. *The African Archaeological Review* 5:29-38.
  1989 The Excavations at 'Ubeidiya in Retrospect: An Eclectic View. In *Investigations in South Levantine Prehistory*, edited by O. Bar-Yosef and B. Vandermeersch, pp. 101-111. BAR International Series, 497, Oxford.
  1991 Stone Tools and Social Context in Levantine Prehistory. In *Paradigmatic Biases in Mediterranean Hunter-Gatherer Research*, edited by G. A. Clark, pp. 371-395. University of Pennsylvania Press, Philadelphia.
Bar-Yosef, O., and A. Belfer
  1977 The Lagaman Industry. In *Prehistoric Investigations in Gebel Maghara, Northern Sinai*, edited by O. Bar-Yosef and J. L. Phillips, pp. 42-84. Institute of Archaeology, Hebrew University, Jerusalem.
Bar-Yosef, O., and N. Goren
  1973 Natufian Remains in Hayonim Cave. *Paléorient* 1 (1):49-68.
  1980 Afterthought Following Prehistoric Surveys in the Levant. *Israel Exploration Journal* 30:1-16.

Bar-Yosef, O., and N. Goren-Inbar
   1993 *The Lithic Assemblages of 'Ubeidiya: A Lower Paleolithic Site in the Jordan Valley.* "Qedem" -
      Monographs of the Institute of Archaeology Vol. 34. The Hebrew University of Jerusalem,
      Jerusalem.
Bar-Yosef, O., and J. L. Phillips (eds)
   1977 *Prehistoric Investigations in Gebel Maghara, Northern Sinai.* Institute of Archaeology, Hebrew
      University, Jerusalem.
Bar-Yosef, O., and E. Tchernov
   1972 *On the Paleo-ecological History of the Site of 'Ubeidiya.* The Pleistocene of the Central Jordan Valley
      Israel Academy of Sciences and Humanities, Jerusalem.
Bar-Yosef, O. and B. Vandermeersch
   1981 Notes Concerning the Possible Age of the Mousterian Layers at Qafzeh Cave. In *Préhistoire du
      Levant,* edited by J. Cauvin and P. Sanlaville, pp. 555-569. Editions CNRS, Paris.
Bar-Yosef O., B. Vandermeersch, B. Arensburg, A. Belfer-Cohen, P. Goldberg, H. Laville, L. Meignen,
Y.Rak, J.D. Speth, E. Tchernov, A-M. Tillier, and S. Weiner
   1992 The Excavations in Kebara Cave, Mt. Carmel. *Current Anthropology* 33:497-550.
Belfer-Cohen, A.
   1988 The Natufian Graveyard in Hayonim Cave. *Paléorient* 14 (2):297-308.
Belfer-Cohen, A., and O. Bar-Yosef
   1981 The Aurignacian at Hayonim Cave. *Paléorient* 7:19-42.
Bergman, C.A.
   1987 *Ksar Akil, Lebanon: A Technological and Typological Analysis of the Later Paleolithic Levels of Ksar Akil.
      Vol. II: Levels XII-VI.* BAR International Series, 329, Oxford.
Binford, L.R.
   1981a *Bones: Ancient Men and Modern Myths.* Academic Press, New York.
   1981b Behavioral Archaeology and the "Pompeii Premise." *Journal of Anthropological Research* 37:195-
      208.
   1987 Searching for Camps and Missing the Evidence? Another Look at the Lower Paleolithic. In *The
      Pleistocene Old World: Regional Perspectives* edited by O. Soffer, pp. 17-31. Plenum Press: New York.
Binford, L.R., and S.R. Binford
   1966 A Preliminary Analysis of Functional Variability in the Mousterian of Levallois Facies. *American
      Anthropologist* 68:238-295.
Blumenschine, R.
   1987 Characteristics of an Early Hominid Scavenging Niche. *Current Anthropology* 28:383-94.
   1988 An Experimental Model of the Timing of the Hominid and Carnivore Influence on
      Archaeological Bone Assemblages. *Journal of Archaeological Science* 15:483-502.
   1989 A Landscape Taphonomic Model of the Scale of Prehistoric Scavenging Opportunities. *Journal of
      Human Evolution* 18:345-71.
Bordes, F.
   1980 Question de Contemporanéité: L'illusion des Remontages. *Bulletin de la Société Préhistorique
      Française* 77 (5):132-133.
Brain, C.K.
   1981 *The Hunters or the Hunted? An Introduction to African Cave Taphonomy.* University of Chicago
      Press, Chicago.
Butzer, K.W.
   1982 *Archaeology as Human Ecology: Method and Theory for Contextual Approach.* Cambridge University
      Press, Cambridge.
Cahen D.
   1984 Interprétations nouvelles pour le site paléolithique final de Meer II, Belgique. In *Upper Paleolithic
      Settlement Patterns in Europe,* edited by H. Berke, J. Hahn and C.J. Kind, pp. 241-250. Verlag
      Archaeologica Venatoria, Institut für Urgeschischte der Universität Tubingen.
Cahen, D., L.H. Keeley, and F.L. Van Noten
   1979 Stone Tools, Toolkits and Human Behavior in Prehistory. *Current Anthropology* 20:661-683.
Cahen, D., and J. Moeyersons
   1977 Subsurface Movements of Stone Artifacts and Their Implications for the Prehistory of Central
      Africa. *Nature* 266 (5605):812-815.

Clark, D.
  1967 The Middle Acheulian Occupation Site at Latamne, Northern Syria (first paper). *Quaternaria* 9:1-68.
  1969 The Middle Acheulian Occupation Site at Latamne (second paper). *Quaternaria* 10:1-76.
Courty, M.A., P. Goldberg, and R. Macphail
  1989 *Soils and Micromorphology in Archaeology.* Cambridge University Press, Cambridge.
Cruze-Uribe, K.
  1991 Distinguishing hyena from hominid bone accumulations. *Journal of Field Archaeology* 18 (4):467-486.
Cziesla E., S. Eickhoff, M. Arts, and D. Winter,
  1990 *The Big Puzzle, International Symposium of Refitting Stone Artifacts.* Studies in Modern Archaeology, Holos, Bonn.
Danin, A.
  1985 Paleoclimates in Israel: Evidence from Weathering Patterns of Stones In and Near Archaeological Sites. *Bulletin of the American Schools for Oriental Research* 259:33-43.
Endo, K.
  1978 Stratigraphy and Paleoenvironments in the Deposits in and Around the Douara Cave Site. *Bulletin of the University Museum, The University of Tokyo* 14:53-81.
Farrand, W.R.
  1979 Chronology and Paleoenvironment of Levantine Prehistoric Sites as Seen from Sediment Studies. *Journal of Archaeological Science* 6:369-392.
Flenniken, J.J., and J.K.C. Haggarty
  1979 Trampling as an Agency in the Formation of Edge Damage: An Experiment in Lithic Technology. *Northwest Anthropological Research Notes* 13:208-214.
Garrod, D.A.E., and D.M. Bate
  1937 *The Stone Age of Mount Carmel.* Vol. Vol. I. Clarendon Press, Oxford.
  1942 Excavations at the Cave of Shukbah, Palestine. *Proceedings of the Prehistoric Society* 8:1-20.
Gifford-Gonzales, D.
  1989 Ethnographic Analogues for Interpreting Modified Bones: Some Cases from East Africa. In *Bone Modification,* edited by R. Bonnichsen and M. H. Sorg, pp. 179-246. Center for the Study of Early Man, Orono.
Gilead, I.
  1988 Le Site Moustérien de Fara II (Néguev septentrional, Israel) et le Remontage de son Industrie. *L'Anthropologie* 92:797-808.
Gilead, I., and C. Grigson
  1984 Farah II: A Middle Paleolithic Open Air Site in the Northern Negev, Israel. *Proceedings of the Prehistoric Society* 50:71-97.
Goldberg, P.
  1979 Micromorphology of Sediments from Hayonim Cave, Israel. *Catena* 6:167-181.
  1980 Micromorphology in Archaeology and Prehistory. *Paléorient* 6: 159-164.
  1986 Late Quarternary environmental history of the Southern Levant. *Geoarchaeology* 1:225-244.
Goldberg, P., and O. Bar-Yosef
  1990 The Effect of Man on Geomorphological Processes Based Upon Evidence from the Levant and Adjacent Areas. In *Man's Role in the Shaping of the Eastern Mediterranean Landscape,* edited by S. Bottema, G. Entjes-Nieborg and W. van Zeist, pp. 71-86. A.A. Balkema, Rotterdam and Brookfield.
Goldberg, P., and H. Laville
  1991 Etude géologique des dépôts de la grotte de Kébara (Mont Carmel): Campange 1982-1984. In *Le squelette Moustérien de Kébara 2,* edited by O. Bar-Yosef and B. Vandermeersch, pp. Editions C.N.R.S. (Cahiers de Paléoanthropologie), Paris.
Goren-Inbar, N.
  1990 *Quneitra: A Mousterian Site on the Golan Heights.* QEDEM, Monographs of the Institute of Archaeology, Hebrew University, Jerusalem.
Goring-Morris A. N.
  1987 *At the Edge: Terminal Hunter-Gatherers in the Negev and Sinai.* BAR International Series 361, Oxford.

1988 Trends in the Spatial Organization of Terminal Pleistocene Hunter-Gatherer Occupations as viewed from the Negev and Sinai. *Paléorient* 14/2:231-244.

Grün, R. and C.B. Stringer

1991 Electron Spin Resonance Dating and the Evolution of Modern Humans. *Archaeometry* 33 (2):153-199.

Hassan, F.A.

1979 Geoarchaeology: The geologist and Archaeology. *American Antiquity* 44:267-270.

Hooijer, D.A.

1961 The Fossil Vertebrates of Ksar 'Akil, a Paleolithic Rock Shelter in Lebanon. *Zoologische Verhandelingen* 49. E. J. Brill, Leiden.

Isaac, G.L.

1967 Towards the Interpretation of Occupation Debris: Some Experiments and Observations. *Kroeber Anthropological Society Papers* 37:31-57.

1984 The Archaeology of Human Origins: Studies of the Lower Pleistocene in East Africa 1971-1981. In *Advances in World Archaeology*, edited by F. Wendorf and A. Close, pp. 1-87. Academic Press, New York.

1986 Foundation Stones: Early Artifacts as Indicators of Activities and Abilities. In *Stone Age Prehistory*, edited by G.N. Bailey and P. Callow, pp. 221-241. Cambridge University Press, Cambridge.

Jelinek, A.J.

1981 The Middle Paleolithic in the Southern Levant from the Perspective of the Tabun Cave. In *Préhistoire du Levant*, edited by J. Cauvin and P. Sanlaville, pp. 265-280. Editions C.N.R.S., Paris.

1982 The Tabun Cave and Paleolithic Man in the Levant. *Science* 216:1369-1375.

Jelinek, A.J., W.R. Farrand, G. Haas, Horowitz, A., and P. Goldberg

1973 New Excavations at the Tabun Cave, Mount Carmel, Israel, 1967-1972; A Preliminary Report. *Paléorient* 1 (2):151-183.

Kersten, A.M.P.

1991 Birds from the Paleolithic Rock Shelter of Ksar 'Akil, Lebanon. *Paléorient* 17:99-116.

Kingery, W.D., R. Vandiver, and M. Prickett

1988 The Production and the Use of Lime Plaster and Gypsum Plaster in the Pre-Pottery Neolithic of the Near East. *Journal of Field Archaeology* 15: 219-244.

Kramer, C.

1982 *Village Ethnoarchaeology.* Academic Press, New York.

Laville, H. and P. Goldberg

1989 The Collapse of the Mousterian Sedimentary Regime and the Beginning of the Upper Paleolithic at Kebara. In *Investigations in South Levantine Prehistory*, edited by O. Bar-Yosef and B. Vandermeersch, pp. 75-95. BAR International Series, 497, Oxford.

Laville, H., J.-P. Rigaud, and J. Sackett

1980 *Rockshelters of the Périgord.* Academic Press, New York.

Leakey, M.D.

1971 *Olduvai Gorge*, Vol. 3, Excavations in Beds I and II, 1960-1963. Cambridge University Press, Cambridge.

Legge, A.J.

1986 Seeds of Discontent: Accelerator Dates on Some Charred Plant Remains from the Kebaran and Natufian Cultures. In *Archaeological Results from Accelerator Dating*, edited by J.A.J. Gowlett and R.E.M. Hedges, pp. 13-22. Oxford University Committee for Archaeology, Oxford.

Leroi-Gourhan, A., and M. Brézillon

1966 L'habitation Magdalénienne no. 1 de Pincevent Près Montereau (Seine-et-Marne). *Gallia Préhistoire* 9 (2):263-385.

1972 *Fouilles de Pincevent: Essai d'Analyse ethnographique d'un habitat Magadalénien.* Supplement à "Gallia Préhistoire" Vol. VIIe. Editions du CNRS, Paris.

MacCurdy, G.G.

1924 *Human Origins, A Manual of Prehistory.* Appeleton and Company, New York.

Marks, A.
  1983 *Prehistory and Paleoenvironments in the Central Negev, Israel. Vol. 3: The Avdat/Aqev Area (Part 3).* Southern Methodist University Press, Dallas.
Martin, G., and O. Bar-Yosef
  1978 Ein Gev III, Israel. *Paléorient* 5:219-220.
Miller Rosen, A.
  1986 *Cities of Clay: The Geoarchaeology of Tells.* The University of Chicago Press, Chicago.
  1989 Ancient Town and City Sites: A View from the Microscope. *American Antiquity* 54 (3):564-578.
Nadel, D.
  1991 Ohalo II - the third Season (1991). *Journal of the Israel Prehistoric Society (Mitekefat Haeven)* 24:158-163.York.
Nadel, D., and I. Hershkovitz
  1991 Ohalo II - A Water Logged Early Epipaleolithic Site in the Jordan Valley, Israel. *Current Anthropology* 32 (5):631-635.
Ohnuma, K.
  1988 *Ksar Akil, Lebanon: A Technological Study of the Earlier Upper Paleolithic Levels at Ksar Akil: Vol. III: Levels XXV-XIV.* BAR International Series, 426, Oxford.
Olami, J.
  1962 Grotte du Sheikh Suleiman (Ornith) Mont Carmel - Israel. In *ATTI Del VI Congresso Internationale delle Scienze Preistoriche E Protostoriche,* Rome.
Petraglia, M. D., and D. T. Nash
  1987 The Impact of Fluvial Processes on Experimental Sites. In *Natural Formation Processes and the Archaeological Record,* edited by D.T. Nash and M.D. Petraglia., pp. 108-130. BAR International Series, 352, Oxford.
Phillips, J. L.
  1988 The Upper Paleolithic of the Wadi Feiran, Southern Sinai. *Paléorient* 14 (2):183-200.
Potts, R.
  1988 *Early Hominid Activities at Olduvai.* Aldine de Gruyter, New York.
Roe, D.
  1983 *Adlun in the Stone Age.* BAR International Series, 159, Oxford.
Ronen, A.
  1991 The Lower Paleolithic Site Evron-Quarry in Western Galilee, Israel. In *Festschrift Karl Brunnacker,* pp. 187-212. Geologisches Institut der Universität zu Köln, Köln.
Ronen, A., and M.Y. Ohel
  1980 Acheulean Artifacts from Two Trenches at Ma'ayan Barukh. *Israel Exploration Journal* 30:17-33.
Sanlaville, P.
  1979 Quaternaire et Préhistoire du Nahr el Kébir Septentrional. In *Collection de La Maison de L'Orient Méditerranéen,* Editions de CNRS. Paris.
Schick, K.D.
  1987 Modeling the Formation of Early Stone Age Artifact Concentrations. *Journal of Human Evolution* 16:789-807.
Schiffer, M.B.
  1976 *Behavioral Archaeology.* Academic Press, London.
Seedan, H.
  1982 Ethnoarchaeological Reconstruction of Halafian Occupational Units in Shams ed-Din Tannira. *Berytus* 30:55-96.
Seedan H., and J. Wilson
  1988 Processes of Site Formation in Villages of the Syrian Gazira. *Berytus* 36:169-188.
Sept, J.M.
  1992 Was There No Place Like Home? A New Perspective on Early Hominid Archaeological Sites from the Mapping of Chimpanzee Nests. *Current Anthropology* 33:187-208.
Skinner, J. D., S. Davis, and G. Ilani
  1980 Bone Collecting by Striped Hyaenas, *Hyeana hyaena,* in Israel. *Paleontologica Africana* 23:99-104.
Sollas, W.J.
  1915 *Ancient Hunters and their Modern Representatives.* Macmillan and Co, London.

Stekelis, M. and D. Gilead
  1966 *Ma'ayan Barukh, A Lower Paleolithic Site in the Upper Galilee.* Mitequfat Ha'even VIII Israel Prehistoric Society, Jerusalem.
Stekelis, M., O. Bar-Yosef, and T. Schick
  1969 *Archaeological Excavations at 'Ubeidiya, 1964-1966.* The Israel Academy of Sciences and Humanities, Jerusalem.
Stevens, D.S., and H.J. Hietala
  1977 Spatial Analysis: Multiple Procedures in Pattern Recognition. *American Antiquity* 42:539-559.
Stiner, M.
  1991 The Faunal Remains from Grotta Guattari: A Taphonomic Perspective. *Current Anthropology* 32:103-117.
Tappan, M.
  1992 *Taphonomy of a Central African Savanna: Natural Bone Deposition in Parc National des Virunga, Zaïre.* Unpublished Ph.D. dissertation, Harvard University, Cambridge, Massachusetts.
Tchernov, E.
  1968 *Succession of Rodent Faunas during the Upper Pleistocene of Israel.* Mammalia Depicta, Hamburg and Berlin.
  1984 Commensal Animals and Human Sedentism in the Middle East. In *Animals and Archaeology,* edited by J. Clutton-Brock and C. Grigson, pp. 91-105. BAR International Series 202, Oxford.
Tchernov, E. (ed.)
  1986 *Les Mammiferes du Pléistocene Inférieur de la Vallée du Jurdain à Oubeidiyeh.* Mémoires et Travaux du Centre de Recherche Français de Jérusalem Association Paléorient, Paris.
  1988 Biochronology of the Middle Paleolithic and Dispersal Events of Hominids in the Levant. In *L'Homme de Néandertal,* edited by M. Otte, pp. 153-168. Etudes et Recherches Archéologiques de l'Université de Liège 34, Liège.
Tixier, J.
  1976 *Le Campement Préhistorique de Bordj Mellala, Ourgla, Algérie.* Editions du Cercle de Recherches et d'Etudes Préhistoriques, Paris.
Toth, N.
  1987 Behavioral Inferences from Early Stone Artifact Assemblages: An Experimental Model. *Journal of Human Evolution* 16:763-787.
Valladas, H., J.L. Joron, G. Valladas, B. Arensburg, O. Bar-Yosef, A. Belfer-Cohen, P. Goldberg, H. Laville, L. Meignen, Y. Rak, E. Tchernov, A.M. Tillier, and B. Vandermeersch
  1987 Thermoluminescence Dates for the Neanderthal Burial Site at Kebara in Israel. *Nature* 330:159-160.
Vandermeersch, B.
  1981 *Les Hommes Fossiles de Qafzeh (Israël).* Editions CNRS.
Villa, P.
  1991 From Debitage Chips to Social Models of Production: The Refitting Method of Old World Archaeology. *The Review of Archaeology* 12 (2):24-30.
Watson, P.J.
  1979 *Archaeological Ethnography in Western Iran.* University of Arizona Press, Tucson: Arizona.
Weiner, S., and O. Bar-Yosef
  1990 States of Preservation of Bones from Prehistoric Sites in the Near East: A Survey. *Journal of Archaeological Science* 17:187-196.
Weiner, S., and P. Goldberg
  1990 On-Site Fourier Transform-Infrared Spectrometry at an Archaeological Excavation. *Spectroscopy* 5:46-50.
Weiner S., P. Goldberg, and O. Bar-Yosef
  in press Bone Preservation in Kebara Cave, Israel: An On-Site Fourier Transform Infrared Spectrometry Study. *Journal of Archaeological Science.*
Wynn, T.
  1981 The Intelligence of Oldowan Hominids. *Journal of Human Evolution* 10:529-41.
Wynn, T., and W.C. McGrew
  1989 An Ape's Eye-View of the Oldowan. *Man* 24:383-98.

3

Cultural and Natural Formation Processes in Late Quaternary Cave and Rockshelter Sites of Western Europe and the Near East

C. Michael Barton
Geoffrey A. Clark
Arizona State University

Caves and rockshelters have played a fundamental role in the demonstration of human antiquity and in the development of prehistoric archaeology. In the 20th Century, they have been important in the development of the cultural and paleoenvironmental sequences that constitute the organizational frameworks for the study of the residues of past human behavior (Daniel 1975; Straus 1979, 1990; Grayson 1983). Especially in the western European "heartland" of paleolithic archaeology, our knowledge of Pleistocene and early Holocene foragers comes largely from cave and rockshelter contexts, to the near exclusion of any other kinds of sites. This has had both good and bad consequences.

We have had the opportunity to "do" cave and rockshelter archaeology in a wide variety of geographic and geomorphological settings in the circum-Mediterranean Old World, spanning time ranges from the beginning of the Upper Pleistocene (ca. 130 kyr B.P.) to the mid-Holocene (ca. 5-6 kyr B.P.). We share briefly here some of the results of this experience. We begin with an overview of the geomorphology of caves and rockshelters in diverse environments and proceed to a discussion of some of the cultural site formation processes associated with the human use of these features of the prehistoric landscape.

Geomorphology and Cave Deposits

From a geological perspective, formation processes in caves and rockshelters are complex and somewhat resistant to generalization (Butzer 1964a: 197-208). What archaeologists call caves and rockshelters represent a wide range of depositional and erosional processes and environments, fully comparable to the geomorphological diversity found in fluvial, lacustrine or glacial deposits (Farrand 1985; Laville et al. 1980:45-73; Straus 1990). Although, from the standpoint of prehistory, rockshelters and the occupiable parts of caves may persist as dynamic features of the landscape for significant, although variable, spans of time, they tend to be short-term phenomena from a geological perspective (Clark 1979, 1983). This is because most such features are in a state of disequilibrium with the geomorphological environment in which they are found.

True caves are formed subareally, primarily through the dissolution of (usually) calcareous bedrock by the action of groundwater as it infiltrates fissures and crevices in the rock. Once a solution cavity has formed and become more or less stabilized (a condition dependent upon the temporal scale of observation), the temperature and relative humidity of cave environments tend to vary little over long periods of time. Percolation through the rock is typically slow and more or less constant, and changes in flow rates tend to take place very gradually. Once opened to the surface through erosion and/or collapse, caves become subject to external environmental conditions quite distinct from those of their formation, including much greater fluctuations in temperature, humidity, and in the quantity and flow rate of surface water. The effects of such episodic changes in the moisture and temperature regimes include roof spalling and collapse, erosion or transport of floor sediments, and the addition of fluvial, colluvial and aeolian sediments from external sources. The end result is often the disappearance of one or several cave entrances through collapse, infilling, or a combination of both.

Rockshelters, on the other hand, tend to result from differential erosion rates, mass wasting, or weathering over a restricted area (e.g., and especially, the formation of an overhang or cornice through differential erosion of relatively soft strata overlain by or interstratified with harder, more resistant ones). These processes can include stream scour at the base of cliffs or differential weathering of rock strata of varying hardness. Over a relatively long time, these differential rates of mass loss will tend to come into equilibrium, resulting in the eventual disappearance of the shelter. Major processes involved here include collapse of a series of retreating overhangs and infilling from fluvial, colluvial, and/or aeolian sources. Although usually of lesser consequence volumetrically, anthropogenic and biogenic contributions to the infilling of both caves and rockshelters are of considerable significance to archaeologists.

Because geomorphological equilibrium generally results in the infilling of these cavities, both caves and rockshelters tend to experience overall aggradational environments. Also, these features often generate their own clastic material (e.g., from roof spall or collapse, carbonate precipitation, or fluvial transport of fine sediments from inside caves) in addition to serving as traps for sediments from external sources. Hence, deposits tend to be a mixture of externally and internally derived sediments.

Finally, the permanent presence of water in heavily karstified terrain (e.g., northern Spain), as well as the springs and streams commonly associated with rockshelters, means that deposits are often strongly altered chemically. This alteration can include eluviation/illuviation of clays and fine clastics, chemical leaching (i.e.,"corrosion") and other forms of *in situ* alteration of minerals, and mineral precipitation. Regularly waterlogged sediments are more susceptible to plastic deformation (e.g., from cryoturbation) and structural collapse (e.g., debris flows).

Archaeologists often seem to assume that, with the exception of block falls and clearly-identifiable episodes of roof collapse, aggradation will be gradual and relatively constant in caves and rockshelters; any other catastrophic alterations of deposits are felt to be erosional in nature. However, on the basis of detailed reanalyses of caves and rockshelters in France and England, Simon Colcutt (personal communication, 1984) suggests that a considerable amount of deposition in rockshelters is episodic and catastrophic in nature, resulting from such processes as slope collapse of mouth cones and mud flows.

Examples of Cave and Rockshelter Depositional Environments

Caves and rockshelters at which we have worked serve to illustrate the diversity of processes responsible for deposits that archaeologists encounter in these features. We emphasize that it is unwise to treat caves and rockshelters as a monolithic class of geomorphic features in which a limited suite of depositional processes are consistently represented. Nevertheless, we believe that cave and rockshelter depositional environments admit to some generalization. Our examples are drawn from opposite ends of the Mediterranean Basin (the Iberian Peninsula, the Levant) and from a variety of environmental settings, including humid karst topography, the Mediterranean coast, upland Mediterranean forest, and semi-arid steppe.

Karstic Systems

La Riera

La Riera cave is located in the town of Posada de Llanes, in the Principality of Asturias, on the north-central Spanish coast (Figure 1). It is a small solution cavity which is part of an extensive karstic system formed in the Lower Carboniferous limestone of the Llera ridge. The cave lies at an elevation of ca. 30 m above present sea level (Figure 2). A steep talus slope descends about 5 m from the cave mouth to the course of the Río Calabres, a small stream that disappears into the Llera ridge about 250 m west of La Riera. At present, the Calabres flows within 40 m of the cave, but during times of protracted, heavy rainfall, it can back up due to partial blockage of its karstic passage, flooding the Posada valley and nearly flooding La Riera. The Río Calabres re-emerges at the Niembro estuary, 1.5 km northeast of La Riera. The present day shore of the Cantabrian Sea is about 1.75 km due

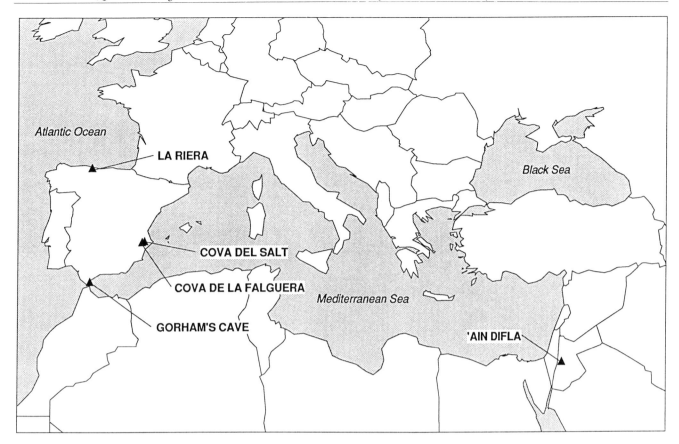

Figure 1. Map of the Mediterranean region, showing sites mentioned in text.

north of the cave. Karstic activity continues today, and the Llera ridge is riddled with a system of narrow galleries that extend over many kilometers.

Most of the archaeological deposits in the cave vestibule were excavated by the Conde de la Vega del Sella in 1917, leaving only restricted intact areas in the cave entrance. These were tested by Clark in 1969, and excavated by Straus and Clark in 1976-1979 (Straus and Clark 1986) (Figure 3). The 1976-1979 excavations revealed a rich and complex Upper and post-Paleolithic archaeological sequence extending in time from ca. 21 kyr B.P. until ca. 7 kyr B.P. (Figure 4). Sedimentological and palynological analyses indicate episodic and differential human use of the cave beginning in the cold, dry Tursac/Laugerie stadial phase, and extending throughout a succession of four additional cold and eight temperate, relatively humid episodes, before the cave was capped with a thick flowstone deposit late in the Boreal Period (Laville 1986; Leroi-Gourhan 1986).

The La Riera deposits present great petrographic, granulometric and morphological diversity due to two overriding characteristics of the cave. The cave was open to the exterior throughout much of its history, and thus was exposed to local climatic variations that affected its depositional environment. These

climatic variations are expressed differentially throughout the deposits as a result of their interaction with processes of sedimentation and alteration. The former include frost-weathering of the limestone roof and walls of the cave, producing *éboulis* of various sizes and shapes, as well as the deposition of colluvial and alluvial deposits from the cave exterior. Alteration processes include secondary fragmentation of limestone debris as they were spalled off or after deposition, cryoturbation of deposits, translocation of fine sediments, and chemical changes in the deposits.

The cave is also part of a vast karstic system, and was thus affected by at least some episodes of that system's reactivation. This had profound effects on both the sediments in the cave mouth and on their subsequent, physical alteration. In particular, the apparently frequent inundation of the cave, the partial removal of deposits by erosion and the leaching and brecciation of many sedimentary units can be attributed to the cave's role in this larger karstic system.

Over the 14,000 years of sporadic human use/occupation, the depositional environment at La Riera was aggradational overall, although interrupted on at least two occasions by erosional events and punctuated by episodes of accelerated frost-weathering, cryoturbation

Figure 2. Entrance to La Riera Cave, Posada de Llanes, Asturias, Spain.

and by the formation of congelifraction layers, and, on at least one occasion, by an apparent, low-energy inundation of the cave mouth, resulting in the deposition of a thick, distinctive yellow clay "marker bed" (Lev. 23/21, Figure 4).

Gorham's Cave

Gorham's Cave offers an example of a cave that experienced a different suite of depositional environments than did La Riera (Figure 1). Located at the southern tip of the Iberian peninsula, Gorham's is one of seven caves cut into the base of cliffs which form

the eastern face of the Rock of Gibraltar (Figures 5, 6). Formed by a combination of erosional, structural, and karstic processes, the cave extends more than 50 m into the rock. Its current floor is about 10 m above sea level, but when first noted by Major A. Gorham in 1907, it was filled with sand to a height of 17 m above sea level. At various times in its long history, springs or seeps have been present in the cave, as they are today (Barton 1987:35-54, 1988:17-30; Waechter 1951; 1964; Zeuner 1953).

Deposits in the inhabited mouth of Gorham's Cave exhibit an unusual variety of sediment sources and

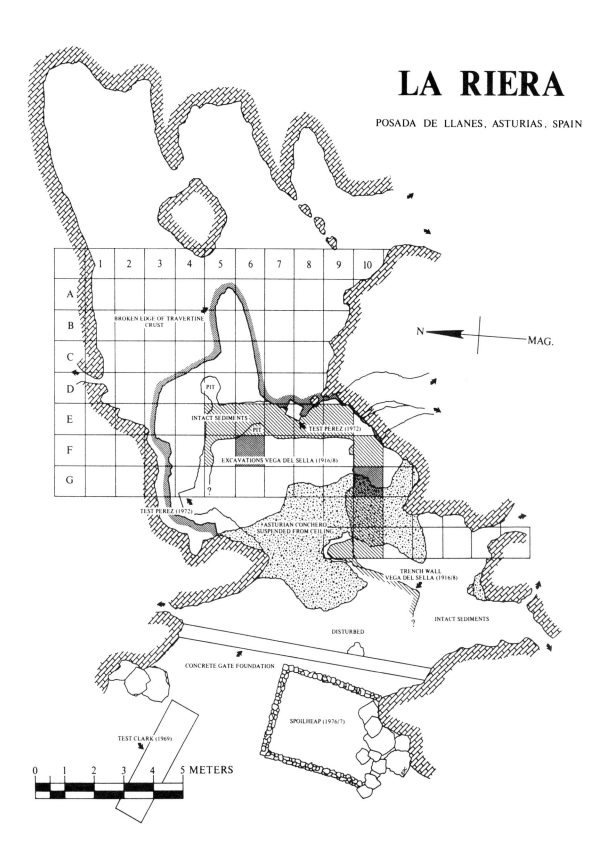

Figure 3. Plan of La Riera (after Straus and Clark 1986:10).

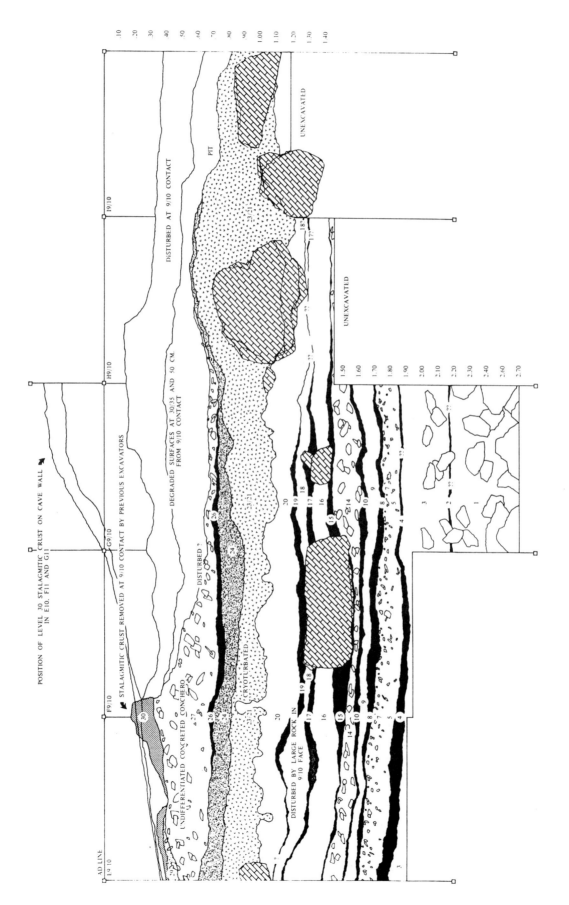

Figure 4. Profile from the 1976-1979 excavations at La Riera. Stratigraphic section at the 9/10 interface in Squares E-I. The arbitrary datum plane is indicated with vertical extent of strata shown on the right. Note cryoturbated Level 20/21 contact (after Straus and Clark 1986:32).

Figure 5. View through entrance to Gorham's Cave, Gibraltar, showing Mediterranean Sea (looking southeast).

transport mechanisms (Figure 7). These include wave-deposited sands and gravels from nearshore and onshore beach sources (often with large amounts of water-worn shell), wind-deposited beach and fore-shore sands, silts and clays from exterior (aeolian) and interior (water-laid) sources, carbonates precipitated from flowing water in the cave interior, and infrequent coarse clastics from roof spalling. Anthropogenic and especially biogenic deposits comprise an important part of the fill. These include

hyena droppings and biogenic carbonates derived in part from moss and algae growth when standing water was present for intervals in the cave (Goldberg and MacPhail 1991). The cave appears to have been scoured during the last maximum sea stand at ca. 120 kyr B.P. and wave erosion may have removed sediments at the entrance during subsequent transgressions. While the volume of sediment lost is unclear, it appears that the cave has not been completely emptied of its contents since the last inter-

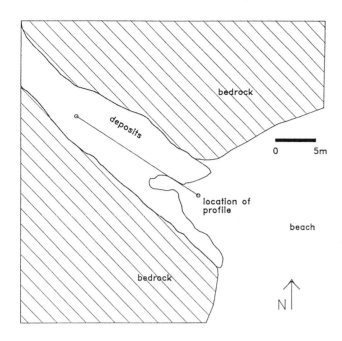

Figure 6. Plan of Gorham's Cave (after Barton 1988: Figure 2.1).

glacial. In addition to erosion, episodes of depositional stability are indicated by zones of carbonate and organic matter accumulation.

Archaeological deposits in Gorham's Cave attest to its episodic occupation by Middle and Upper Paleolithic humans at various times since the last interglacial. It is possible that it was also occupied earlier, but scouring during the last interglacial has removed any evidence of that.

In summary, the depositional environments at Gorham's Cave seem to have been generally aggradational throughout the Upper Pleistocene and Holocene. The overall rate of aggradation was slow (i.e., 8 m in ca. 120 kyr, or about .0067 cm/year), punctuated by episodes of erosion and stability.

Rockshelters

Cova del Salt

Cova del Salt is located about 2 km southwest of the city of Alcoi, in eastern Spain (Figure 1). Both a cave and a Middle Paleolithic archaeological site have formed within a very large rockshelter created by an extinct fall of the Río Barxell, which now flows a short distance to the southwest (Figure 8). Originally, the

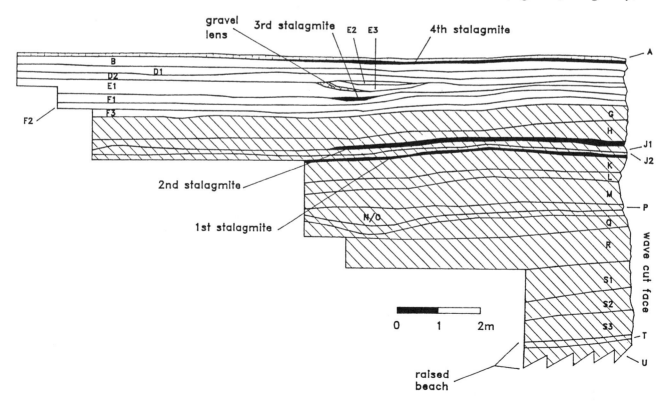

Figure 7. Stratigraphy of Gorham's Cave exposed by Waechter's 1948-1954 excavations (after Waechter 1964). See Barton (1988:21) for descriptions of deposits.

Figure 8. Cova del Salt, Alcoi, Alicante, Spain (looking west).

shelter was filled with a talus cone that reached at least to the elevation of the cave. The upper part of this accumulation was removed in this century to provide *abono* (rich, organic, garden soil) (Barton 1987:68-90, 1988:37-52; Villaverde 1984:280).

Cova del Salt reflects the potential diversity of rockshelter deposits (Figure 9). The angularity of the coarse gravels and blocks in the upper series indicates that they are largely a product of mass wasting (i.e., collapse of the shelter overhang). However, part of these deposits also may have been reworked by slumping and contain clastics that may derive from the Polop/Barxell valley above the shelter. The lower deposits are much finer, well sorted, and laminated, suggesting transport over considerable distance and deposition by water. An intervening bed consists of fine sediments trapped behind a large block and cemented by spring carbonates. It is likely that the site experienced considerable erosion between the deposition of the lower and upper series of sediments.

The lower series of deposits contain Middle Paleolithic artifacts assigned a late Early Glacial-early Pleniglacial age (i.e., oxygen isotope stages 5a-4) on the basis of geomorphic evidence (Barton 1987:80-86, 1988:40-48) and uranium series dating (Bischoff, personal communication, 1992). The upper series was probably deposited during the Pleniglacial. As it is unlikely that coarse gravel would make good *abono*, the uppermost sediments removed during terracing were probably similar in character to those of the lower series. Furthermore, because subrecent ceramics are embedded in the top of the coarse gravels, these lost sediments were probably Holocene in age and reflected present-day conditions of occasional, low-energy flows of water over the extinct falls.

Depositional environments have varied significantly, then, at Cova del Salt over the past 80,000 years. Early in the rockshelter's history, aggradation—possibly relatively slow—seems to have predominated. This was followed by a significant

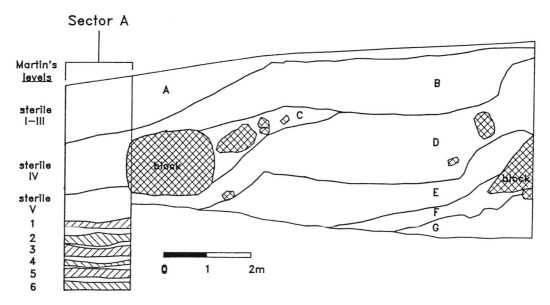

Figure 9. Profile of Cova del Salt deposits exposed by 1961 excavations (after Barton 1988:43). See Barton (1988:41-42) for descriptions of deposits.

erosional episode of unknown duration and extent. While the overall effect of Pleniglacial environments was aggradational in these western Mediterranean caves and shelters, aggradation was almost certainly episodic and interrupted by numerous erosional intervals.

Cova de la Falguera

Cova de la Falguera is located a few kilometers upstream from Salt in a montane *barranco*—the Barranc de Coves—in the Sierra Carrascola (Figure 1). It was formed by lateral stream erosion of the limestone cliffs of the *barranco* wall and is, therefore, a more "typical" rockshelter with respect to its origins (Figures 10, 11). Its 2.5 m stratigraphic section appears to be a mix of roof spall and coarse, subangular fluvial gravels (Barton et al. 1990; Domenech 1991; Rubio Gomís and Barton 1990). The sediments are almost certainly of local provenance as erosion of the upper reaches of the *barranco* is the most likely source for the fluvial gravels. Even the fine sediments were probably derived from further upslope on the Sierra Carrascola, the crestline of which is less than 2 km distant.

Immediately below the shelter, large blocks choke the *barranco*. Below these blocks, the *barranco* is deeply incised; other rockshelters cut into the *barranco* walls have been almost completely emptied of sediments. It is uncertain at present whether the blocks, by damming the *barranco*, caused Falguera (and the nearby shelter of Cova de la Figuera) to fill with sediments, or whether the blocks have simply protected the deposits from erosion. In any case, the fill of

Falguera is relatively recent. A radiocarbon determination from near the base of the deposits gave a date of 7,410 ± 70 B.P. (AA2295) and the top of the fill appears to be late Neolithic in age (i.e., ca. 5,500 B.P.) on the basis of ceramic evidence (Barton et al. 1990; Domenech 1991; Rubio Gomís and Barton 1990).

Falguera's deposits, then, appear to result from a brief (i.e., ca. 2 kyr) interval of aggradation in a generally erosional regime in the Barranc de Coves. Deposition greatly slowed or halted altogether following the Neolithic because stream entrenchment had reached the base of the blocks choking the *barranco* at the site, and because the sediments trapped behind the blocks had accumulated to their top. It is unlikely that further deposition will occur under present conditions. In fact, the deposits at Falguera may well be lost to erosion over the course of the next few millennia.

'Ain Difla

'Ain Difla comprises a small pocket of sediment preserved under a rockshelter located at ca. 780 m above sea level in the Wadi Ali, a southern tributary of the Wadi Hasa in west-central Jordan (Figure 1). The site is a remnant of a much larger rockshelter (Figure 12), the contents of which have mostly been removed by fluctuations in the course of the Wadi Ali, now located some 12 m below it. The rockshelter probably formed during the late Middle Pleistocene in a series of interbedded sandstones and limestones of Lower Cretaceous age. Originally (i.e., at some point in the early Upper Pleistocene), the site might have

Figure 10. Cova de la Falguera, Barranc de Coves, Alcoi, Alicante, Spain (looking north).

extended for as much as 150 m to the west of the preserved remnant, since the shelter itself extends at least that far. The site covers about 50 m². The talus deposits in front of the rockshelter are steeply sloped (ca. 30-35°). Due to a paucity of vegetation cover, erosional processes continue to act on the remaining sediments.

Excavations were conducted at 'Ain Difla in 1984, 1986 and 1992 (Lindly and Clark 1987; Clark et al. 1988, 1992). Although the natural stratigraphy is not particularly well-defined, 16 depositional units were identified provisionally in Trench A, which was divided into upslope and downslope steps, each 4 x 1 m in extent (Figure 13). Surface sediments in the upslope portion (Lev. 1) are 10-20 cm thick and consist of loose, grey and light brown, powdery fine silts and sandy silts. Lacking sedimentary structure, they have probably suffered postdepositional disturbance due to the activities of burrowing animals and sporadic use of the shelter overhang by shepherds. The block of sediments underlying the surface deposit ranges in thickness from 20 to 60 cm. These sediments are all of

colluvial origin and are more consolidated than those of Level 1. They appear to be *in situ*, roughly horizontal lenses (they follow the inclination of the slope), brecciated in places due to percolation and subsequent evaporation of lime-charged water. The brecciated pockets suggest paleoclimatic episodes substantially wetter than the present, since they do not form in the area today.

In the lower, downslope part of the trench, differences other than the degree of consolidation are not so clearly marked. At the base of the test is a clayey silt that is more reddish brown than the overlying sediments. A concentration of large roof-fall blocks about three-quarters of the way downslope probably represents a major collapse of a part of the shelter overhang.

Surficial deposits contained no temporal or cultural diagnostics of periods later than the Middle Paleolithic, thus indicating that the shelter was a concentrated locus of sporadic human activity only during some part of the long Levantine Middle Paleolithic time span (ca. 230-45 kyr B.P., Bar-Yosef et

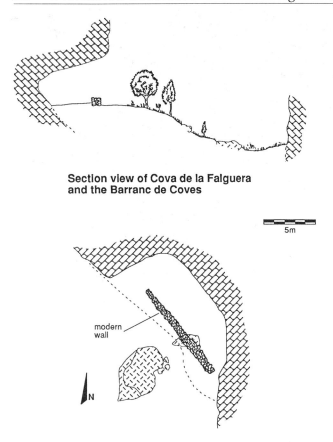

**Section view of Cova de la Falguera
and the Barranc de Coves**

5m

Plan View of Cova de la Falguera

Figure 11. Profile and plan views of Cova de la Falguera.

al. 1992). Since the site is under a cornice at one end of the shelter, it probably became filled with cultural and natural debris during the Middle Paleolithic and could no longer be used as a habitation or campsite during subsequent periods.

There is one TL date for 'Ain Difla — an Oxford determination on burnt flint from Level 5 (105 ± 15 kyr B.P.). However, the date is at variance with the 'Ain Difla pollen data. Although Levantine paleoenvironmental data are extremely "coarse-grained" relative to those of Europe, cool, relatively mesic paleoenvironments are suggested for the 127–90 kyr B.P. interval (Besançon and Sanlaville 1990; Besançon et al. 1990; Horowitz 1979). Pollen evidence from 'Ain Difla indicates that human use/occupation of the site coincided with a cool, *dry* interval, with an absence of trees and a chenopodia/artemesia-dominated NAP fraction that suggests a later date for the site (S. Fish, personal communication, 1989).

Artifact and faunal densities were relatively high throughout the deposits in the upslope exposure in Trench A. The downslope area showed a decrease in artifact densities in the lower levels, indicating either more concentrated human activity upslope, under the

(present) overhang, or, perhaps more likely, removal of downslope deposits by continuing lateral erosion of the talus deposits below the shelter by the Wadi Ali, which presently flows almost directly below 'Ain Difla. Bedrock was not exposed in any of the excavations, and it is estimated that 3-4 m of deposits remain intact under the present shelter.

Site contextual integrity is exceptionally high at 'Ain Difla, allowing for the reconstruction of 12 cores- an astonishing number in light of the very limited area tested. This suggests that the excavated deposits at 'Ain Difla represent a restricted period of occupation during the early Pleniglacial, followed by fairly rapid burial of cultural debris and minimal postdepositional disturbance. The infrequency of retouched pieces and the lack of edge damage also attests to a limited span of occupation, and minimal post-occupational surface exposure (Potter 1991). The implied rapidity of sediment accumulation is consistent with the primarily colluvial character of the deposits. On the other hand, the lack of sediments in the remainder of the shelter indicates the predominantly erosional character of the local geomorphological regimen after ca. 100,000 years ago.

Site Formation Processes in Caves and Rockshelters

Natural Site Formation Processes

One of the reasons that cave and rockshelter sites are often grouped together with respect to excavation methods and interpretations is because there is a general preconception that they share a number of characteristics with respect to formation processes. With regard to natural formation processes, these assumed similarities include a consistently aggradational depositional regime, a slow rate of deposition, and the protection of deposits (and their "cultural" contents) from erosion, weathering, or other forms of alteration.

The examples presented, however, indicate the great variety of depositional environments that can occur in these features. While the deep interiors of true (i.e., karstic) caves may be characterized by environments of slow, relatively continuous aggradation, the mouths of caves and rockshelters (i.e., those parts normally used by humans and thus of interest to archaeologists) tend to have much more complex and idiosyncratic depositional histories. As with any other geomorphic setting, rockshelters and inhabitable cave mouths variously experience deposition by wind, water, gravity, and chemical precipitation; alternating

Figure 12. 'Ain Difla (a). View of the rockshelter from a fragment of the 27m terrace preserved on the north wall of the wadi, above the site (looking southwest). (b). 'Ain Difla as seen from the 3 m terrace on the south bank of the wadi (looking north).

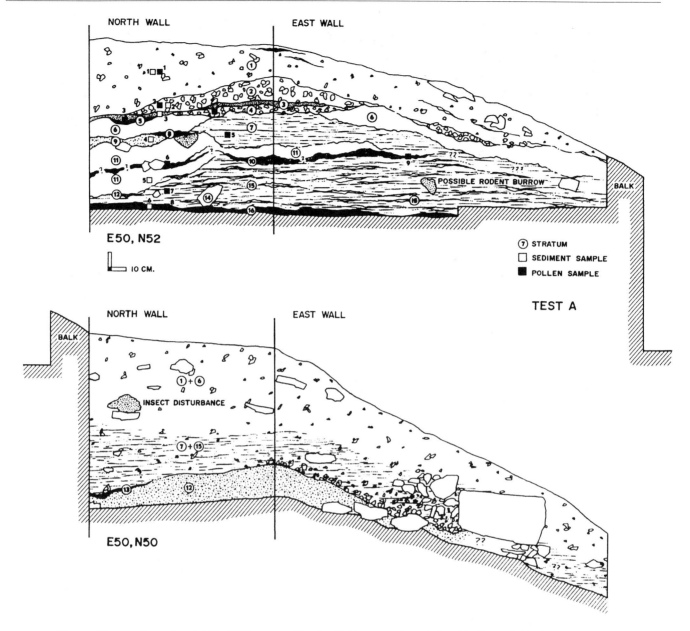

Figure 13. Stratigraphy at 'Ain Difla exposed in the 1984 excavations (after Lindly and Clark 1987:283).

episodes of erosion and deposition; and varying rates of deposition and erosion.

This makes it dangerous to generalize *across regions* about the long-term character of depositional processes in these features. A classic example is the wide-spread application of cryogenic models of clastic accumulation developed in southwestern France (e.g., Laville et al. 1980), but applied to caves and rockshelters in other, and quite different, climatic and geomorphic settings (see Butzer 1964b; Colcutt 1979; Petraglia 1987). The diversity of geomorphic processes affecting caves and rockshelters requires that each site be approached individually, and in much the same way that these processes are (or should be) treated at open sites. This is not to say that there are never depositional similarities among cave and rockshelter sites. Similar deposits result from parallel depositional histories, however, and not simply from the fact that the sites involved are caves or rockshelters.

As with cultural formation processes, discussed below, some biogenic and anthropogenic aspects of cave and rockshelter deposits permit a somewhat greater degree of generalization. For example, these solution cavities were, and continue to be, attractive to non-human animals for many of the same reasons that they have been attractive to humans (i.e., as a ready-made shelters). While not invariably occupied, carnivores especially often use caves and rockshelters for dens and lairs of various kinds and at various seasons of the year, for caches, and for nests (in the case of raptors, bats). The analysis of the remains of carnivore meals (bones, coprolites, raptor pellets, bat droppings) can lead to a better understanding of the biological component of cave and rockshelter deposits (Binford 1981; Brain 1981). If not distinguished from the remains of human prey, however, these remains can easily distort reconstructions of human subsistence activities (Stiner 1991). For example, the presences of hyena coprolites in Gorham's Cave makes it difficult to assess, in default of a complete reanalysis of the fauna, the extent to which it can be attributed to Middle Paleolithic hunting and/or scavenging, or kills by non-human predators (Goldberg and MacPhail 1991).

Cultural Site Formation Processes

Caves and rockshelters also share a suite of characteristics affecting cultural formation processes that differentiate them from many open sites. Primary among these are the results of spatial constraint of human activities and their residues by the walls of these features. Constraint affects site structure and discard patterns and, in association with variability in aggradation rates, affects artifact morphology (Straus 1979, 1990).

In open sites, the primary locus of human activity practically always shifts over time, even when sites are reoccupied at relatively short intervals. This has several generalizable consequences. One of them is that, the greater the frequency of reoccupation, the greater the horizontal dispersion of the artifact scatters. Another is that patterned residues of different activities, which can sometimes shed light on task organizational structure, tend to be more distinct and easier to associate with individual occupation episodes. This is because spatial patterning is often clearer when features and artifact associations are horizontally distributed in a relatively thin veneer, rather than superimposed, and because, in a spatially unconstrained open site, each subsequent occupation has a reduced probability, *vis à vis* caves, of disturbing evidence from previous occupations.

The situation at many caves and rockshelters is, of course, quite different. Except in very large rockshelters, the walls of these features bound both human activities and their residues (Straus 1990). When inevitable, even minor, shifts in the spatial distribution of activities with each subsequent reoccupation of a site are combined with very slow aggradation rates and the resolution of current archaeological techniques, it may be virtually impossible to recover meaningful information about site structure. In truth,

this is often problematic in open sites as well (Binford 1982; Coinman et al. 1989). Compounding this problem is the fact that caves and rockshelters are "long-term" features of the human landscape (albeit not of the geological one) and can serve repeatedly as foci of human settlement. Thus, the direct superpositioning of activities and their residues, and the subsequent perturbation of the latter, are much more likely in the confined spaces of caves and rockshelters than they are at open sites. Assuming correct interpretation of (often complex and convoluted) stratigraphy, this is why caves serve so well for chronology building. However, it also makes isolation of individual occupation episodes difficult to achieve and to interpret in behavioral terms.

Artifact (especially lithic) morphology also can be affected differentially by both natural and cultural formation processes that take place in caves and rockshelters. As discussed above, deposition and erosion rates can vary greatly over the long term in rockshelters and in cave mouths. However, in those situations where sedimentation is relatively slow and accumulation of cultural debris relatively rapid, artifacts can comprise a significant component of these deposits, and can remain exposed for long periods of time. Cultural residues also can be exposed (or be repeatedly re-exposed) over long time periods on stable or deflationary land surfaces, especially in arid environments like those of the desert Southwest or the Middle East, where the surface is armored by a gravel veneer or "desert pavement". The effects of long exposure on site formation are exacerbated, however, in situations where repeated reoccupations of the same locality are more likely. In addition to producing palimpsests of multiple occupations, discussed above, this has several predictable consequences for artifact morphology.

Artifacts may, for example, be altered postdepositionally by trampling or burning. While the potential effects of trampling have long been recognized (Neilsen 1991), potential problems associated with postdepositional burning of lithics and ceramics have only appeared with attempts to evaluate recent advances in analytical techniques, especially dating methods. Measurements of thermoluminescence (TL) and electron spin resonance (ESR) have been used recently to date burned artifacts in a variety of contexts ranging from Middle and Upper Pleistocene hominid localities in Africa and in the Near East to refired potsherds less than 1,000 years old (Aitken 1985, 1989; Dreimanis et al. 1985; Grün and Stringer 1991; Ikeya 1985). If the artifacts have only been burned once, and at a time close to their interval of manufacture and use (e.g., lithic debris burned in a hearth shortly after manufacture, or ceramics when initially fired), these techniques have the potential to provide useful age estimates for associated human activities (but see Jelinek 1992 for a critique of TL and ESR dating methods in ancient contexts). However, if artifacts remain at or near the surface, they may be reheated by fires of subsequent reoccupations of a site. Because of the greater potential for direct superimposition of activities, this is far more likely to occur in caves and rockshelters than in open sites. Such reheating can release trapped electrons in the artifact, effectively "resetting" the TL and ESR "clocks" (Aitken 1985; Dreimanis et al. 1985). It is important to note that this resetting can be either complete or partial, depending upon the temperature and duration of heating. The overall effect is to produce dates younger than the original manufacture/use date of the artifact. The amount of time lost will depend on the time elapsed between the initial and last firings, and the TL effects of each firing (which are multiple and complex). In the case of repeated cave or rockshelter occupations over long periods of time, TL (or ESR) values recorded from a burned flake or sherd may show little relationship to the time of manufacture and use of the artifact. Dating artifacts recovered from widely spaced sample points within a deposit could help to control for such problems, as could more rigorous adherence to the many constraints of TL and ESR sampling procedures (see Aitken 1985 for a discussion of these). Often, however, neither solution is feasible due to excavations of restricted horizontal extent or to the ever-present limitations of time and funding.

To make matters even more complicated, long-term exposure to sunlight can also decrease the accuracy of TL/ESR determinations (Dreimanis et al. 1985; Yanchou et al. 1988). A worst-case scenario might be artifacts periodically re-exposed by erosion and/or human activity long after manufacture on a stable surface in a south-facing rockshelter or in an open site. These conditions are frequently encountered in the Middle East.

Another consequence of lengthy artifact exposure is that they tend to be reused more by subsequent occupants of a site. Again this is a possibility at any site where the depositional environment leaves cultural residues exposed on the surface but is perhaps more likely in caves and rockshelters where the same locality is a highly visible feature of the landscape and may be repeatedly reoccupied over many millennia. Although, in theory, practically any artifact has the potential for reuse, reuse is probably most likely in the case of lithics due to their ability to be preserved in usable condition over extremely long time periods, and the tendency to discard them prior to exhaustion in many contexts where curation is not a high priority (Barton 1990; Kuhn 1990, 1991). The

end result of significant reuse of chipped stone, especially when accompanied by edge rejuvenation, is an increase in the frequency of retouched pieces in assemblages and an increase in the intensity of retouch (Barton 1988, 1990, 1991; Clark 1989; Dibble 1988; Rolland 1981; Rolland and Dibble 1990; Jelinek 1988). Some of these arguments about pattern also apply to ground stone. Increased reuse of ground stone should be signaled by size reduction, increased regularity in form, and possibly increased breakage.

An important implication of greater reuse is that lithic assemblages from cave and rockshelter contexts may differ systematically from those at open sites, even though an identical activity suite may have taken place in both cases (see, e.g., Henry 1989; Coinman 1990; Potter 1991 for Levantine examples). Also, due to the processes just mentioned, the "grain" of cave and rockshelter archaeological assemblages may vary according to the aggradation rate, with the frequency and intensity of retouch inversely related to the rate of deposition (Jelinek 1988). Because the rate of deposition may, in part, be a function of local and regional geomorphic processes affected by climate and vegetation, it may appear that there is a more direct relationship between lithic variability and environmental change (e.g., behavioral adaptation to climatic change) than is actually the case.

In addition to the effects of deposition rates and re-occupation on artifact assemblages, caves and rockshelters might have played consistent roles in regional settlement-subsistence systems over fairly long periods of time (e.g., Bordes [1972] at Combe Grenal; cf. Clark [1989]; Straus and Clark [1986] for changing site function over time at La Riera). If consistency in site function can be demonstrated, however, it probably had more to do with the topographic settings of caves and rockshelters than with the fact that they *are* caves and rockshelters (cf. Binford 1978, 1980). As would be expected, many of these features occur in vertical or near vertical bedrock outcrops, most commonly along upper valley margins (Cova del Salt, 'Ain Difla), in ravines and canyons (Cova de la Falguera), and along or near sea coasts (Gorham's Cave, La Riera).

Discussion and Conclusions

In summary, we have tried to point out some of the salient features of caves and rockshelters as loci for concentrated prehistoric human activities. Although these features share some characteristics, their deposits represent a wider variety of geomorphic processes than is commonly recognized. We have tried to indicate the range of this geomorphological diversity with capsule discussions of natural formation processes at five cave and rockshelter sites from opposite ends of the Mediterranean.

With respect to cultural formation processes, caves and rockshelters share at least two characteristics that are much less commonly found at open-air sites. The first is that the rock walls of these features constrain the spatial distribution of human activities and their residues to relatively small spaces, and these spaces are often utilized repeatedly, although intermittently, over long time intervals. The second and related characteristic is that, because of physical constraint, cave and rockshelter reoccupations tend to result in direct superimposition and subsequent perturbation of the residues of human activities, thus creating stratigraphies that are typically more complex than those of open sites. Both characteristics have important implications for interpreting spatial patterning, artifact morphology and diversity, and even the results of some dating techniques.

We think it is especially important to try to distinguish between natural and cultural formation processes at cave and rockshelter sites (Schiffer 1987). To fail to do so can easily lead us to confound the effects of these two major kinds of processes. It also appears unwise to try to make broad generalizations about natural formation processes at caves and rockshelters simply because they are located in natural catchments. These features often have complex and diverse depositional histories that must be studied on a case-by-case basis. On the other hand, there are generally recognized geomorphological processes that can affect material culture residues in the same or similar ways. Because caves and rockshelters are relatively easy to locate and often contain deeply stratified residues of human activity accumulated over long time periods, these "paleoanthropological resources", as Straus (1979) called them, will continue to be of considerable importance to prehistoric archaeology in the foreseeable future. Hopefully, archaeologists will maintain a balanced perspective in investigating them, recognizing the limitations as well as the advantages of these site contexts for providing information about the human past.

Acknowledgments

Work at Cova del Salt and Gorham's Cave was supported in part by grants from the University of Arizona; research at Cova de la Falguera was supported in part by a grant from Arizona State University. Barton wishes to thank the Museu d'Arqueologic of Alcoi and the Gibraltar Museum for their invaluable assistance. Clark wishes to acknowledge the support of the National Science Foundation (Grant Nos. BNS76-08382 and BNS86-06658) in regard to the work at La Riera, and the support of the National Geographic Society (Grant No. 2915-84), the National Science Foundation (Grant Nos. BNS84-05601, BNS89-21863, and BNS90-13972), and the Arizona State University Research Vice-President's Office (Grant No. 90-0729) for underwriting the continuing research program at 'Ain Difla.

References Cited

Aitken, M.J.M.
  1985 *Thermoluminescence Dating*. Academic Press, London.
  1989 Luminescence dating: a guide for non-specialists. *Archaeometry* 31:147.
Bar-Yosef O., B. Vandermeersch, B. Arensburg, A. Belfer-Cohen, P. Goldberg, H. Laville, L. Meignen, Y.Rak, J.D. Speth, E. Tchernov, A-M. Tillier, and S. Weiner
  1992 The excavations in Kebara Cave, Mt. Carmel. *Current Anthropology* 33:497-549.
Barton, C.M.
  1987 *An Analysis of Lithic Variability from the Middle Paleolithic of the Iberian Peninsula*. Ph.D. dissertation, University of Arizona. University Microfilms, Ann Arbor.
  1988 *Lithic Variability and Middle Paleolithic Behavior: New Evidence from the Iberian Peninsula*. BAR International Series, 408, Oxford.
  1990 Stone Tools and Paleolithic Settlement in the Iberian Peninsula. *Proceedings of the Prehistoric Society* 56:15-32.
  1991 Retouched tools: fact or fiction? Paradigms for interpreting paleolithic chipped stone. In *Perspectives on the Past: Theoretical Biases in Mediterranean Hunter-gatherer Research*, edited by G.A. Clark, pp. 143-163. University of Pennsylvania Press, Philadelphia.
Barton, C.M., F. Rubio Gomís, C.A. Miksicek, and D.G. Donahue
  1990 Domestic Olive. *Nature* 346:518, 519.

Besançon, J., and P. Sanlaville
1990 L'évolution géomorphologique du Bassin d'Azraq (Jordanie) depuis le Pléistocène Moyen. In *Préhistoire du Levant: Processus des Changements Culturels*, edited by O. Aurenche et al., pp. 23-30. Editions du CNRS, Paris.

Besançon, J., L. Copeland, and P. Sanlaville
1990 Réflexions sur les prospections géo-préhistoriques au Proche-Orient. In *Préhistoire du Levant: Processus des Changements Culturels*, edited by O. Aurenche et al., pp. 31-39. Editions du CNRS, Paris.

Binford, L.R.
1978 Dimensional Analysis of Behavior and Site Structure: Learning from an Eskimo Hunting Stand. *American Antiquity* 43:330-361.
1980 Willow smoke and dogs' tails: hunter-gatherer settlement systems and site formation. *American Antiquity* 45:4-20.
1981 *Bones: Ancient Men and Modern Myths.* Academic Press, New York.
1982 The Archaeology of Place. *Journal of Anthropological Archaeology* 1:5-31.

Bordes, F.
1972 *A Tale of Two Caves.* Harper and Row, New York.

Brain, C.K.
1981 *The Hunters or the Hunted? An Introduction to African Cave Taphonomy.* University of Chicago Press, Chicago.

Butzer, K.W.
1964a *Environment and Archaeology.* Aldine, Chicago.
1964b Pleistocene and cold climate phenomena on the Island of Mallorca. *Zeitschrift für Geomorphologie* 8:7-31.

Clark, G.A.
1983 *The Asturian of Cantabria: Early Holocene Hunter-Gatherers in Northern Spain.* Anthropological Papers of the University of Arizona No. 41. University of Arizona Press, Tucson.
1989 Romancing the stones: biases, style and lithics at La Riera. In *Alternative Approaches to Lithic Analysis*, edited by D. Henry and G. Odell, pp. 27-50. Archeological Papers of the American Anthropological Association No. 1, Washington.

Clark, G.A. (editor)
1979 The North Burgos Archaeological Survey: Bronze and Iron Age Archaeology on the Meseta del Norte (Province of Burgos, North-Central Spain). *Arizona State University Anthropological Research Paper* No. 19. Tempe, Arizona.

Clark, G.A., J. Lindly, M. Donaldson, A. Garrard, N. Coinman, J. Schuldrenrein, S. Fish, and D. Olszewski
1988 Excavations in Middle, Upper, and Epipaleolithic sites in the Wadi Hasa, west-central Jordan. In *The Prehistory of Jordan*, edited by A. Garrard and H.-G. Gebel, pp. 209-285. BAR International Series 396, Oxford.

Clark, G.A., M. Neeley, B. MacDonald, J. Schuldrenrein, and K. 'Amr
1992 Wadi Hasa Paleolithic project – 1992: preliminary report. *Annual of the Department of Antiquities of Jordan* 36:13-23.

Coinman, N.
1990 *Rethinking the Levantine Upper Paleolithic.* Ph.D dissertation, Arizona State University. University Microfilms, Ann Arbor.

Coinman, N., G.A. Clark and M. Donaldson
1989 Aspects of structure in an Epipaleolithic occupation site in west-central Jordan. In *Alternative Approaches to Lithic Analysis*, edited by D. Henry and G. Odell, pp. 213-235. Archeological Papers of the American Anthropological Association No. 1, Washington.

Colcutt, S.N.
1979 The Analysis of Quaternary Cave Sediments. *World Archaeology* 10:290-301.

Daniel, G.
1975 *A Hundred and Fifty Years of Archaeology.* Gerald Duckworth, London.

Dibble, H.L.
1988 Typological aspects of reduction and intensity of utilization of lithic resources in the French Mousterian. In *Upper Pleistocene Prehistory of Western Eurasia*, edited by H.L. Dibble and A. Montet-White, pp. 181-197. The University of Pennsylvania Museum, Philadelphia.

Domenech Faus, E.M.
1991 Aportaciones al Epipaleolítico del norte de la Provincia de Alicante. *Alberri* 3:15-166.

Dreimanis, A., G. Hutt, A. Raukas, and P.W. Whippey
1985 Thermoluminescence Dating. In *Dating Methods of Pleistocene Deposits and their Problems*, edited by N.W. Rutter, pp. 1-7. Geoscience Canada Reprint Series No. 2. Geological Association of Canada, Ottawa.

Farrand, W.R.
1985 Rockshelter and cave sediments. In *Archaeological Sediments in Context*, edited by J.K. Stein and W.R. Farrand, pp. 21-40. Center for the Study of Early Man, Institute for Quaternary Studies, University of Maine, Orono.

Goldberg, P., and R.I. McPhail
1991 Sedimentary processes in Gorham's Cave, Gibraltar. Paper presented at the 56th Annual Meeting of the Society for American Archaeology, New Orleans.

Grayson, D.
1983 *The Establishment of Human Antiquity*. Academic Press, New York.

Grün, R., and C.B. Stringer
1991 Electron spin resonance dating and the evolution of modern humans. *Archaeometry* 33:153.

Henry, D.
1989 *From Foraging to Agriculture: the Levant at the End of the Ice Age*. University of Pennsylvania Press, Philadelphia.

Horowitz, A.
1979 *The Quaternary of Israel*. Academic Press, New York.

Ikeya, M.
1985 Electron Spin Resonance. In *Dating Methods of Pleistocene Deposits and their Problems*, edited by N.W. Rutter, pp. 73-87. Geoscience Canada Reprint Series No. 2. Geological Association of Canada, Ottawa.

Jelinek, A.J.
1988 Technology, Typology, and Culture in the Middle Paleolithic. In *Upper Pleistocene Prehistory of Western Eurasia*, edited by H.L. Dibble and A. Montet-White, pp. 199-212. The University of Pennsylvania Museum, Philadelphia.
1992 Problems in the Chronology of the Middle Paleolithic and the First Appearance of Early Modern *Homo sapiens* in Southwest Asia. In *The Evolution and Dispersal of Modern Humans in Asia*, edited by T. Akazawa et al., pp. 253-276. Hokusen-sha, Tokyo.

Kuhn, S.
1990 A Geometric Index of Reduction for Unifacial Stone Tools. *Journal of Archaeological Science* 17:585-593.
1991 "Unpacking" Reduction: Lithic Raw Material Economy in the Mousterian of West-central Italy. *Journal of Anthropological Archaeology* 10:76-106.

Laville, H.
1986 Stratigraphy, Sedimentology and Chronology of the La Riera Cave Deposits. In *La Riera Cave: Stone Age Hunter-Gatherer Adaptations in Northern Spain*, edited by L. Straus and G.A.Clark, pp. 25-56. Anthropological Research Papers No. 36. Arizona State University, Tempe.

Laville, H., J.-P. Rigaud, and J. Sackett
1980 *Rock Shelters of the Périgord*. Academic Press, New York.

Leroi-Gourhan, A.
1986 The Palynology of La Riera cave. In *La Riera Cave: Stone Age Hunter-Gatherer Adaptations in Northern Spain*, edited by L. Straus and G.A.Clark, pp. 59-64. Anthropological Research Papers No. 36. Arizona State University, Tempe.

Lindly, J. and G.A. Clark
1987 A Preliminary Analysis of the Mousterian Site of 'Ain Difla (WHS Site 634) in the Wadi Ali, West-central Jordan. *Proceedings of the Prehistoric Society* 53:279-292.

Nielsen, A.E.

1991 Trampling the Archaeological Record: an Experimental Study. *American Antiquity* 56:483-503.

Petraglia, M.

1987 *Site Formation Processes at the Abri Dufaure.* Ph.D. dissertation, University of New Mexico. University Microfilms, Ann Arbor.

Potter, J.M.

1991 *Middle Paleolithic Settlement Pattern and Assemblage Variability in West-central Jordan.* Unpublished M.A. Thesis, Arizona State University, Tempe.

Rolland, N.

1981 The Interpretation of Middle Palaeolithic variability. *Man* 16:15–42.

Rolland, N., and H.L. Dibble

1990 A New Synthesis of Middle Paleolithic Variability. *American Antiquity* 55:480-499.

Rubio Gomís, F., and C.M. Barton

1990 Abric de la Falguera: avance préliminar. Ms. on file, Museu d'Arqueologic, Alcoi, Spain.

Schiffer, M.

1987 *Formation Processes of the Archaeological Record.* University of New Mexico Press, Albuquerque.

Stiner, M.

1991 The Faunal Remains from Grotta Guattari: a Taphonomic Perspective. *Current Anthropology* 32:103-117.

Straus, L.G.

1979 Caves: a Palaeoanthropological Resource. *World Archaeology* 10:331-339.

1990 Underground archaeology: perspectives on caves and rockshelters. In *Archaeological Method and Theory*, vol. 2, edited by M.B. Schiffer, pp. 255-304. University of Arizona Press, Tucson.

Straus, L.G., and G.A. Clark (editors)

1986 *La Riera Cave: Stone Age Hunter-gatherer Adaptations in Northern Spain.* Anthropological Research Papers No. 36. Arizona State University, Tempe.

Villaverde Bonilla, V.

1984 *La Cova Negra de Xátiva y el Musteriense de la región central del Mediterráneo Español.* Serie de Trabajos Varios No. 79. Servicio de Investigación Prehistorica, Valencia.

Waechter, J. d'A.

1951 Excavations at Gorham's Cave, Gibraltar. *Proceedings of the Prehistoric Society* 17:83-92.

1964 The excavation of Gorham's Cave, Gibraltar, 1951-54. *Institute of Archaeology Bulletin* 4:189-221.

Yanchou, Lu, J.R. Prescott, and J.T. Hutton

1988 Sunlight bleaching of the thermoluminescence of Chinese loess. *Quaternary Science Reviews* 7:335.

Zeuner, F.

1953 The chronology of the Mousterian at Gorham's Cave, Gibraltar. *Proceedings of the Prehistoric Society* 19:180-188.

4

Archaeological Contexts in Deep Cave Sites: Examples from the Eastern Woodlands of North America

George M. Crothers
Patty Jo Watson
Washington University

"Deep cave sites" consist of a set of archaeological sites in the karst regions of the Eastern Woodlands, set apart from the more familiar bluff-face natural shelters or cave opening habitation sites. Prehistoric human activity in the dark zones of deep caves, once thought to be a novelty or an oddity of the archaeological record, is now known to have been widespread in the Eastern Woodlands. At some times and places, this activity was intensive and reflects systematic use or exploitation of the cave environment by indigenous populations (Crothers 1987; Faulkner 1986, 1988; Kennedy 1990; Munson and Munson 1990; Munson et al. 1989; Watson 1969, 1974).

Although there are many thousands of limestone caves in the Eastern Woodlands, relatively few are documented prehistoric archaeological sites. This is partially due to the dynamic hydrological processes that characterize many cave environments, often not conducive to the preservation of residues of human activity. It is also the case that few systematic efforts have been made to locate these sites.

We describe the range of contexts that characterize cave environments before summarizing the specific research we have conducted in five different caves: Jaguar, Saltpetre, and Big Bone caves in central Tennessee, and Mammoth and Salts caves in west central Kentucky (Figure 1).

Cave environments tend to fall near the ends of a hydrological energy spectrum that directly affects the formation, preservation, and transformation of archaeological deposits. The ends of this spectrum are the active or dynamic cave passage and the abandoned or arrested cave passage, respectively (Figure 2). We use the term "cave" in the strict sense of a subsurface conduit created by subterranean stream invasion of soluble carbonate bedrock (Crawford 1982; Sweeting 1973:130). The active subsurface conduit is a high energy environment characterized by periodic chemical solution and mechanical abrasion of the cave walls, collapse of the cave roof or breakdown, deposition of the subterranean-stream suspended load, and precipitation of groundwater carbonate solutions. Active caves are not favorable for the preservation or even burial of evidence of human activity. Rather, most such evidence is periodically flushed from the cave environment.

Advanced karst valley development, however, will result in the formation of abandoned or upper level cave passages by some combination of uplift, downcutting of the stream base level, and further subterranean stream invasion. Given the appropriate geological situation—massively bedded carbonate rocks capped by less permeable formations—these abandoned cave passages will maintain virtually constant atmospheric conditions. It is this latter end of the hydrological

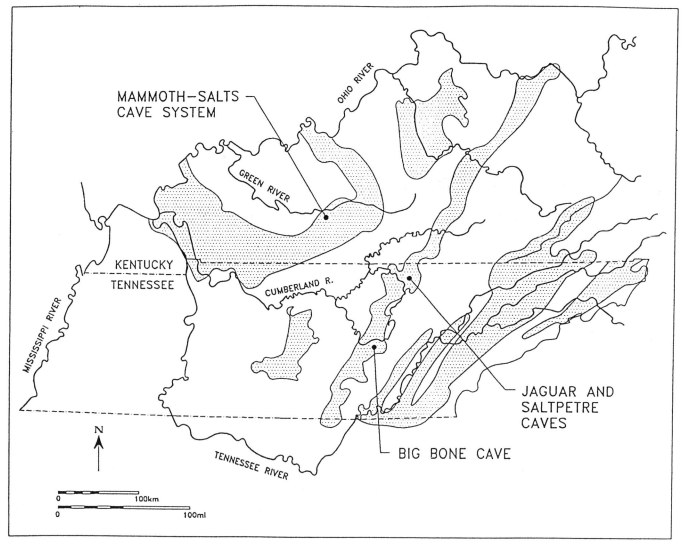

Figure 1. Karst regions of Kentucky and Tennessee (stippled), showing locations of cave sites discussed in the text.

energy spectrum, abandoned subsurface conduits, that characterizes the limited set of archaeological deep cave sites. The arrested cave environment also preserves perishable archaeological remains where these hydrologically abandoned caves are capped by impermeable sandstone or shale, as is the case for Big Bone Cave and the Mammoth-Salts cave system.

The Active Cave Environment

Human entry into the cave environment is made through openings to the surface at swallets, resurgences, or collapsed sinks (Figure 2). The entrances to Mammoth, Big Bone, and Saltpetre caves are abandoned stream resurgences. The entrance to Jaguar Cave is an active resurgence, and the Salts Cave entrance is a collapsed sink. Cave openings are high energy depositional environments, subject to an array

of geological and biological, as well as humanly derived, depositional factors. Natural shelters and the processes affecting interpretation of their deposits are better known to archaeologists, who more commonly work in rockshelter and cave opening sites (e.g., Straus 1990). However, of the five cave sites we describe, only the entry chamber (vestibule) of Salts Cave retains evidence of prehistoric occupation. The depositional characteristics of Salts Cave Vestibule have been the subject of several investigations that are described elsewhere (Gardner 1987; Kennedy 1990; Redman 1969; Watson 1974).

Another type of archaeological site in the active portions of caves is the vertical shaft or pit cave used prehistorically in the Eastern Woodlands as a repository for the dead (Haskins 1988; Oakley 1971; Turner 1984; Willey and Crothers 1986; Willey et al. 1988). Approximately 30 to 40 of these sites have been

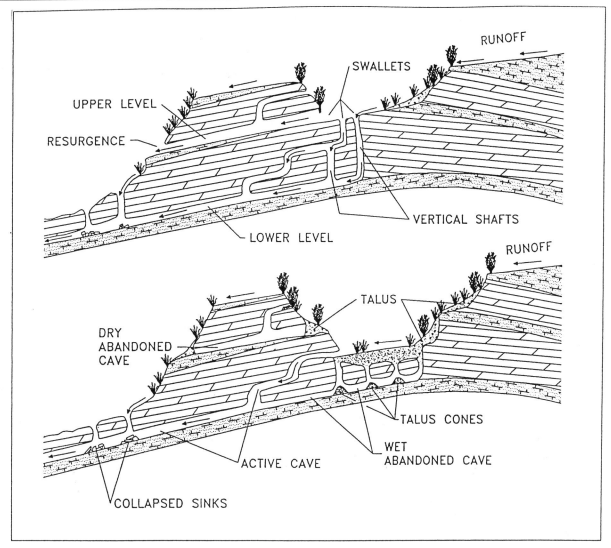

Figure 2. Schematic representation of subterranean stream invasion and advanced karst valley development (after Crawford 1982:Figure 11).

recorded, a few have been dug by nonarchaeologists and received minimal recording with some of the osteological remains being described, but many more have been extensively looted and the materials lost. Few systematic excavations of any of these sites have been made and little is known of their specific depositional characteristics.

Generally, it appears that the bodies (presumably dead) were dropped through the surface openings, where they became incorporated into the active talus cone that forms at the base of the vertical shaft. The main processes acting on these deposits are body decomposition, scavenging by small animals (primarily woodrats), down slope movement of the remains, and burial by other debris entering the pit. The remains may be exposed by subsequent erosion of the talus cone and then redeposited repeatedly by active stream flow or flooding in the cave. Burial pit

caves present highly complex site formation processes. However, the much needed, thorough investigation of such sites will be a formidable undertaking because of the dynamic depositional environment and the logistical problems of excavating in an active cave setting.

The Arrested Cave Environment

Abandoned subsurface conduits maintain relatively constant temperature and humidity. If these abandoned caves are formed beneath an impermeable cap-rock, then the passages may also be completely dry, preserving perishable archaeological materials. In either case, dry or wet, preservation of even the most fragile evidences of human activity is possible. Herein lies the greatest contextual problem of the hydrologically abandoned cave passage: there is no stratigraphic context in the normal sense. The ancient walking surface of the cave passage is also the modern walking surface. The simple fact of our physical presence in the cave may be enough to obliterate or seriously alter evidence of prehistoric human activity that has persisted undisturbed for several millennia. Undoubtedly many such sites were destroyed by modern exploration and other activity in caves. It is rare when these sites are recognized and even rarer when they are preserved to be studied by archaeologists.

The archaeological record in Jaguar Cave, which is several miles long, illustrates the fragile nature of these cave environments. In a remote passage of the cave, 272 complete human footprints in the soft clay floor have been mapped (Robbins et al. 1981; Watson et al., in prep.). The prints, together with a sparse trail of torch charcoal and smudges on the cave walls, comprise the only evidence of prehistoric activity. Radiocarbon determinations on torch charcoal indicate the footprints have been preserved in the still pliable mud for 4,600 years, making this the earliest evidence of activity in any deep cave environment in Eastern North America.

Based on dimensions and morphology of the footprints, physical anthropologist Louise Robbins determined that nine individuals were responsible for the prints; at least two of the individuals may have been female and one of the individuals an adolescent. Close examination of the individual prints revealed differences in the rate of patination of the mud among footprints, consistent superposition of specific prints, and other micro-topographic and micro-erosional features that led her to conclude that the prints represent at least two separate trips through the passage, presumably many years apart (Robbins et al. 1981).

Jaguar Cave is remarkable not only for the fragile evidence of aboriginal caving trips recorded in its soft clay floor, but also because it unequivocally conveys to us the skill of these prehistoric cave explorers. On two occasions small parties of aboriginal explorers, composed of men, women, and adolescents, penetrated a remote section of the cave not rediscovered until the mid-1970s. They explored in a seemingly casual way to the end of the remote passage and then retraced their route to the main cave. We suspect that the Jaguar Cave archaeological remains are indicative of rather routine prehistoric exploration of deep caves. But the record of such activity is only occasionally preserved in deep cave environments, rarely recognized before it is obliterated by modern cavers, and even less often recorded in sufficient detail (e.g., mapping of each distinguishable imprint) to allow resolution of individual events like those still interpretable in Jaguar Cave (Watson et al., in prep.)

A site near Jaguar Cave in north central Tennessee, known as Saltpetre Cave, has a more complex archaeological record. In a remote, upper-level portion of this cave, approximately 150 meters of two intersecting passages have been mined for high quality chert nodules (Ferguson 1982). Pits dug into the sandy sediments of the floor, small hearths, chalcedony hammerstones, and debitage from the primary reduction of the cobbles, effectively create an impression that the activity took place only yesterday. Yet the pooled mean of four radiocarbon determinations date the intensive utilization of the cave to approximately 2900 B.P. (950 B.C.; Crothers 1987:Table 4). A fifth determination—4350 ± 60 b.p. (2400 B.C.)—from a section of the cave between the entrance and the chert quarry indicates there may have been earlier exploration in Saltpetre Cave approximating the time of that in Jaguar Cave.

It is parsimonious and also plausible to link the pits, debitage, hearths, and hammerstones as a set of consistent activities or residues. However, and quite unexpectedly, a series of petroglyphs was also found on the low ceiling in the chert quarry passage. The glyphs include a prominent sun symbol, concentric circles, and series of wavy lines. Patination of the limestone surface indicates that the glyphs are not recent, and it seems reasonable to link the glyphs with the mining activity. If these activities were indeed linked, then the glyphs are among the earliest known such markings in the Eastern Woodlands.

The scale of chert mining in Saltpetre Cave suggests that it was visited on repeated occasions over some unknown period of time. Cobble reduction appears to be limited to decortication and early stage biface manufacture. Interpretation of the Saltpetre Cave site is still in progress, but the point we wish to make here is that owing to its location within an arrested cave environment the entire site context is exposed to us. There is no indication that the integrity of the prehistoric deposits has been altered by processes other than the original acts of quarrying and cobble reduction. Such an archaeological situation is extremely rare and extremely valuable.

Big Bone Cave, Tennessee is our third example of an archaeological deep cave site in an arrested cave environment. Historically, the ten mile long cave was well known as an archaeological site because of the ordinarily perishable remains still present, well known as a paleontological site because of an articulated ground sloth found in one passage, and well known as a commercial saltpetre mine during the nineteenth century. In 1896, this information led Henry C. Mercer from the University of Pennsylvania to examine the stratigraphic relation in this cave of

Indian remains to the Pleistocene ground sloth (Mercer 1896, 1897).

In one day of excavation Mercer was able to distinguish four stratigraphic layers. Layer 1 had a depth of 2 to 3 inches and contained objects of later age than the bones, or of "doubtful antiquity". Layer 2 had a thickness of 2 to 2.5 feet and contained ground sloth bones and objects as old as the bones. Layers 3 and 4 contained objects older than the bones. Mercer established that the debris left by the saltpetre miners and by the Indians who preceded them was all contained in Layer 1, distinct from and younger than the sloth remains. He further believed that among the variety of torch debris in the cave, charred, resinous pine splints were historic because they showed cut marks made by iron tools, whereas at least some of the cane had been "cast away at the spot by Indians" (Mercer 1897:43).

We have been concerned to document the distribution of prehistoric material in the cave as well as the nature of the activity that produced this material. Approximately 1000 m of passage contain aboriginal remains relatively undisturbed by historic saltpetre mining and other activity in the cave. Nine radiocarbon determinations, primarily on wood and cane torch debris, date the prehistoric use of the cave to within a few hundred years of 2200 B.P. (250 B.C.; Crothers 1987:Table 1). An additional date on a pine splint was assayed as 440 ± 55 years B.P. (A.D. 1510) supporting Mercer's suggestion that such splints are historic period artifacts.

The range of prehistoric material in Big Bone Cave, including digging sticks, bottle gourd and pepo gourd container fragments, and a woven bag associated with extensive selenite crystals in the gypsiferous cave sediment suggests that Big Bone was mined for these minerals in much the same manner as Mammoth and Salts caves were (Munson et al. 1990). However, the saltpetre mining has destroyed considerable portions of the original cave deposits, and only in small, remote passages have the aboriginal materials remained in their original context.

Selenite and gypsum mining in those portions of the world's longest cave (minimally 335 mapped miles) known as Mammoth and Salts caves, Kentucky, has been well documented (Munson et al. 1990; Watson 1969, 1974). Although extensive areas of the cave have been disturbed by saltpetre mining and other activities, prehistoric and historic materials can usually be distinguished. Evidence of selenite and gypsum mining is present in several thousand meters of passage in each cave. The quantity of prehistoric debris associated with this mining is still impressive despite nearly 200 years of collecting and destruction. Twenty-two radiocarbon determinations range between 1900 and 4100 years B.P. (Kennedy 1990:Table

1). However, most of the cave activity appears to have been between 2400 and 2900 years B.P.

During Watson's work in Salts Cave in the 1960s, a small test unit (designated Test A) was dug in a portion of the passage that was filled with sediment, a situation not common in Upper Salts, which is characterized by breakdown nearly everywhere and hence is very rocky (Watson 1969:20). At this time it was known that prehistoric battering or scraping of gypsum crust from the cave wall was common through large portions of the cave. However, it was surprising to find prehistoric material buried at least 150 cm below the present surface of this unit. The total depth of deposit is unknown because breakdown blocked further excavation of the test unit.

The sediments in Upper Salts are Pleistocene in age, possibly early Pleistocene. Yet the excavation revealed seven distinct ash layers, some with *in situ* burning, the last at a depth of 140 cm. Interspersed among the ash layers were considerable quantities of torch and fire debris. It seemed a little perplexing but not totally implausible that the 150 cm plus of deposit could have been built up through repeated use of this cave locale by people scuffing about in the fine-grained and wholly unconsolidated sediment, by sediment filtering down through the loosely consolidated breakdown, and by deliberate burial of old hearths to facilitate reuse of the same spot by the prehistoric cavers (Watson 1969:21). In light of more recent work in the Mammoth-Salts system (Munson et al. 1990), we now think that the context represented in Salts Cave Test A is probably aboriginal selenite and satinspar mining (Kennedy 1990:75).

Selenite and satinspar, as well as gypsum crust are all forms of hydrous calcium sulfate, $CaSO_4 \cdot 2H_2O$. However, selenite is distinctive because it occurs as single, large translucent crystals in the dry, sulfate-rich cave sediments. The extraction of selenite requires digging into these deposits, as appears to have been done extensively in Upper Salts and Mammoth caves (Munson et al. 1990).

The archaeological context in Salts and Mammoth, where historic saltpetre mining has not taken place, is completely attributable to aboriginal digging and movement of the breakdown within the passage. Saltpetre mining does not extend far beyond the historic entrance area in Mammoth Cave, and never occurred in Salts. Given the extensive evidence of this activity through the cave and the intensity of mining represented in Salts Test A, one concludes that the quantity of selenite, satinspar, and gypsum removed from the cave would be measured in tons.

Both the quantity of material mined in the Mammoth-Salts cave system and the range of radiocarbon dates indicate that these caves were explored and worked over several hundred years. Because of the lack of geological stratification in the cave we cannot subdivide this activity into finer chronological units. However, the sequence of radiocarbon dates does suggest that portions of the cave may have been mined or explored in a linear fashion.

Kennedy (1990) suggests, based on a recent analysis of the radiocarbon chronology, that portions of the cave may have been systematically used earlier and then abandoned. She notes that the lower passages in both Mammoth Cave and Salts Cave, contain the earliest dates. Further radiocarbon dating and statistical analysis of the determinations is needed to test her hypothesis, but if she is correct, then we may be able to detect a linear sequence in the use of cave passages through time.

Our interest in providing finer chronologic resolution of aboriginal activities in the cave is centered upon the paleofecal specimens left there by the prehistoric miners. The paleofeces analyzed so far appear to be primarily Early Woodland in age, although use of the cave begins at least as early at the Late or Terminal Archaic Period. The Mammoth-Salts fecal specimens are important in defining the indigenous Eastern Woodlands horticultural complex. If we can isolate portions of the caves as having been used at the early end of the time sequence, then associated paleofecal specimens may provide detailed information not otherwise available about the origins of plant cultivation in this portion of the Eastern Woodlands.

Summary

Archaeological sites in active or dynamic cave environments in Eastern North America include human occupational debris in cave openings, and osteological remains in vertical shafts or pit caves. The complex formation processes occurring in cave openings are familiar to archaeologists and have received considerable attention. Talus deposits in pit caves are equally complex, but few thorough or systematic studies of such sites have been made.

Arrested or hydrologically abandoned cave passages are remarkable for the kinds of human activity preserved, but the interpretation of these sites requires minute, small-scale observation. Soot, patination, micro-erosion, and superposition of features indicate varied and subtle formation processes in such environments. Prehistoric activity in deep caves ranges from isolated, short-term events like the exploration of Jaguar Cave and quarrying of chert in Saltpetre Cave to extensive alteration of the cave envi-

ronment like the mining of sulfate minerals in Big Bone, Salts, and Mammoth caves.

The prehistoric activity in these caves—minimally: chert, gypsum, and selenite mining— has caused considerable impact on the arrested cave environment. The ancient activities can usually be distinguished from historic saltpetre mining and other recent uses of the cave, leaving us with an extensive record of relatively intact prehistoric remains. The evidence of mining in Big Bone, Salts, and Mammoth caves indicates rather systematic and possibly long term use. Additional AMS radiocarbon dating is being undertaken to provide greater resolution of spatial patterning in these caves, and to indicate how use of them has changed through time.

Jaguar Cave, Tennessee, is the earliest known record of prehistoric cave exploration in the Eastern Woodlands. The preservation of dozens of human footprints in the arrested cave environment at this site is extremely rare. Careful observation of the differences in patination, superposition, and micro-erosional features of the various prints has allowed us to interpret individual events that comprise the archaeological record, a situation seldom possible for prehistoric archaeologists. Places such as Jaguar Cave may lie outside the mainstream of archaeological significance, but the site conveys to us in a manner that few sites can, the intensity and skill with which aboriginal inhabitants of eastern North America pursued knowledge of their physical environment.

Acknowledgments

We are grateful to Dave Nash and Mike Petraglia for inviting us to join the original S.A.A. symposium, to contribute to the resulting volume, and for editorial suggestions on the manuscript. We are indebted to volume editor Paul Goldberg and reviewer Michael Schiffer for their advice about revising the draft paper. Nick Crawford kindly gave us permission to use a modified version of his karst valley development diagram, which appears here as Figure 2. As has been the case for many years, the Cave Research Foundation and the local National Park Service officials supported our research in Mammoth Cave National Park, for which we thank them. The field work and analyses referred to in this paper were funded in part by the Cave Research Foundation, the National Speleological Society, the Smithsonian Institution Laboratory of Radiobiology, the Tennessee Department of Conservation, and Washington University in St. Louis.

References Cited

Crawford, N. C.
  1982 *Karst Hydrogeology of Tennessee*. Guidebook prepared for Karst Hydrogeology Workshop, Nashville, Tennessee. Copies available from the Center for Cave and Karst Studies, Department of Geography and Geology, Western Kentucky University, Bowling Green.
Crothers, G. M.
  1987 *An Archaeological Survey of Big Bone Cave, Tennessee and Diachronic Patterns of Cave Utilization in the Eastern Woodlands*. Unpublished Master's thesis, Department of Anthropology, University of Tennessee, Knoxville.
Faulkner, C. H. (editor)
  1986 *The Prehistoric Native American Art of Mud Glyph Cave*. University of Tennessee Press, Knoxville.
  1988 A Study of Seven Southeastern Glyph Caves. *North American Archaeologist* 9:223-246
Ferguson, L. G.
  1982 A Preliminary Report of Archaeological Investigations at a Chert Quarry Cave in Fentress County, Tennessee. Ms. on file, Department of Anthropology, University of Tennessee, Knoxville.
Gardner, P. S.
  1987 New Evidence Concerning the Chronology and Paleoethnobotany of Salts Cave, Kentucky. *American Antiquity* 52:358-366.
Haskins, V.
  1988 *The Prehistory of Prewits Knob, Kentucky*. Unpublished Master's thesis, Department of Anthropology, Washington University, St. Louis.
Kennedy, M. C.
  1990 *An Analysis of the Radiocarbon Dates from Salts and Mammoth Caves, Mammoth Cave National Park, Kentucky*. Unpublished Master's thesis. Department of Anthropology, Washington University, St. Louis.
Mercer, H. C.
  1896 Cave Exploration by the University of Pennsylvania in Tennessee. *The American Naturalist* 30:608-611.
  1897 The Finding of the Remains of the Fossil Sloth at Big Bone Cave, Tennessee, in 1896. *Proceedings of the American Philosophical Society* 36:36-70. Philadelphia.
Munson, P. J. and C. A. Munson
  1990 *The Prehistoric and Early Historic Archaeology of Wyandotte Cave and Other Caves in Southern Indiana*. Prehistoric Research Series, Vol. VII, No. 1. Indiana Historical Society, Indianapolis.
Munson, P. J., K. B. Tankersley, C. A. Munson, and P. J. Watson
  1989 Prehistoric Selenite and Satinspar Mining in the Mammoth Cave System, Kentucky. *Midcontinental Journal of Archaeology* 14:119-145.
Oakley, Jr., C. B.
  1971 *An Archaeological Investigation of Pinson Cave (1Je20)*. Unpublished Master's thesis, Department of Anthropology, University of Alabama, University.
Redman, C. L.
  1969 *Context and Stratigraphy: The Need for Observations*. Unpublished Master's thesis, Department of Anthropology, University of Chicago.
Robbins, L. M., R. C. Wilson, and P. J. Watson
  1981 Paleontology and Archeology of Jaguar Cave, Tennessee. *Proceedings of the Eighth International Congress of Speleology* 1:377-380. Bowling Green, Kentucky.
Straus, L. G.
  1990 Underground Archaeology: Perspectives on Caves and Rockshelters. In *Archaeological Method and Theory*, Volume 2, edited by M. B. Schiffer, pp. 255-304. University of Arizona Press, Tucson.
Sweeting, M. M.
  1973 *Karst Landforms*. Columbia University Press, New York.
Turner, K. R.
  1984 Report on the Human Skeletal Materials from Loyd's Pit (Site 1Ja212). Ms. on file, Laboratory of Human Osteology, Department of Anthropology, University of Alabama, Tuscaloosa.

Watson, P. J.
    1969 *The Prehistory of Salts Cave, Kentucky.* Report of Investigations No. 16. Illinois State Museum, Springfield.
    1974 Excavations in the Vestibule of Salts Cave. In *Archaeology of the Mammoth Cave Area*, edited by P. J. Watson, pp. 71-82. Academic Press, New York.
Watson, P. J. (editor)
    1974 *Archaeology of the Mammoth Cave Area.* Academic, New York.
Watson, P. J., M. C. Kennedy, P. Willey, L. M. Robbins, and R. C. Wilson
    in prep. Prehistoric Footprints in Jaguar Cave, Tennessee. For submission to the *Journal of Field Archaeology.*
Willey, P., and G. Crothers
    1986 *Archaeological and Osteological Survey of Bull Thistle Cave (44Tz92), Virginia.* Midsouth Anthropological Research Corporation. Submitted to Virginia Division of Historic Landmarks, Richmond.
Willey, P., G. Crothers, and C. H. Faulkner
    1988 Aboriginal Skeletons and Petroglyphs in Officer Cave, Tennessee. *Tennessee Anthropologist* 13:51-75.

5

Formation Processes of Acheulean Localities in the Hunsgi and Baichbal Valleys, Peninsular India

K. Paddayya
Deccan College

Michael D. Petraglia
Smithsonian Institution

Stone Age investigations in India commenced one hundred and thirty years ago with the pioneering discoveries of Robert Bruce Foote around Madras (Foote 1916). Since that time, many important discoveries have been made, and important information about the Lower, Middle and Upper Paleolithic has been gathered. For the past three decades, and up to the present day, intensive regional studies have been performed in many parts of India, leading to an understanding of the geographical distribution of Paleolithic localities, Stone Age technology, and the stratigraphic context of finds (for backgrounds, see Sankalia 1974; Jacobson 1979; Paddayya 1984; Misra 1987, 1989).

While much has been learned about the distribution and nature of Acheulean occurrences in India, little information about hominid behavior and activity has been acquired. This has primarily been due to the traditional emphasis placed on culture-stratigraphic relationships and the lack of large scale excavations at Paleolithic localities in non-fluvial contexts.

Behavior-oriented archaeologists in India have recognized that transported sites like those associated with high-energy river sediments and gravels do not help to reconstruct aspects of hominid activity. Emphasizing the discovery and investigation of localities in non-fluvial contexts, Jacobson (1970, 1975, 1985) and Paddayya (1977a, 1978, 1982) systematically investigated localities in non-fluvial contexts, conducting large-scale, valley-wide surveys to reconstruct Acheulean activities. This represented an important departure from many other Paleolithic investigations in India, and it became apparent that in order to better understand Acheulean settlement and activity, not only did basin-wide surveys have to be carried out, but localities in their original depositional contexts had to be identified. Moreover, in order to analyze hominid activities, it has been realized that lateral excavations were needed to expose Paleolithic occupation surfaces (Corvinus 1968, 1973, 1981, 1983).

With the increased desire to understand intra-site and inter-site patterns, it was clear that more sophisticated approaches had to be used to decipher site formation processes. Most recently, Paddayya (1987a) has drawn attention to the multitude of processes that created the Stone Age archaeological record in India, broadly equivalent to formation process studies in other parts of the world (Schiffer 1976, 1987; Binford 1981; Isaac 1989). For the first time in Indian Stone Age archaeology, emphasis was placed on the significance of site formation research.

This chapter expands upon the site formation approach in India and discusses the joint investigation of Acheulean localities located in the Hunsgi and Baichbal Valleys, southern India. To illustrate the various problems and issues raised by site formation

61

processes, a representative sample of the Acheulean localities from the Hunsgi Valley (Gulbal II, Hunsgi II, Hunsgi V) and from the Baichbal Valley (Mudnur VIII, Mudnur X, Yediyapur I, Yediyapur IV, Yediyapur VI, Fatehpur V) was selected for comparison. Where appropriate, other Acheulean localities from the Hunsgi and Baichbal Valleys are mentioned to further illustrate problems and issues. The goal of this study is to place the localities on a relative, interpretive scale, assessing the degree to which natural processes influenced the composition and condition of the artifact accumulations and to infer the type and extent to which behavioral information was preserved at these localities.

Regional Background

The Hunsgi and Baichbal Valleys are located in the Gulbarga District of Karnataka. Although the valleys are separated from each other by a narrow remnant strip of a shale-limestone plateau, they still constitute a single erosional basin of Tertiary age (Mahadevan 1941; Mukherjee 1941). The basin contains the headwaters of a minor stream called the Hunsgi nullah, one of the minor left-bank feeders of the major Krishna River. The basin has a maximum length of 30 km (north-south) and measures about 500 square kms in extent (Figure 1). The basin is flanked by shale-limestone plateaus (at places capped by the Deccan Trap) on the southern and western sides and by low hills and outcrops of the Archaean formations (hornblende schist and granite) on the northern and eastern sides. The basin floor itself is made up of granite gneiss and associated ridges of quartz, pegmatite and dolerite. The patches of limestone and shale occasionally found on the valley floor mark the remnants of erosion which carved out the basin. The enclosing of the valley by steep-sided escarpments on all sides and the lack of a direct relationship with a major river mark the basin off as a distinct and separate geographical unit.

The area forms part of the semi-arid and drought prone Deccan, with an average annual rainfall of about 65 cm, contributed by the southwest monsoon. The monsoonal climate came into existence in Peninsular India by the early part of the Pleistocene (Joshi 1970). During the height of the wet, monsoonal season, the drainage pattern of the valley is dendritic, flowing towards the east and southeast. The seasonality of rainfall during the year largely governs the water flow in the beds of the nullahs and streams; the nullahs carry water only during the wet season. During the wet season, numerous rills flow off the escarpments and drain towards the valley floor. Shallow but perennial water bodies occur in the area

due to the activity of seep-springs emanating from the junction of shale and limestones with the underlying granite formations. The occurrence of thick and extensive travertine deposits proves that the activity of seep springs is of high antiquity based on uranium-series dates (Szabo et al. 1990).

Far from being a plainland, the valley floor presents a gently rolling topography resulting from the existence of a series of flattened, tongue-shaped sweeps of land separated from one another by shallow, linear-shaped depressions (8 to 10 km long and up to 1 km in breadth) marking the ancient drainage tracts that carve out the valley floor. The present-day nullahs occupy the bottom portions of these depressions, with the gently rising sweeps of land along them serving as their inter-flueves. Many of the Acheulean localities found in the area occur on the upward sloping sides along the streams.

The Hunsgi-Baichbal Valleys have been under cultivation for at least two millennia, and more intensive cultivation for the last several hundred years. The vegetation today is characterized as a pseudo-steppe environment with low scattered shrubs (Gaussen et al. 1965). The discovery of small amounts of fauna at the Acheulean localities, including *Bos, Bubalus, Elephas,* and *Equus,* suggests that the area was a savanna woodland with sources of standing water (Paddayya 1985).

Stone Age research in the Hunsgi-Baichbal Valleys has been conducted since 1974 (Paddayya 1977a, 1977b, 1979, 1982, 1987a, 1987b, 1987c, 1989, 1991). These prolonged investigations have brought to light a wealth of data pertaining to the Lower, Middle and Upper Paleolithic of the region. One important and significant difference in the distribution of these localities is that all Acheulean occurrences discovered to date are situated on the valley floor. After fifteen years of intensive survey, no Acheulean localities have been found on the plateaus above the valley floor and only Middle and Upper Paleolithic occurrences occur on the surrounding plateaus.

Based upon seven uranium-series dates, the Acheulean localities have been dated from 150,000 B.P. to a minimum of 350,000 years B.P. (Szabo et al. 1990; Mishra 1992). Thus, the Acheulean localities date from the Middle Pleistocene to the early Late Pleistocene. Based upon currently accepted hominid chronologies this occupation may belong to an advanced form of *Homo erectus* or early representatives of *Homo sapiens.*

As stated above, surveys in the Hunsgi-Baichbal Valleys have emphasized the discovery of localities away from major river valleys for reconstructing the settlement of Stone Age cultures (Paddayya 1978, 1982). This was in contrast to the then dominant

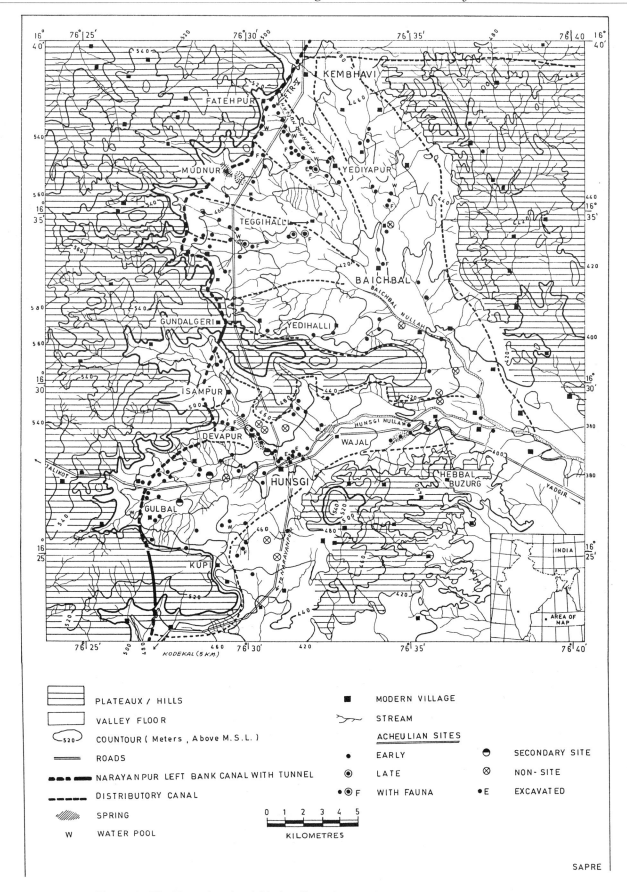

Figure 1. The Hunsgi and Baichbal Valleys showing location of Acheulean localities.

research paradigm in Indian Stone Age research which concentrated on the construction of regional culture-sequences based on the study of secondary localities, such as those associated with river sections. Investigations in the Hunsgi Valley from 1974 to 1982 brought to light about 60 localities belonging to the Acheulean. Barring a dozen localities, all artifacts were discovered in non-fluviatile sedimentary contexts, and were therefore described as "primary" sites.

The implement-bearing horizon of the primary localities measured up to 25 cm in thickness and was usually overlain by a black soil, measuring up to half a meter in thickness. Based upon the estimated horizontal extent and composition of artifact clusters, these localities were divided into four groups: small (up to 25 specimens), medium (between 26 and 100 specimens), large (between 101 and 200 specimens), and very large (above 200 specimens). Two of these so-called primary localities near Hunsgi (Localities Hunsgi V and Hunsgi VI) were excavated in an attempt to achieve a better understanding of the depositional context of the occupation horizon and its spatial extent (Paddayya 1977b, 1979).

While this approach was generally welcomed and seen as a necessary departure in Indian prehistoric research, some doubts were also expressed about the "primary" character of the Acheulean localities of the area. In a review of the monograph dealing with the Hunsgi Valley study, Straus (1983) wondered whether or not the granite surface on which the Acheulean horizon occurs could have been an ideal situation for spatial preservation without alteration. In addition, J.D. Clark (personal communication, 1986) felt that the artifactual levels at these localities were colluvial in origin, implying that the artifacts were transported. A short time later, Lewis Binford (personal communication, 1986) remarked that the sites were deflated, meaning that originally the localities had a fairly thick sedimentary cover which was eroded over the course of time.

At about the same time these arguments were made, Paddayya (1987a) supported the perspective that the archaeological record should not be viewed simply as a dichotomy between primary or secondary sites, but rather as a continuum of sites with lesser or greater degrees of preservation by natural and cultural processes (cf. Schick 1986, 1987). The need for applying this concept in future investigations of the Acheulean localities was therefore fully recognized and accepted.

Accordingly, some attention was given to the problem of site formation in subsequent field investigations in the Baichbal Valley. Studies from 1983 to 1989 consisted of an intensive survey of the valley floor leading to the discovery of over 50 Acheulean localities (Paddayya 1987b, 1991). As was the case for the Hunsgi Valley localities, the Baichbal localities also showed a distinct tendency to cluster along the sloping sides of inter-fluves, which together with ancient drainage tracts, contributed to the gently rolling topography of the valley floor. The cluster of localities along the Fatehpur nullah is the richest group known from the area and consists of about 20 Acheulean localities in a stretch of about 3 to 4 kms (Paddayya 1989). One of these localities lying at Yediyapur (Locality VI) was excavated (Paddayya 1987c). In these studies, information was obtained about the environmental context of these localities—their relation to stream courses and/or the foothill zones, the nature of the local geological formation, the flat/sloping nature of the terrain around occurrences, and the nature of the sediment cover enveloping the artifactual material. Secondly, observations were also made about the horizontal integrity of the artifact scatters and about aspects of the lithic assemblages (e.g., number of artifacts, tool types, raw material composition). To investigate the potential disruptive effects of natural processes and the effects of surface run-off, an experimental station at Kembhavi in the Baichbal Valley was established.

The main conclusion resulting from the archaeological observations and from the experimental study is that gross categories like "primary" and "secondary" are certainly not meaningful for discussion about the Acheulean occurrences (see Schick 1987). Rather, it is more appropriate to conceive of these localities as representing various stages of preservation along a continuum, where there is a great degree of variability in natural and cultural formation processes. This variability in natural and cultural formation processes is the subject of the remainder of this chapter.

Natural Formation Processes

Depositional Contexts

An increasing number of actualistic studies are documenting the general relationship between the depositional context of a site and the preservation of spatial patterns (e.g., Isaac 1967; Rick 1976; Gifford and Behrensmeyer 1977; Harris 1978; Bowers et al. 1983; Frostick and Reid 1983; Schick 1984, 1986, 1987; Petraglia and Nash 1987). In order to characterize the general depositional context of the Hunsgi-Baichbal localities, and to understand the potential postdepositional processes which contributed to their formation, the localities were classified into the four following broad categories: a) fluvial occurrences, b) colluvial occurrences, c) sheetwash occurrences, and d) deflationary occurrences. Localities within the category of fluvial occurrences have traditionally been classified as "secondary" occurrences while localities within the categories of colluvial, sheetwash and deflationary occurrences would have been classified as "primary" occurrences. The localities have been divided into these four broad categories based upon their geomorphic and sedimentological contexts. While the relationship between depositional context and integrity has been generally supported, the same studies often show that there can be tremendous variation in stratigraphic integrity within the same depositional context. Nevertheless, the distinction between the four categories should be a useful starting point for characterizing the differences between the localities, and assessing the degree to which the patterns are a result of cultural and natural processes.

Fluvial Occurrences

There are over a dozen localities belonging to this category. Most of these occurrences lie in the southwestern part of the Hunsgi Valley; they are distributed over a distance of two kilometers from the shale-limestone plateau flanking the valley on the western side. Artifactual materials occur in fluvial gravels at all of these localities.

Gulbal II is the best known example of a fluvial conglomerate containing artifactual material. At this location a sheet-like limestone boulder and cobble conglomerate is exposed over an area measuring approximately a square kilometer in extent. In the gully sections exposed by present-day nullahs, the deposit was found to be about two meters thick. The deposit consists of sub-rounded to rounded cobbles and boulders, usually measuring up to 35 cm along their long axes. The conglomerates are set in a matrix of kankary silt and are fully cemented. Features such as size-sorting and orientation of rock pieces along their long axes can be observed in the deposit. The horizontal, sheet-like form of this conglomerate and the incipient nature of size-sorting and orientation of clastic units along their long axes suggest that this deposit was laid down as a valley floor filling by sheet-floods. Rubble accumulations derived from the plateaus and kankar conglomerates (ancient slope deposits of pre-Acheulean age) probably served as the sources for the derivation of this deposit. In this connection, two to three meter thick kankar conglomerate deposits, with Acheulean artifactual materials on its surface, were discovered in the foothill zone between the villages of Gulbal and Maralbhavi. While these localities often occur in stream channels, it should be noted that the origin of these materials cannot be far from their source, since the streams are within the valley floor, and these do not flow off the

surrounding plateaus. In fact, it is also possible that some of the artifacts within the fluvial conglomerates are discarded objects in paleo-stream settings.

Colluvial Occurrences

There are about half a dozen localities belonging to this category. These localities are located in or close to the foothill zone of the plateaus. The best examples are provided by a locality near Kembhavi in the Baichbal Valley and at Wajal VIII in the Hunsgi Valley. At both of these locations the implement-bearing deposit measures more than a meter thick and is exposed as patches measuring 50 to 80 meters across. The deposit consists of angular limestone debris with some of the blocks measuring over a half-meter across. The limestone blocks and debris are set in a matrix of consolidated kankary silt. Unlike the fluviatile conglomerates, these deposits are poorly sorted and the rock fragments still preserve angular features on their surfaces. The artifacts locally occur throughout the sedimentary deposits. Thus, these deposits are not tied to fluvial activity; rather, these likely represent debris flow pediment surfaces.

Sheetwash Occurrences

Sheetwash occurrences are common in the Hunsgi-Baichbal Valleys. The wide spread of the artifactual material at the localities appears to have been displaced by surface run-off. Consequently, it is likely to have suffered some degree of horizontal displacement, particularly in situations where it occurs on sloping surfaces. Fatehpur VIII in the Baichbal Valley is one of the best examples of this situation, consisting of a discrete area of artifacts, but low in density and distributed over a large area. This situation would primarily occur in areas lacking vegetation cover, on localities which were not originally buried, or at localities which have been exposed to the surface by deflation. This category occupies an intermediate position between transported assemblages and deflated occurrences.

Deflationary Occurrences

These are the most common types of localities encountered in the Hunsgi-Baichbal Valleys, occurring in both the foothill area and on the valley floor. Many localities were probably formerly covered with a black soil which, on account of erosion and agricultural activities, has been loosened and removed by surface runoff. This probably caused a portion of the artifactual material to be winnowed away, while the remainder of the assemblage settled in the same spot.

Although deflationary occurrences are inferred to represent areas of hominid activity, there are differences among these localities with respect to their depositional contexts and the degree of postdepositional disturbances. Based upon their depositional contexts and the arrangement of material items, the localities appear to have undergone a variable degree of artifactual rearrangement due to agencies like overbank flooding and surface runoff. For example, Hunsgi II and V are located close to a perennial stream, and thus flooding may have affected intra-site patterns. In contrast, Fatehpur V does not rest along a perennial stream, but in the foothill zone, just below the shale and limestone plateaus (Figure 2). At Fatehpur V, at least eight separate clusters of artifacts were identified along rills over a large area (Figure 3), each consisting of distinct assemblages (Figure 4). Because each of these separate clusters contain assemblages without apparent size sorting, these appear to represent remnant areas of hominid activity rather than transported assemblages. At Fatehpur V colluvial processes and low energy surface runoff from the plateau probably caused some rearrangement of material prior to burial. Deflated localities occur directly on bedrock, on travertine surfaces, or remnant sediments.

Localities exist both along the Devapur-Hunsgi nullah in the Hunsgi Valley and along the Fatehpur nullah in the Baichbal Valley where the artifactual horizon rests on bedrock. At Yediyapur I the artifactual horizon rests directly on weathered granitic gruss, overlain by a shallow black soil measuring 25-30 cm in thickness. At Hunsgi V, and in several other localities, the artifactual material appears to have been originally in a matrix of kankary moorum derived from the weathering of bedrock subsequent to the desertion of the locality by the Acheulean occupants.

In the Hunsgi Valley, there are more than half a dozen localities at Devapur and Kaldevanhalli where the artifactual material occurs on the top surface of a travertine deposit formed in pre-Acheulean times. Wherever the artifactual horizon was subsequently covered by the black sediment (e.g., Devapur I) the archaeological material is still well preserved. At other localities, sediments have been entirely removed, leading to settling of artifacts on the travertine surface, where exposure has led to postdepositional changes in the material as a consequence of surface runoff and gully erosion.

In the third major category of deflationary occurrences, the artifactual horizon is associated with fine-grained sediments. The artifactual material appears to be better preserved due to the presence of a sedimentary cover. There are several localities in the Baichbal Valley where the artifactual material occurs as a distinct lense (10 to 15 cm thick) in a brownish clay deposit overlain by a black soil, consisting of locally derived granitic detritus derived from *in situ* weathering. In some places artifacts are contained in

Figure 2. View looking towards plateau, Cluster 4, Fatehpur V.

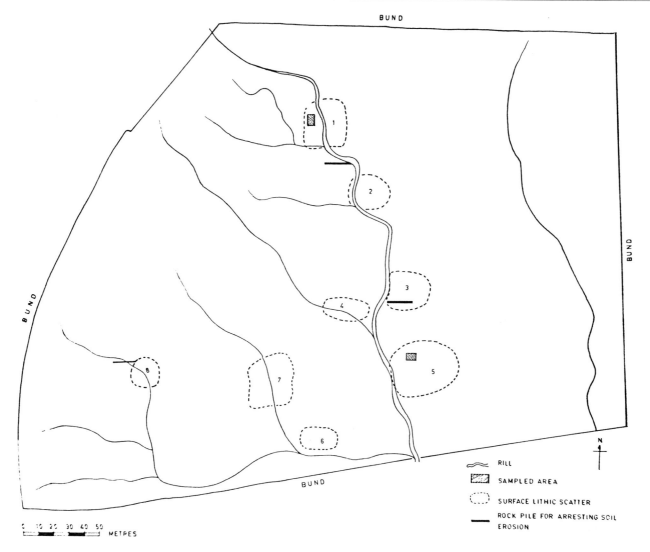

Figure 3. Fatehpur V showing clusters.

the black soil, which measures up to 3 meters in thickness. The brown clay and black soil can be found at Mudnur VIII, Mudnur X, Yediyapur IV, and Yediyapur VI.

Artifact Analyses

In order to supplement the depositional information and to examine aspects of site formation, artifact analyses were performed including study of artifact size, rounding, patination, and weathering. Each of these variables was considered useful for evaluating the contribution of natural processes on the formation of the localities, although it was recognized that multiple sets of criteria, rather than any one single variable, would be most useful for assessing site formation.

The following section compares 3 Acheulean localities from the Hunsgi Valley (Gulbal II, Hunsgi II,

Hunsgi V) and 6 localities from the Baichbal Valley (Mudnur VIII, Mudnur X, Yediyapur I, Yediyapur IV, Yediyapur VI, and Fatehpur V). As described above, Gulbal II was classified as a fluvial occurrence; the other eight localities were classified as deflationary occurrences, situated on bedrock, on travertine or in fine-grained sediments. Thus the goal of the following analysis is two-fold: a) to distinguish how Gulbal II, a fluvial occurrence, differs from the localities which may be classified as deflationary occurrences, and b) to examine the variability between the localities classified as deflationary occurrences. Unfortunately, at the time of this analysis, no information was collected on localities that could be classified as colluvial or sheet-wash occurrences.

Artifact Size Distributions

Archaeologists have recognized that artifact size distributions may be used to indicate the role of

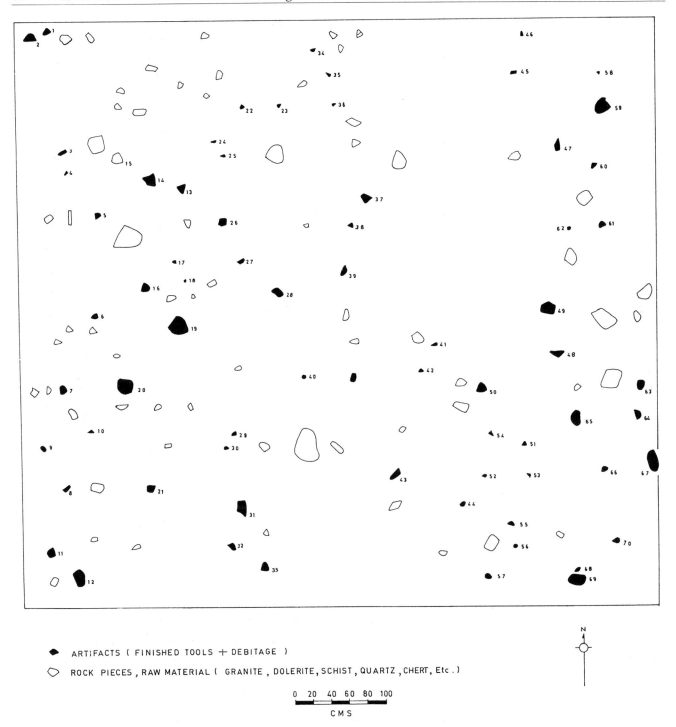

Figure 4. *Plan of Cluster 5, Fatehpur V.*

natural processes in sorting archaeological assemblages (cf. Schiffer 1983, 1987). Investigators have shown that artifact assemblages may be sorted by natural processes, and small items may be selectively removed from sites by gravity, sheetwash, and fluvial processes (e.g., Isaac 1967; Rick 1976; Harris 1978; Frostick and Reid 1983; Schick 1984, 1986, 1987;

Petraglia and Nash 1987; Petraglia 1987; Petraglia and Potts n.d.). However, as a single variable, caution should be exercised since the same studies have sometimes shown that small items may remain at a site despite the operation of natural processes.

Two Acheulean assemblages from the Hunsgi-Baichbal Valleys have been excavated (Hunsgi V,

Yediyapur VI), and one locality (Fatehpur V) was intensively collected. Unfortunately, quantification of the artifact size variability is not possible for the remainder of the Hunsgi-Baichbal localities. Many of the Acheulean localities were discovered during surface surveys and only general estimates of the number of artifacts were obtained. In many cases, only the temporally diagnostic tools were collected, thus artifact size distributions are not possible.

The average weight of the three classifiable lithic assemblages was 438 gms for Hunsgi V, 280 gms for Fatehpur V, and 321 gms for Yediyapur VI. As has been traditionally the case, the sediments in these localities were not screened, thus it should be realized that not all of the smaller artifacts were identified. The percentage of artifacts below 50 gms was calculated for the three localities. Fatehpur V (31%, n=134) contained the greatest percentage of items falling below 50 gms, followed by Yediyapur VI (29%, n=73) and Hunsgi V (18%, n=79). While it is possible that natural processes such as water flow and sheetwash may have removed items from the localities, some percentage of the assemblage remained within the localities. The presence of small items at the localities also suggests that a greater percentage of the original set of larger, heavier items remained in the localities (cf. Harris 1978; Schick 1986; Petraglia and Nash 1987).

Artifact Rounding

Artifact rounding and abrasion has traditionally been used to assess the degree to which sites have been transported by water flow (Singer et al. 1973; Shackley 1974, 1978; Wymer 1976). Despite various attempts to classify artifact rounding, little substantive research has been conducted to establish how artifact rounding occurs and the rate at which it develops. Little is known about how mechanical and chemical processes produce artifact rounding. Moreover, numerous factors probably influence rounding rates, such as raw material types, the size and shape of artifacts, the geologic context, and sedimentary conditions.

Realizing the complexity of rounding, and the probability that the Hunsgi-Baichbal artifacts were affected by mechanical transport and chemical processes, a rounding model was adopted to assess the kinds of natural processes acting on the localities and the potential impact of these processes. Petraglia and Potts (n.d.) have hypothesized that as an artifact is transported by water flow over a fine substrate, contact with sedimentary particles can cause rounding of flake scar facets, on ridges between the facets, and along the edges of an artifact. Due to contact of all artifact surfaces with the substrate, rounding of the entire artifact may occur during transport. An exception to this

is artifact transport with coarse load over a gravel bed. In coarse-grained beds, transported artifacts may sometimes become chipped through contact with other particles, resulting in the production of some "fresh" edges (Harding et al. 1987).

A different pattern of rounding may result when flowing water travels over stable or partially buried objects or when *in situ* chemical processes interact with artifact surfaces. Water flow over partially buried artifacts or chemical interactions with partially buried or buried artifacts can be presumed to produce differential rounding. A variable degree of rounding on the dorsal and ventral faces and edges of an artifact should be expected (cf. Petraglia and Potts n.d.). General rounding of artifacts in stable contexts would only occur in the most severe cases, where artifacts were exposed to the surface for long periods of time, or where chemical alterations were most serious.

This model therefore implies that different types of artifact rounding can be expected for transported assemblages versus those on stable land surfaces. While it is clear that rounding is a complex subject, with many variables influencing rounding types and rates, there should be a relationship between artifact rounding and differing depositional contexts and conditions.

In order to begin to distinguish between artifacts that may have been rounded during transport versus those rounded as a result of exposure to the ground surface or by diagenetic processes, rounding information was gathered on the dorsal face, the ventral face, and on the edges of the Hunsgi-Baichbal artifacts. The artifacts were classified according to three major types of rounding: fresh to slight, moderate, and heavy. An example of the distinction between a heavily rounded and a fresh artifact is shown in Figure 5. Table 1 lists artifact rounding by locality.

Patination

The causes of lithic patination are numerous and may include a variety of geological and chemical processes (e.g., Rottländer 1975; Goffer 1980). Upon initial review of the Hunsgi-Baichbal assemblages, it was noted that there was variation in patination between localities. Variation in patination was hypothesized to be useful for further differentiating the localities and their depositional environments, although the exact causes for lithic patination are unknown.

Artifacts were classified according to the four following patination categories: none, slightly stained (original surface visible), moderately stained, and heavily stained (original surface entirely obliterated with significant color change). The degree of artifact patination by locality is summarized in Table 2.

Figure 5. "Heavily rounded" limestone artifact from Gulbal II and "fresh" limestone artifact produced by experimental replication.

Weathering

Weathering is the natural decomposition of material through physical, chemical, and biological processes (cf. Ritter 1978). Physical and chemical weathering often operate simultaneously on rocks and minerals, and are therefore the processes are difficult to distinguish. Physical weathering consists of the collapse of material and its breakdown in size, the dimunition in size occurring when stress is exerted along zones of weakness in the material. Very little research has been devoted to lithic artifact weathering by archaeologists. However, faunal remains have been classified according to weathering stages, which incorporate characteristics of bone cracking, exfoliation, and splintering which result from the length of time bones are exposed to subaerial processes, and features such as abrasion, which relate to other processes that affect bone surfaces (e.g., Miller 1975; Behrensmeyer 1978; Potts 1986, 1988).

Upon initial review of the Hunsgi-Baichbal assemblages, it was noted that many lithic artifacts had some degree of surface cracking, probably due to a combination of physical and chemical processes near the surface. It was hypothesized that the degree to which an artifact was cracked may refer to the length of time it was exposed to the surface, although experimental rates for lithic artifact cracking and the causes have not been documented. Three weathering stages were codified as follows: none to slight, moderate, and heavy. Heavily weathered artifacts were typified by numerous cracks with pieces falling away, most often on the granite artifacts (Figure 6). Table 3 lists the weathering stage data.

Discussion

The depositional contexts of the Hunsgi-Baichbal localities and the results of the foregoing artifact analyses suggest that the localities vary in the degree to

Table 1. Artifact Rounding by Locality.

Locality	Face*	Fresh to Slight	Moderate	Heavy
Gulbal II	DFR	13 (32.5%)	3 (7.5%)	24 (60%)
	VFR	13 (35%)	3 (8%)	21 (57%)
	ER	1 (14%)	3 (43%)	3 (43%)
Hunsgi II	DFR	-	6 (13%)	40 (87%)
	VFR	-	9 (20%)	37 (80%)
	ER	-	1 (3%)	30 (97%)
Hunsgi V	DFR	27 (7%)	241 (59%)	138 (34%)
	VFR	16 (8%)	122 (61%)	63 (31%)
	ER	37 (14%)	184 (67%)	53 (19%)
Mudnur VIII	DFR	6 (67%)	3 (33%)	-
	VFR	8 (89%)	1 (11%)	-
	ER	8 (89%)	1 (11%)	-
Mudnur X	DFR	6 (50%)	4 (33%)	2 (17%)
	VFR	2 (28.5%)	3 (43%)	2(28.5%)
	ER	7 (78%)	2 (22%)	-
Yediyapur I	DFR	1 (4%)	5 (23%)	16 (73%)
	VFR	1 (5%)	7 (33%)	13 (62%)
	ER	-	10 (83%)	2 (17%)
Yediyapur IV	DFR	-	9 (43%)	12 (57%)
	VFR	-	13 (65%)	7 (35%)
	ER	8 (36%)	14 (64%)	-
Yediyapur VI	DFR	39 (21%)	78 (42%)	69 (37%)
	VFR	9 (12%)	35 (45%)	33 (43%)
	ER	39 (22%)	119 (68%)	17 (10%)
Fatehpur V	DFR	5 (4%)	89 (76%)	23 (20%)
	VFR	3 (7.5%)	23 (57.5%)	14 (35%)
	ER	6 (6%)	90 (91%)	3 (3%)

*Dorsal Facet Rounding (DFR), Ventral Facet Rounding (VFR), and Edge Rounding (ER)

Table 2. Artifact Patination by Locality.

Locality	No Staining	Slightly Stained	Moderately Stained	Heavily Stained
Gulbal II	-	5 (13%)	20 (51%)	14 (36%)
Hunsgi II	-	-	14 (30%)	33 (70%)
Hunsgi V	2 (.5%)	53 (12%)	244 (56%)	138 (31.5%)
Mudnur VIII	-	9 (100%)	-	-
Mudnur X	-	9 (75%)	3 (25%)	-
Yediyapur I	-	8 (36%)	10 (46%)	4 (18%)
Yediyapur IV	-	9 (39%)	12 (52%)	2 (9%)
Yediyapur VI	22 (9%)	40 (16%)	95 (38%)	93 (37%)
Fatehpur V	2 (2%)	29 (22%)	77 (57%)	26 (19%)

Figure 6. Heavily weathered granite artifact.

Table 3. Artifact Weathering by Locality.

Locality	None to Slight	Moderate	Heavy
Gulbal II	39 (98%)	1 (2%)	-
Hunsgi II	46 (98%)	-	1 (2%)
Hunsgi V	401 (92%)	30 (7%)	6 (1%)
Mudnur VIII	9 (100%)	-	-
MudnurX	11 (92%)	1 (8%)	-
Yediyapur I	16 (73%)	6 (27%)	-
Yediyapur IV	21 (88%)	2 (8%)	1 (4%)
Yediyapur VI	219 (88%)	22 (9%)	9 (3%)
Fatehpur V	117 (87%)	7 (5%)	10 (8%)

which they are preserved and altered by natural processes. The analyses tend to support the distinction made between fluvial occurrences (Gulbal II) and deflationary occurrences, although the variability in preservation among the deflationary occurrences appears considerable.

The artifact analyses tend to support that Gulbal II is a transported fluvial occurrence. The locality consists of artifacts within a 2 meter thick limestone conglomerate. The artifacts appear to be size sorted and exhibit preferred orientations. Large bifaces are usually retrieved from these thick deposits, and few small artifacts have been observed. These objects are almost always isolated, and are never concentrated. The pattern of highly rounded artifacts and a percentage of "chipped" artifacts at Gulbal II holds with the model of transported assemblages in coarse-grained stream beds. The lower proportion of weathered artifacts in this assemblage either indicates burial of the artifacts once they were deposited, or general smoothening of these predominantly lime-stone objects by water flow.

In contrast to Gulbal II, the deflationary occur-rences appear to be assemblages that have retained some degree of depositional integrity, although the degree to which they have been modified by natural processes varies.

Two localities situated in fine-grained sediments, Mudnur VIII and Mudnur X, appear to have retained the greatest degree of depositional integrity. The favorable depositional setting and the artifact anal-yses appear to indicate well preserved assemblages, not seriously sorted by natural processes. The artifacts from the Mudnur localities are usually fresh in appearance, and are infrequently patinated and weathered. Pedestrian survey over Mudnur X revealed a wide distribution of artifacts, with variable clusters of material, consisting of both small and large artifacts. Mudnur VIII consisted of a small number of standardized handaxes in a confined area, standing apart from all other Acheulean localities. The fine-grained deposits, the artifact analyses and the presence of an unusual set of Acheulean artifacts would imply that the Mudnur localities retain a high degree of behavioral integrity.

The Yediyapur VI assemblage occurs in a weath-ered granite gruss, partially covered by a black soil. The artifact analyses imply that Yediyapur VI retains some degree of integrity, but preservation is not as good as that noted at the Mudnur localities. A propor-tion of the smaller artifacts is present, implying that if winnowing occurred, it was not severe. Yediyapur VI displays variation in the degree of rounding on arti-facts, suggesting that rounding has occurred as a result of long-term exposure to the surface rather than from transport. Indeed, the high percentage of weathered pieces supports the notion that artifacts were exposed to the surface for some length of time. Despite being covered by black soil, the presence of weathered arti-facts suggests that the assemblage was exposed on the surface before final burial, and thus postdepositional processes may have acted on this locality.

In the case of Hunsgi V and Fatehpur V, the sedi-ments were probably eroded away along with a proportion of the artifacts, the assemblages coming to rest on or near bedrock surfaces. At these localities a proportion of the smaller artifacts is still found, suggesting that not all of the smaller elements have been winnowed from the locality. These two localities do not contain large percentages of fresh artifacts nor highly rounded artifacts suggesting that rounding has

occurred as a result of long-term exposure to the surface rather than from transport. While Fatehpur V contains high percentages of eroded pieces, the dorsal and ventral rounding values are quite different, arguing for exposure of artifacts rather than transport. The presence of some weathered pieces supports the notion that artifacts were exposed to the surface for some length of time.

Yediyapur I and Hunsgi II appear to be most affected by postdepositional processes, consisting of either severe *in situ* processes or possibly transport. These localities are close to bedrock, and they have been exposed by erosion. Yediyapur I and Hunsgi II have high percentages of heavily rounded artifacts, suggesting the possibility of transport, the operation of long-term diagenetic processes, or exposure to the surface. Transport may be indicated by the high percentage of dorsal and ventral rounding and the high percentage of edge rounding. Hunsgi II displayed the greatest percentage of patinated pieces, further signalling the operation of postdepositional processes. Yediyapur I contains a high percentage of weathered pieces, implying long-term exposure to the surface.

Yediyapur IV appears to occupy an intermediate position between the deflated sites. At this locality, the artifacts show signs of moderate rounding and weathering.

The sedimentary contexts and artifact analyses suggest that the integrity of the Acheulean localities varies considerably. In order to put the Acheulean localities in a proper comparative framework, the localities were ranked according to the degree to which they have been modified by natural processes. The localities may be viewed on different interpretive scales, including basin-wide and intra-site scales.

Basin-Wide Scale

The Hunsgi and Baichbal Valleys took their basic geological configuration during the Tertiary. Since that time, there has been overall geological stability, and no evidence for tectonic movements. The basin has also been generally stable, indicated by an unchanging basin configuration, the limited evidence for major fluvial activity, and the gentle gradient of the valley floor. These factors account for the preser-vation of the Acheulean localities to a degree not normally seen in high energy fluvial contexts.

The Hunsgi and Baichbal Valleys are not part of a large river valley with a deep channel, but rather the valleys occur in the headwater zone of the major Krishna drainage. There are no major rivers in the valley that could have caused long distance transport of the artifactual material. The Acheulean localities occur within distances varying from a few hundred meters to a few kilometers from the foothill zone and, as a result, the question of long-distance transport cannot be supported.

Since the Acheulean localities occur in the headwater zone, the operation of low order alluvial processes has meant that the Acheulean localities have not been subject to fluvial processes of the magnitude experienced in major river valleys. However, because of their location, there was little source for sediment accumulation, and thus the localities were not deeply buried.

Archaeological evidence may be used to support the lack of wholesale assemblage transport. The fact that there are Middle and Upper Paleolithic occupations on the plateaus is significant, and means that the basin has certainly taken on its configuration at least since the Middle Paleolithic. That is, if there was continuous erosion from the plateaus since the Middle Paleolithic, there would be little evidence of intact localities on these surfaces.

The Acheulean localities on the valley floor are distinct, localized occurrences, and certain patterns to be discussed below suggest they are the product of Acheulean activity, rather than transported accumulations. Factors such as surface runoff, minor stream action, and colluvial processes surely caused spatial alterations at the localities. However, the magnitude of these natural processes were partially offset by factors like gentle slope of the valley floor and the presence of vegetation, particularly the grass cover which responds quickly to the availability of soil moisture.

Many of the Acheulean localities in the Hunsgi-Baichbal Valleys, and in many other valleys in India, occur in plowed fields. The denudation of artifactual levels could have been a serious factor especially in the last half century or so on account of vegetation clearance and reclamation of the land for agricultural purposes. It should be noted that in the Hunsgi-Baichbal Valleys, the effects of traditional Indian plowing have certainly been less disturbing than mechanical techniques. As such, the scope for displacement, both vertically and horizontally, of artifacts is not as severe. This is particularly true in the case of Acheulean localities which tend to yield high percentages of large, heavy artifacts.

Site Scale

A major question raised in this study is the implication of the depositional contexts of the localities for understanding spatial integrity. The distinction between spot provenience and point provenience seems useful to bear in mind. In the former case the artifact assemblage is still confined to the spot or locality, whereas point provenience refers to the original positions in which the individual items at a locality are still preserved.

Judging the Acheulean localities of the area in terms of these parameters, one can say that the localities in fluviatile and colluvial situations lack both spot provenience and point provenience. The assemblages have clearly been displaced from their original positions. Nevertheless, considering the enclosed topographical setting of the area and the short distance that the assemblages could travel, ranging from a few tens of meters to a few kilometers of displacement, these localities are far less secondary than true river cliff sections such as those found on the Narmada river valley and other rivers throughout India. As a result, these localities are useful for purposes of general reconstruction, for example, typo-technological studies and raw material variability. This is particularly true of colluvial situations since these localities tend also to produce raw material blocks and debitage along with finished tools.

Localities subjected to a variable degree of modification by surface runoff occupy an intermediate place between purely fluviatile and colluvial contexts on the one hand, and deflationary contexts on the other. While it is true that these localities have suffered alteration in respect to both spot provenience and point provenience, one cannot overlook the fact that these localities still preserve a large portion of the original artifactual material and at spots lying close to the original localities. Hence they have a place of their own in the reconstruction of past hominid activities.

Localities that have been classified as deflationary occurrences are characterized by spot provenience. Here the artifactual material is still preserved within the confines of their original localities. Even allowing some margin for time lapse between location desertion and its burial by sediments, these localities do not appear to have undergone an extreme amount of distortion by high energy natural processes. This is reflected in the lower energy depositional contexts, dense concentration of artifacts, occurrence of raw material blocks, variability in artifact types within and among localities, occurrence of small components of debitage, and the results of the artifact analyses. The effects of surface runoff, the most likely geomorphic agency acting on these surfaces, is an important consideration and indeed runoff likely affected the localities to variable degrees. However, the effects of surface runoff would have been counterbalanced by grass cover, ground vegetation and topographic conditions which tend to hold artifacts in place. The Kembhavi experimental plot set up by the authors has shown a lack of artifact displacement despite several monsoon seasons. None of the pieces planted on this plot, including the small pieces, has moved outside of the plot boundaries even after three annual seasons of the Indian monsoon. On the contrary, the bottoms of large objects and the edges of smaller pieces have developed a tendency to become embedded in the sediments.

Even granting the inference that some of the localities are on or close to original spots of hominid activity, it is an altogether different matter with regard to point provenience. In a majority of the cases the individual pieces forming part of the Acheulean floors could have and probably indeed did suffer intra-site displacement ranging from a few centimeters to many meters. It is likely that smaller artifacts were winnowed from the localities and original spatial patterns were probably altered. Thus, intra-site patterns probably no longer can be directly interpreted to be the result of hominid activities. This means that extreme caution should be exercised when attempting site structural interpretations.

Cultural Formation Processes

Based upon the variable preservation of the Acheulean localities, it should be possible to compare the localities for their ability to yield information about hominid activities. While transported and severely sorted localities would be limited in their ability to provide information about Acheulean technology and activity, a conclusion of this study is that some of the localities are not deposited far from their original spots, and certain other localities occur on or close to their original spots. Transported sites would therefore allow for comparisons to be made between aspects of stone tool technology and functional variability.

Technology

Table 4 lists the handaxe dimensions from each of the localities. The Yediyapur I and Fatehpur V handaxe weights were low and the width to length ratios were high, indicative of short, and stout objects. On the other hand, the Mudnur VIII handaxes were heavy and had low width to length ratios, indicative

of elongate objects. The two Mudnur X handaxes were small and had high thickness to width ratios [also evidenced by finds in the field], perhaps indicative of a special handaxe type, or perhaps heavy reworking.

Differences in handaxe ratios among the localities may partially be the result of stylistic variations. There is ample typo-technological evidence from the Hunsgi and Baichbal Valleys for distinguishing two stone tool stylistic variations within the Acheulean assemblages. While an explanation is not readily apparent, these two stylistic variations appear to correlate with sediment types. The stylistic variation consists of a crude tradition as represented by localities where the artifactual horizon usually occurs on bedrock and a more developed or refined tradition as revealed by assemblages associated with brownish clay deposits. The possibility is that the temporally earlier localities may have been deflated, while the later localities are still contained in non-eroded sediments.

This stylistic variation not only occurs between localities, but within localities. Yediyapur IV in the Baichbal Valley may be regarded as the most representative for demonstrating these two stylistic traditions within one locality. In one part of Yediyapur IV, an Acheulean assemblage based on the working of granite and dolerite and characterized by rough outlines of artifacts, pointed handaxes with thick cross-sections were found on the weathered granite surface. In another part of the Yediyapur IV, a brownish clay (1 to 1.5 meter thick) yielded an artifactual assemblage of limestone and dolerite with artifacts showing fine flaking, thin cross-sections and reduction in overall size.

Raw Material Variability

Table 5 presents the raw material breakdown for each of the Hunsgi-Baichbal localities. Limestone is the principal raw material employed at localities in the Hunsgi Valley. Limestone was obtained as

Table 4. Handaxe Dimensions by Locality.

Locality	No.	Mean Length (cms)	Mean Width (cms)	Width/ Thick (cms)	Thick/ Length (cms)	Mean Width (cms)	Mean Weight (gms)
Gulbal II	12	15	9	5	.60	.55	902
Hunsgi II	18	17	10	5	.58	.50	1042
Hunsgi V	43	15	9	5	.60	.55	682
Mudnur VIII	9	23	11	6	.47	.54	1302
Mudnur X	2	12	6	4	.50	.66	265
Yediyapur I	10	12	8	4	.66	.50	443
Yediyapur IV	11	14	8	4	.57	.50	627
Yediyapur VI	21	13	8	4	.61	.50	591
Fatehpur V	11	12	8	4	.66	.50	455

nodules from slope wash deposits and kankar conglomerates and as river cobbles. In the Baichbal Valley artifacts are produced from a variety of materials. At certain localities granite and dolerite predominate, while at others, limestone predominates. Thus there is variation between the two valleys and between localities in the use of raw material.

Functional Variability Among Localities

Suggesting functional variability, artifact density and diversity varied among the localities in the Hunsgi and Baichbal Valleys. Based on estimates obtained during surface walkovers, Mudnur VIII can be classified as a small locality (1-25 artifacts); Hunsgi II, Mudnur X, Yediyapur I, and Yediyapur IV as medium localities (12-100 artifacts); and Hunsgi V, Yediyapur VI, and Fatehpur V, as very large localities (>200 artifacts).

Many of the localities measure 50 to 60 square meters in extent, often occurring as scatters of stone material owing to their exposure by sedimentary deflation and modern land use activities. There are some localities, like Fatehpur V, which cover a much larger area. The Fatehpur V locality covers a total area of more than two hectares and contains as many as eight surface clusters.

Table 6 lists the recovered artifact types from the localities. The diversity of artifact types may signal some functional differences among localities. Mudnur VIII is set apart from the other localities with respect to the recovery of only handaxes and the complete absence of other tools or debitage. The sample from Mudnur X is more diverse, the assemblage consisting of both tools and debitage. At Yediyapur I, handaxes and a broad array of other tools are found, but debitage is absent. Yediyapur IV is similar to Yediyapur I in terms of the dominance of handaxes, although there is not as much diversity in tool types, and some debitage is present. Yediyapur VI, Hunsgi V, and Fatehpur V contain a broad spectrum of tool types and debitage. Hunsgi V contains a larger number of scrapers, perhaps indicating specialized activity at this locality. Yediyapur VI, Hunsgi V, and Fatehpur V contain flake cores, flakes, and hammerstones, demonstrating that stone tool reduction took place at these locations.

Table 7 is a summary of the cortical percentages for tools and debitage by locality. Few objects were completely cortical or completely thinned to remove all signs of cortex. Cortical percentages vary among the Valleys and between the localities, signalling some differences in tool manufacture and reduction. The Hunsgi sites contain the highest percentage of cortical artifacts, whereas the Baichbal sites contain the least, particularly at the Mudnur localities.

In terms of the utilization of stone tools, the edges of all implements were examined to determine if any smaller flake scars, indicative of use or secondary stage technological shaping, were visible. As noted earlier, many of the artifacts were rounded and signs of smaller flake scars were sometimes obscured. Although many artifacts bore edge rounding, smaller flake scars were often visible, if sometimes rounded. Nevertheless, upon examination of the edges of the stone tools, many bore signs of smaller flake scars, 100% at Mudnur VIII, 86% at Yediyapur IV, 67% at Mudnur X, 67% at Yediyapur I, 63% at Hunsgi V, 45% at Fatehpur V, 44% at Yediyapur VI, and 36% at Hunsgi II. This analysis could not demonstrate if the smaller flake scars were the result of stone tool reduction practices, use, or natural processes. However, the evidence does suggest that microwear analysis may help to elucidate the function of stone tools.

A number of localities in the Hunsgi-Baichbal Valleys, including Yediyapur IV and Fatehpur V, are located on topographical eminences along streams and produce a large number of artifacts, together with raw material blocks and debitage. These localities appear to represent multipurpose activities where tool-making, food processing activities, and repeated artifact discard took place. Further, there are certain features such as differential weathering and reflaking of artifacts which suggest that some of these localities witnessed multiple episodes of occupation and use.

There is another class of localities represented by Hebbal Buzburg II, Teggihalli II, Yediyapur XII which have produced limited numbers of finished tools along with faunal material. The faunal material consists of both dental and post-cranial remains of animals species belonging to the *Bos, Bubalus, Elephas,* and *Equus* groups (Paddayya 1985). The proximity of these spots to large localities and the lack of raw material blocks and debitage suggest that these localities experienced specialized activity, perhaps food processing activities.

There are a few localities which seem to bear evidence of artifact curation, important to our understanding of the ability of early hominids for long-term planning (Binford 1987) and caching (Potts 1988). In the Hunsgi-Baichbal Valleys, the best example of a curated assemblage is provided by Mudnur VIII where massive handaxes of limestone (Figure 7) were found in a small area, without any signs of any other accompanying artifacts or debitage. Apparently, the locality represents a cache meant for future use, but never revisited. The standard size and shape of the artifacts (Table 8), and the spatial clustering of these artifacts, suggests the hominids cached the items, intending to re-visit this location. This would provide evidence for some degree of planning depth during the Acheulean.

Table 5. Raw Materials by Locality.

	limestone	quartzite	chert	sandstone	shale	granite	dolerite	schist	filite	quartz
Gulbal II	22		18							
	(55%)	(45%)								
Hunsgi II	43	2	1			1				
	(92%)	(4%)	(2%)			(2%)				
Hunsgi V	353	11	61	3	1	2	1	3	1	1
	(80.5%)	(2.5%)	(13.5%)	(.5%)	(.5%)	(.5%)	(.5%)	(.5%)	(.5%)	(.5%)
Mudnur VIII	9									
	(100%)									
Mudnur X	9	2				1				
	(75%)	(17%)				(8%)				
Yediyapur I	7		1			11	8	3		
	(23%)		(3%)			(37%)	(27%)	(10%)		
Yediyapur IV	11					5	6	3		
	(44%)					(20%)	(24%)	(12%)		
Yediyapur VI	12	6	42	3		116	61	5		5
	(5%)	(2%)	(17%)	(1%)		(46.5%)	(24.5%)	(2%)		(2%)
Fatehpur V	1		26			77	18	2		10
	(1%)		(19%)			(58%)	(13%)	(2%)		(7%)

Table 6. Number of Artifact Types by Locality.

	chopper	handaxe	cleaver	pick	knife	polyhedron	spheroid	end scraper	side scraper
Gulbal II	8	12	2	2	1				1
Hunsgi II	5	18	13		1				1
Hunsgi V	27	43	53	23	29	8	4	1	22
Mudnur VIII		9							
Mudnur X		2			1				
Yediyapur I	1	10	6	3	2	2	2		1
Yediyapur IV	1	11	6		3				
Yediyapur VI	23	21	17	8	9		1		3
Fatehpur V	10	11	11	3	4	2			3

	end/ side scraper	hammer stone	utilized material	discoid	biface	prepared butt	backed tool	flake core	flake	angular debris
Gulbal II			7					5	2	
Hunsgi II			2		2			4	1	
Hunsgi V	7	7	2	2	2	2	1	38	122	8
Mudnur VIII										
Mudnur X		1		1	1			2	4	
Yediyapur I			3						4	
Yediyapur IV									4	
Yediyapur VI		7	2	5	11			17	121	4
Fatehpur V	2	5	1	1	2			3	75	1

Finally, there are many instances of the occurrence of one or of a few tools in an area. These instances are spread all over the valley floor in a random fashion, perhaps indicating hominid activity over the entire landscape as has been examined in non-site approaches (e.g., Thomas 1975; Foley 1981a, 1981b; Isaac 1984; Ebert 1991). These finds may represent satellites of activity between larger localities. In some cases, these isolated artifacts may represent single-episode events involving an individual or a small group, perhaps for food collecting or processing activities.

Conclusions

The foregoing attempt to examine the Acheulean localities of the Hunsgi-Baichbal Valleys is a provisional model concerning the relative roles played by natural and cultural formation processes. We hope that from this account it is clear that the Acheulean localities vary considerably in their preservation. These varied contexts are probably best understood by treating them as the end-product of the interplay of two opposite sets

Figure 7. Large Handaxes from Mudnur VIII.

Table 7. Cortical Percentages by Locality.

Locality	0%	1-25%	26-50%	51-75%	76-99%	100%
Gulbal II	4 (10%)	14 (35%)	8 (20%)	6 (15%)	8 (20%)	-
Hunsgi II	-	8 (42%)	4 (21%)	4 (21%)	3 (16%)	-
Hunsgi V	44 (11%)	166 (41%)	78 (19%)	57 (14%)	49 (12%)	14 (3%)
Mudnur VIII	-	9 (100%)	-	-	-	-
Mudnur X	1 (9%)	6 (55%)	3 (27%)	-	1 (9%)	-
Yediyapur I	-	16 (67%)	5 (21%)	3 (12%)	-	-
Yediyapur IV	3 (19%)	10 (63%)	2 (12%)	1 (6%)	-	-
Yediyapur VI	66 (36%)	60 (33%)	21 (12%)	7 (4%)	18 (10%)	9 (5%)
Fatehpur V	37 (33%)	47 (43%)	13 (12%)	4 (4%)	5 (4%)	4 (4%)

Table 8. Handaxe Dimensions from Mudnur VIII.

Length	Width	Thickness	Weight
23	9	7	1190
25	11	6	1500
25	11	6	1475
21	9	6	975
21	11	6	1160
23	12	7	1560
24	10	7	1450
22	11	6	1245
21	12	4	1140

of processes operating on the landscape—one set of factors tending to preserve the features of the landscape and the other set tending to alter the localities.

While this study needs to be pursued further and put on a sounder footing by undertaking more detailed and systematic field and laboratory analyses, one could probably say with justification that it has already served the purpose of exposing the hollowness of oft-repeated classification of sites in India into the simple dichotomy of primary and secondary types. In a larger sense the prolonged research in the Hunsgi-Baichbal Valleys serves to emphasize the potential of the lateral approach in which emphasis is placed on the selection of areas away from major rivers and the investigation of non-riverine sites.

Although the Acheulean localities of the Hunsgi-Baichbal valleys have undergone some alteration due to natural processes, the basin-wide survey has proven to be useful for establishing Acheulean settlement patterns. Clearly, the most important precondition for attempting settlement system reconstructions rests firmly on an understanding of formation processes.

Peninsular India surely has numerous untapped regions and sites similar to that presented by the Hunsgi-Baichbal Valleys. Given the lack of deep burial of Acheulean localities in India, it is possible to reconstruct settlement patterns, unlike in other parts of the world, where exposures in rivers and gullies present the only chance for discovering sites. This site formation study is the first attempt of its kind in Indian Stone Age archaeology. We hope that it will be followed by similar studies in other parts of Peninsular India, so that Indian prehistory can eventually formulate its own 'Rosetta Stones', rather than continue to blindly use yardsticks adopted from other parts of the Old World.

Acknowledgments

K. Paddayya gratefully acknowledges the prolonged financial support provided by Deccan College, Pune, and the University Grants Commission, New Delhi. The joint research presented here was first discussed during K. Paddayya's travel to the U.S. as a Senior Fulbright Fellow. K. Paddayya is grateful to the International Council for the Exchange of Scholars, Washington, D.C., and the United States Educational Foundation in India, New Delhi, for providing this opportunity. M. Petraglia's studies in India would not have been possible without the generous support provided by the Smithsonian Institution's Special Foreign Currency Program, and the kind assistance of the director of the Office of International Relations, F. Berkowitz. Support for M. Petraglia's research was also provided by the L.S.B. Leakey Foundation, the Boise Foundation, and the Smithsonian's Human Origins Program. The authors are grateful to R. Korisettar, P.C. Venkata Subbaiah and R. Jhaldiyal for their help in setting up and monitoring the experimental station at Kembhavi. Thanks are extended to D. Nash for his assistance in the analysis of lithic assemblages at Deccan College, to T. Plummer for assistance in the analysis of the data set at the Smithsonian, and to C. Martin for Plates 2 and 3. P. Goldberg, D. Nash, and M. Schiffer provided valuable comments on a draft of this chapter. M. Petraglia gratefully acknowledges the support and assistance provided to him by colleagues at Deccan College, especially V.N. Misra, S.N. Rajaguru, G.L. Badam and R. Korisettar. Friends at the World Centre of Girl Guides and Girl Scouts are thanked for their warm hospitality.

References Cited

Behrensmeyer, A.K.
1978 Taphonomic and Ecologic Information from Bone Weathering. *Paleobiology* 4:150-162.
Binford, L.R.
1981 *Bones: Ancient Men and Modern Myths*. Academic Press, New York.
1987 Searching for Camps and Missing the Evidence? Another look at the Lower Paleolithic. In *The Pleistocene Old World: Regional Perspectives*, edited by O. Soffer, pp. 17-31. Plenum Press, New York.
Bowers, P.M., Bonnichsen, R., and D.M. Hoch
1983 Flake Dispersal Experiments: Noncultural Transformation of the Archaeological Record. *American Antiquity* 48:553-572.
Corvinus, G.K.
1968 An Acheulian Occupation Floor at Chirki-on-Pravara, India. *Current Anthropology* 9:216-218.
1973 Excavations at an Acheulean Site at Chirki-on-Pravara in India. In *South Asian Archaeology*, edited by N. Hammond, pp. 13-28. Duckworth, London.
1981 *A Survey of the Pravara River System in Western Maharashtra, India, Vol. 1: The Stratigraphy and Geomorphology of the Pravara River System*. Institut für Urgeschichte, Tubingen.
1983 *A Survey of the Pravara River System in Western Maharashtra, India, Vol. 2: The Excavations of the Acheulian Site of Chirki-on-Pravara, India*. Institut für Urgeschichte, Tubingen.
Ebert, J.
1991 *Distributional Archaeology*. University of New Mexico Press, Albuquerque.
Foley, R.
1981a Off-Site Archaeology: An Alternative Approach for the Short-Sited. In *Pattern of the Past: Studies in Honour of David L. Clarke*, edited by I. Hodder, G. Isaac, and N. Hammond, pp. 157-183. Cambridge University Press, Cambridge.
1981b *Off-Site Archaeology and Human Adaptation in Eastern Africa: An Analysis of Regional Artefact Density in the Amboseli, Southern Kenya*. BAR International Series 97, Oxford.
Foote, R.B.
1916 *The Foote Collection of Indian Prehistoric and Protohistoric Antiquities: Notes on Their Ages and Distribution*. Government Museum, Madras.
Frostick, L., and I. Reid
1983 Taphonomic Significance of Sub-Aerial Transport of Vertebrate Fossils on Steep Semi-Arid Slopes. *Lethaia* 16:157-164.
Gaussen, H., P. Legris, and M. Viart
1965 International Map of Vegetation and of Environmental Conditions - Notes on the Sheet Godavari. Indian Council of Agricultural Research, New Delhi.
Gifford, D.P., and A.K. Behrensmeyer
1977 Observed Formation and Burial of a Recent Human Occupation Site in Kenya. *Quaternary Research* 8:245-266.
Goffer, Z.
1980 *Archaeological Chemistry: A Sourcebook on the Applications of Chemistry to Archaeology*. Wiley, New York.
Harding, P., Gibbard, P.L., Lewin, J., Macklin, M.G., and E.H. Moss
1987 The Transport and Abrasion of Flint Handaxes in a Gravel-Bed River. In *The Human Uses of Flint and Chert*, edited by G. De G. Sieveking and M.H. Newcomer, pp. 115-126. Cambridge University Press, Cambridge.
Harris, J.W.K.
1978 *The Karari Industry, its Place in East African Prehistory*. Ph.D. Dissertation, University of California, Berkeley, University Microfilms, Ann Arbor.
Isaac, G.Ll.
1967 Towards the Interpretation of Occupation Debris: Some Experiments and Observations. *Kroeber Anthropological Society Papers* 37:31-57.
1984 The Archaeology of Human Origins: Studies of the Lower Pleistocene in East Africa 1971-1981. In *Advances in World Archaeology*, edited by F. Wendorf and A. Close, pp. 1-87. Academic Press, New York.

1989 *The Archaeology of Human Origins: Papers by Glynn Isaac*. Cambridge University Press, Cambridge.

Jacobson, J.

1970 On Palaeolithic Occupation Floors in India. *Current Anthropology* 11:483.

1975 Early Stone Age Habitation Sites in Eastern Malwa. *Proceedings of the American Philosophical Society* 119:280-297.

1979 Recent Developments in South Asian Prehistory and Protohistory. *Annual Reviews of Anthropology* 8:467-502.

1985 Acheulian Surface Sites in Central India. In *Recent Advances in Indo-Pacific Prehistory*, edited by V.N. Misra and P. Bellwood, pp. 49-57. Oxford and IBH, New Delhi.

Joshi, R.V.

1970 The Characteristics of the Pleistocene Climatic Events in the Indian Subcontinent - A Land of Monsoon Climate. *Indian Antiquary* 4:53-63.

Mahadevan, C.

1941 Geology of the South and Southwestern Parts of Surapur Taluk of Gulbarga District. *Journal, Hyderabad Geological Survey* 4:102-161.

Miller, G.J.

1975 A Study of Cuts, Grooves, and Other Marks on Recent and Fossil Bone: II Weather Cracks, Fractures, Splinters, and Other Similar Natural Phenomena. In *Lithic Technology*, edited by E.H. Swanson, pp. 211-226. Mouton, The Hague.

Misra, V.N.

1987 Middle Pleistocene Adaptations in India. In *The Pleistocene Old World: Regional Perspectives*, edited by O. Soffer, pp. 99-119. Plenum Press, New York.

1989 Stone Age India: An Ecological Perspective. *Man and Environment* 14:17-64.

Mishra, S.

1992 The Age of the Acheulian in India: New Evidence. *Current Anthropology* 33:325-328.

Mukherjee, S.K.

1941 Geology of Parts of Surapur and Shahpur Taluks, Gulbarga District. *Journal, Hyderabad Geological Survey* 4:9-54.

Paddayya, K.

1977a An Acheulian Occupation Site at Hunsgi, Peninsular India: A Summary of the Results of Two Seasons of Excavation (1975-6). *World Archaeology* 8:344-355.

1977b The Acheulian Culture of the Hunsgi Valley (Shorapur Doab), Peninsular India. *Proceedings of the American Philosophical Society* 121:383-406.

1978 New Research Designs and Field Techniques in the Palaeolithic Archaeology of India. *World Archaeology* 10:94-110.

1979 Excavation of a New Acheulian Occupation Site at Hunsgi, Peninsular India. *Quartar* 29/30:139-155.

1982 *The Acheulian Culture of the Hunsgi Valley (Peninsular India): A Settlement System Perspective*. Deccan College, Poona.

1984 India. In *Neue Forschungen Zur Altsteinzeit*, edited by O. Bar Yosef, et al., pp. 345-403. Verlag C.H. Beck, Munich.

1985 Acheulian Occupation Sites and Associated Fossil Fauna from the Hunsgi-Baichbal Valleys, Peninsular India. *Anthropos* 80:653-658.

1987a The Place of the Study of Site Formation Processes in Prehistoric Research in India. In *Natural Formation Processes and the Archaeological Record*, edited by D.T. Nash and M.D. Petraglia, pp. 74-85. BAR International Series 352, Oxford.

1987b The Stone Age Cultural Systems of the Baichbal Valley, Gulbarga District, Karnataka - A Preliminary Report. *Bulletin of the Deccan College Research Institute* 46:77-100.

1987c Excavation of an Acheulian Occupation Site at Yediyapur, Peninsular India. *Anthropos* 82:610-614.

1989 The Acheulian Culture Localities Along the Fatehpur Nullah, Baichbal Valley, Karnataka (Peninsular India). In *Old Problems and New Perspectives in the Archaeology of South Asia*, edited by J.M. Kenoyer, pp. 21-28. University of Wisconsin Press, Madison.

1991 The Acheulian Cultural Phase in the Baichbal Valley, Peninsular India. In *Indian Archaeological Heritage (Shri K.V. Soundara Rajan Festschrift)*, Volume 1, edited by C. Margabandhu, K.S. Ramachandran, A.P. Sagar, and D.K. Sinha, pp. 55-61. Agam Kala Prakashan, Delhi.

Petraglia, M.D.

1987 *Site Formation Processes at the Abri Dufaure: A Study of Upper Paleolithic Rockshelter and Hillslope Deposits in Southwestern France*. Ph.D. Dissertation, University of New Mexico, University Microfilms, Ann Arbor.

Petraglia, M.D., and D.T. Nash

1987 The Impact of Fluvial Processes on Experimental Sites. In *Natural Formation Processes and the Archaeological Record*, edited by D.T. Nash and M.D. Petraglia, pp. 108-130. BAR International Series 352, Oxford.

Petraglia, M.D., and R. Potts

n.d. Water Flow and the Formation of Early Pleistocene Artifact Sites in Olduvai Gorge, Tanzania. Manuscript in possession of authors.

Potts, R.

1986 Temporal Span of Bone Accumulations at Olduvai Gorge and Implications for Early Foraging Behavior. *Paleobiology* 12:25-31.

1988 *Early Hominid Activities at Olduvai*. Aldine de Gruyter, Chicago.

Rick, J.W.

1976 Downslope Movement and Archaeological Intrasite Spatial Analyses. *American Antiquity* 41:133-144.

Ritter, D.F.

1978 *Process Geomorphology*. Wm. C. Brown Company Publishers, Dubuque.

Rottländer, R.

1975 The Formation of Patina on Flint. *Archaeometry* 17:106-110.

Sankalia, H.D.

1974 *The Prehistory and Protohistory of India and Pakistan*. Deccan College Postgraduate and Research Institute, Poona.

Schick, K.D.

1984 *Processes of Palaeolithic Site Formation: An Experimental Study*. Ph.D. Dissertation, University of California, Berkeley, University Microfilms, Ann Arbor.

1986 *Stone Age Sites in the Making: Experiments in the Formation and Transformation of Archaeological Occurrences*. BAR International Series 319, Oxford.

1987 Experimentally-Derived Criteria for Assessing Hydrologic Disturbance of Archaeological Sites. In *Natural Formation Processes and the Archaeological Record*, edited by D.T. Nash and M.D. Petraglia, pp. 86-107. BAR International Series 352, Oxford.

Schiffer, M.B.

1976 *Behavioral Archeology*. Academic Press, New York.

1983 Toward the Identification of Formation Processes. *American Antiquity* 48:675-706.

1987 *Formation Processes of the Archaeological Record*. University of New Mexico Press, Albuquerque.

Shackley, M.L.

1974 Stream Abrasion of Flint Implements. *Nature* 248:501-502.

1978 The Behaviour of Artefacts as Sedimentary Particles in a Fluviatile Environment. *Archaeometry* 20:55-61.

Singer, R., Wymer, J., Gladfelter, B.G., and R.G. Wolff

1973 Excavation of the Clactonian Industry at the Golf Course, Clacton-On-Sea, Essex. *Proceedings of the Prehistoric Society* 39:6-74.

Straus, L.G.

1983 Review of *The Acheulian Culture of the Hunsgi Valley* by K. Paddayya's. *Journal of Anthropological Research* 39:447-449.

Szabo, B.J., C. McKinney, T.S. Dalbey, and K. Paddayya

1990 On the Age of the Acheulian Culture of the Hunsgi-Baichbal Valleys, Peninsular India. *Bulletin of the Deccan College Post-Graduate and Research Institute* 50:317-321.

Thomas, D.H.

1975 Non-Site Sampling in Archaeology: Up the Creek Without a Site? In *Sampling in Archaeology*, edited by J.W. Mueller, pp. 61-81. University of Arizona Press, Tucson.

Wymer, J.J.

1976 The Interpretation of Palaeolithic Cultural and Faunal Material found in Pleistocene Sediments. In *Geoarchaeology: Earth Science and the Past*, edited by D.A. Davidson and M.L. Shackley, pp. 327-334. Duckworth, London.

Section II

The Intra-Site Scale

The chapters in the previous section presented examples of how the effects of formation processes can be evaluated at sites occurring in similar geomorphic contexts (e.g., caves) and at sites occurring in the same region. While the inter-site approach is valuable for assessing how sites may compare, the inter-site perspective also demonstrates that models obtained from a region, specific site, or even from one area of a single site may or may not be applicable to other similar contexts. The chapters in this section demonstrate that individual sites must be rigorously evaluated on their own terms. The chapters deal with a diverse set of specific analytical and interpretive problems frequently associated with formation processes at the level of the deposit.

The chapter by William Farrand examines the issue of assessing depositional sequences and integrity. Farrand examines a deep cave sequence in Greece and attempts to document an important topic in site formation, that of stratigraphic hiatuses and discontinuity. Following this chapter, Michael Petraglia examines the role of natural and cultural processes in the formation of a rockshelter and slope site in France. This study employs a number of variables in order to show how the intra-site patterns were created and altered, and how the resolution of the deposits varies, preserving both short- and long-term processes.

In a study of a rockshelter in France, Todd Koetje tackles a common problem in archaeology, that of analyzing a thick, seemingly undifferentiated deposit.

Analytical techniques are used to evaluate cultural formation processes, enabling the archaeological deposit to be reliably divided into a number of distinct behavioral depositional episodes. By subsequently comparing the contents of these sub-levels, new insights concerning site function and the nature of resource and landscape use through time was obtained. In the final chapter of this section, David Nash attempts to distinguish culturally produced artifacts from naturefacts in a cave located in the western United States. Nash draws attention to the ambiguity that may be present in lithic assemblages and conducts rockfall experiments to suggest how artifacts and naturally modified stone may be distinguished.

While the problems laid out in the following chapters may be specific to each of the sites discussed, these issues may be expected to occur in varying forms and degrees at many sites. Dealing with each of these major problems, as well as others relating to the formation of the archaeological record at the intra-site level, requires that first they be anticipated prior to the initiation of a research program, so that an appropriate research strategy dealing with these problems can be devised and implemented.

The chapters in this section present specific case examples of why potential sources of ambiguity or lack of information should be anticipated, and how to identify and resolve this ambiguity. In this light it formulates implications for developing behavioral interpretations of human activity at the intra-site scale.

6

Discontinuity in the Stratigraphic Record: Snapshots from Franchthi Cave

William R. Farrand
University of Michigan

Currently, one of the hot topics in stratigraphy, geological as well as archaeological, is that of the continuity of the record. How much of the prehistoric past is actually preserved and potentially recoverable, even in the most meticulous excavations? This is not the same question as that of differential preservation of perishable and non-perishable artifacts or body parts, but one that deals with the complete absence in a stratigraphic sequence of a part of sedimentary matrix that potentially enclosed artifacts, bones, or features. These gaps, hiatuses, or unconformities may result from non-deposition of sediments during a period of time or from physical removal of sediments, either by natural erosion or anthropogenic disturbance. I will illustrate the limitations that such gaps impose on the stratigraphic record at one particular site, and then conclude with some remarks on the general nature of this problem.

In 1976 Thomas Jacobsen published an overview of Indiana University excavations in Franchthi Cave titled "17,000 Years of Greek Prehistory." One major importance of this work was documentation of the essentially continuous record of cultural change found in a single site, spanning later Paleolithic, Mesolithic, and Neolithic times. Recently, the Franchthi chronology has been extended even farther back in time, and Jacobsen could modify his title to read "More than 25,000 years of Greek Prehistory."

However, when one examines the physical stratigraphy closely—on the basis of sedimentological studies that had not yet been completed in 1976—the continuous nature of the Franchthi record comes into question.

In this paper I will document some six or seven identifiable gaps in this 25,000-year time span, and there are probably others, totaling more than 50 per cent (or 8300 years) of the Franchthi record between 22,330 and 6000 B.P. Most of these gaps are not self-evident in the physical stratigraphy, but are revealed only by detailed analysis of subtle sedimentary features (see below), combined with the chronometric record of some 50 radiocarbon dates. Owing to the idiosyncratic nature of cave sedimentation, these gaps may not have correlates in any other sites. Indeed, some of them are not found in different areas of the same cave. Unfortunately several major gaps coincide with times of significant cultural change, begging the question of continuity in regional cultural evolution across the Paleolithic/Mesolithic and Mesolithic/Neolithic boundaries.

This paper will focus on these gaps, the missing record, in an effort to determine how much is missing, and when? However, events that occurred during those time gaps are not totally without record. In some cases, weathering, erosion, and possible human disturbance during the time gaps can be detected by their effects imprinted on the underlying sediments, those that accumulated prior to the gap. In fact, weathering and erosion imply the presence of a hiatus in the sedimentary record. Weathered sediments and soils underlying unweathered deposits imply a period of time when the now-weathered sediments lay exposed on the surface subject to physical and chemical weathering processes. From the kind and degree of development of weathering features one can infer the kind, intensity and/or duration of the weathering interval, which was ultimately terminated by renewed sedimentation. Erosional gaps, produced by physical removal of previously deposited sediment, are commonly difficult to detect in the sedimentary record because unweathered sediment may directly overlie other unweathered sediment. Erosion is obvious where there is an angular discordance between the underlying and overlying sediments, but that discordance carries no inherent information about the duration of the gap. Erosional hiatuses may commonly be detected by discontinuities in biostratigraphic or ethnostratigraphic sequences, or by offsets in a series of radiometric dates, as will be shown below.

I want to stress that my reconstruction of the sequence of events is based on (a) sedimentological analyses, (b) lithostratigraphy, and (c) chronometric control, all of which can be dealt with independently of the archaeological and biological succession in the same strata. Later, one can include the ethnostratigraphy and various kinds of biostratigraphy, and use each one of them to supplement, to readjust (or fine-tune), and to complete the overall chronological sequence.

Lithostratigraphy

Lithostratigraphy is the sequence of sediments preserved in a site, defined on the basis of sediment type (lithology) and boundary relations, and is the fundamental framework of all other stratigraphies for a given site (see also Stein 1987, 1990). A lithostratigraphic unit, called stratum, layer, bed, or lens, is characterized by uniformity of its sediment type, which is different from the sediment above, below and/or lateral to it. Such units commonly cannot be delineated immediately as they are excavated because the exposure in a typical 1 x 1 or 2 x 2 meter trench is too limited. The importance of a change in sediment type encountered by the excavator can be evaluated later when the exposure is expanded or additional trenches are dug, and then a lithostratigraphic unit can be synthesized from excavation units (see below) and section drawings. Lithostratigraphy constitutes the physical entity in which everything else is found—e.g., artifacts, features, fossils, radiocarbon

samples. This does not mean, however, that ethno- and biostratigraphic boundaries have to coincide with lithostratigraphic boundaries, but they must be referenced to them.

More elemental (or primary) is the excavation stratigraphy, comprising excavation units, as they are called at Franchthi Cave, that is, the smallest volumes of sediment removed during excavation and given a single identifying name or number (Fedele 1984). These are also called cuts, spits, and passes, and are the most basic sedimentary entities to which all the various kinds of materials recovered can be provenienced, short of piece-plotting each find. Excavation units provide the finest degree of stratigraphic resolution for all materials, especially microfauna, microflora, and microartifacts, that are recovered by sieving or flotation. However, they are not fundamental in the same sense as lithostratigraphy. Excavation units may be arbitrary 5- or 10-cm passes, or they may parallel natural strata, but in the latter case they may be thicker or thinner than natural strata. Moreover, excavation units may crosscut the natural stratigraphy, even in the best-controlled excavations. I emphasize excavation units at this point because they are the sole means for determining the co-occurrence of various kinds of recovered cultural and biological materials and their sedimentary context.

Franchthi Cave

Setting

Franchthi Cave is a horizontal karstic cavern, about 150 meters long, situated within 50 to 60 meters of the present coast of the Gulf of Argos in the southern Peloponnese, Greece (see Jacobsen and Farrand [1987] for detailed description and stratigraphic sections). Today the interior of the cave is dominated by a huge mound of very large limestone blocks resulting from ceiling collapse that opened a large "window" to the sky in the center of the cave (Figure 1). However, at the end of the Neolithic occupation, about 5000 B.P., the cave floor was marked by much less topographic relief, as far as we can tell, lying about ten to twelve meters above present sea level. Prior to that time the cave had accumulated sediments in excess of twelve meters thick, that is, extending well below present sea level, as determined by resistivity soundings.

Excavations were carried out, beginning in 1967, in a number of locations, both inside and outside the cave. However, the two most important trenches, in terms of excavation procedures and stratigraphic depth, are located in the forward part of the cave between the entrance and the large breakdown pile. These are referred to as Trench FA and Trench HH1,

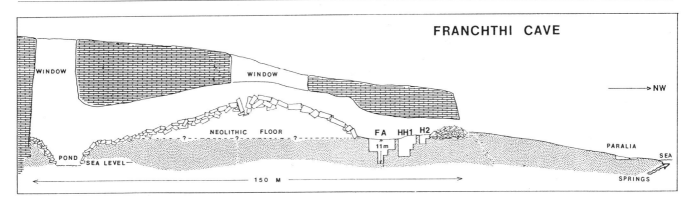

Figure 1. Schematic longitudinal profile of Franchthi Cave. HH1 and FA are the principal excavated trenches discussed in the text. "Paralia" indicates an open-air Neolithic site just above the present beach.

which were excavated down to sea level and to +2.5 m above sea level, respectively. These trenches are about 14 meters apart, Trench FA being rather close to the western cave wall and Trench HH1 more or less along the centerline of the cave. The general relations of the two trenches is shown in Figure 2, including the present configuration of the cave floor and the interpreted correlations between the trenches. Note that the cave floor in the center of the cave (in the vicinity of Trench HH1) has always stood higher than the floor nearer the west wall (at Trench FA) over the last 25,000 or 30,000 years. The upper two or three meters of the deposits throughout the excavated area were strongly disturbed in historic times, presumably by mining of the sediments for manure or saltpeter and the use of the cave as a refuge for sheep and goats.

Archaeological Sequence

Very briefly, the cultural manifestations in Franchthi Cave include the following main events. The chipped stone artifacts begin with a microscale Upper Paleolithic assemblage dominated by backed bladelets (Perlès 1987), followed by a Mesolithic assemblage that is at first non-microlithic, then microlithic, and finally non-microlithic in its final phases (Perlès 1991), all of which is overlain by a thick Neolithic sequence comprising a good pressure blade industry (Perlès, n.d.). The Paleolithic tools are mostly of local chert, but obsidian appears somewhat before 10,000 B.P., increases in abundance throughout the Mesolithic assemblages, and dominates the lithic artifacts in the Neolithic. The obsidian is known to have been imported from the island of Melos, separated from the Greek mainland by deep water, thus requiring some sort of seafaring capability by the Franchthi inhabitants or some unknown contemporaries. This conclusion is reinforced by the abundance of large marine fish vertebrae (tunny) in the cave, especially in Mesolithic layers.

Pottery is rare and possibly intrusive in the earliest Neolithic deposits ("Initial Neolithic" of Perlès 1991), but becomes abundant thereafter (K.D. Vitelli 1993). Seed analysis reveals the abrupt appearance of domesticated emmer wheat in small quantity at the onset of the Initial Neolithic. Fully domesticated barley and lentils appear only about 1000 years later. During the Mesolithic occupation there was extensive gathering of wild plants—oats, peas, barley, and lentils (Hansen 1978, 1991). Among the larger mammals, horse and cattle were dominant in the earlier Upper Paleolithic record, indicating open grassland habitats, but they were gradually replaced by red deer suggesting increasing brush and woodland landscapes. At the end of the Mesolithic, deer comprised some 90 per cent of the large mammals, but there was an abrupt shift to some 90 per cent sheep and goats at the beginning of the Initial Neolithic (Payne 1982 and personal communication).

Land snails were a conspicuous component of the final Paleolithic and Mesolithic diets. Thick middens of whole shells of *Helix* cf. *pomatia* (perhaps *H. figulina* [N. Whitney-Desautels, personal communication]) occur in the final Upper Paleolithic, and crushed snail shells are pervasive in much of the Mesolithic sequence. However, marine mollusks are also abundant from late Upper Paleolithic times onward, although the shells are dispersed throughout the strata in contrast to the land snail concentrations (Shackleton 1988). It should be noted that Franchthi Cave was not very close to the marine coast throughout the times of Upper Paleolithic and Mesolithic occupations. The marine mollusks collected at the shoreline had to be transported some two to six kilometers back to the cave. Submarine investigations have led to a hypothesis of changing shoreline habitats with concomitant fluctuations in the availability of different marine molluscan species through time (Shackleton and van Andel 1986; Shackleton 1988).

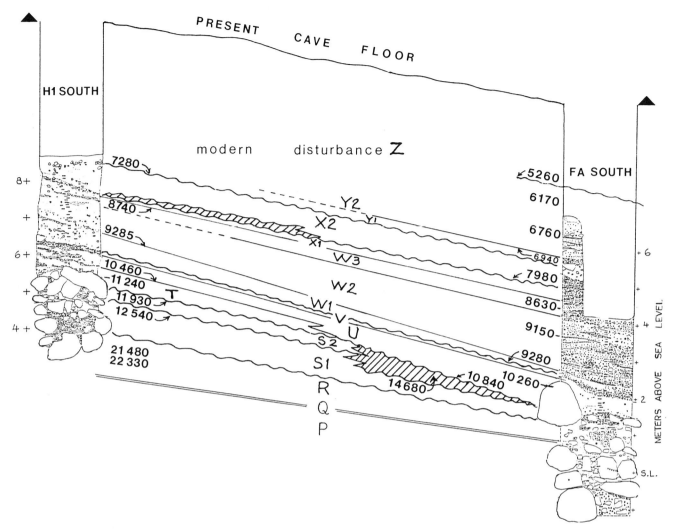

Figure 2. Correlation between Trenches HH1 and FA in Franchthi Cave, illustrating the principal lithostratigraphic units, the presence of unconformities (wavy lines), and key radiocarbon dates (in B.P.). The section is transverse to the long axis of the cave, HH1 situated near the center of the cave floor and FA near the west wall. (See Jacobsen and Farrand 1987 for detailed plans and section drawings.)

Lithostratigraphy

The principal lithostratigraphic units identified in Franchthi Cave are shown in Figure 2. They are assigned capital letters in reverse alphabetical order from the top down. Layer Z is the stratum of modern disturbance, two to three meters thick in this part of the cave, and will not be subdivided. Complete descriptions of the strata are being prepared (Farrand, n.d.), but the principal layers can be characterized briefly, based on excavators' notes, as follows:

Y2	Red and gray "clay" with hearths
Y1	Rocky lenses with ash
X2	Gray clay, charcoal, and shells (mostly snails)
X1	Rocky red sediment
W3	Sediment with much crushed snail shell
W2	Red sediment with shell lenses, hearths, and bones
W1	Homogeneous red brown loam with few rocks
V	Rocky layer with shells
U	Hard "clay" with "white rocks" (chalky surfaces)
T3	(Upper) snail midden
T2	Intermidden lens
T1	Snail midden (multiple?)
S2	Rockfall, variable amount of matrix, bones, few snails
S1	Rockfall with "white rocks" and loamy matrix
R	Rockfall with wet clay loam
Q	Tephra (volcanic ash)
P	Rockfall with wet clay loam

In Trench FA, Layers T1, T2, and T3 are not found, and Layers S1 and S2 are much reduced in thickness in comparison to Trench HH1. On the other hand, Layers Y1 and Y2 are strongly disturbed in Trench HH1, where modern potsherds occur throughout the Neolithic strata (K. D. Vitelli, 1993).

Lithologic correlation between the two trenches was based initially on the unique volcanic tephra, Layer Q, and on two, relatively distinct rocky layers, X1 and V, which happen to coincide closely with the Neolithic/Mesolithic and Mesolithic/Paleolithic boundaries in this site, although they were not chosen for that reason. Additional, and finer-scale correlation was based on the sedimentological character of the deposits as revealed by laboratory analyses described below (Figure 3), and controlled by radiocarbon dates. Unconformities indicated by horizontal wavy lines in Figure 3 generally were not obvious in the field, although the excavators did recognize "white rocks" in some places, which are an indication of weathering, and elsewhere they noted abrupt changes in color or compactness, which may indicate a change in depositional type potentially associated with gaps.

The lithostratigraphy was evaluated by means of four classes of criteria. First were the observations of the excavators as recorded in the field notes, as alluded to in the preceding paragraphs.

Secondly, the section drawings of the walls of the trenches were important. These drawings were made by excavators, but not necessarily the same persons who had excavated a given trench, and in any case the drawings were usually done well after the trench was dug. Thus, there is a certain independence of the information from the excavators' notes and the drawn sections. Additionally, all the drawings were compared in the field to the actual walls still standing in 1979 by myself and the draftsman (D. J. Pullen) who prepared the final drawings.

Thirdly, the results of laboratory analysis (Figure 3) of sediment samples collected from four different columns in Trenches FA and HH1 provided subtle details not immediately evident in the field. Laboratory analyses include grain-size measurements (sieving and pipette), chemical analysis ($CaCO_3$, pH), and observations of the surface conditions of rock particles (roundness, weathered surfaces). These are required because sediment as one sees it in the field, even with careful trowel and brush work, is an intimate mixture of all its components. One cannot do a quantitative grain-size analysis in the trench, and the finer particles mask the character of the larger ones. (See Farrand 1975a for a more complete discussion of this kind of analysis.) For example, in Figure 3 Layer V is characterized by an abundance of coarse rock fragments (32-128 mm) and very little clay-sized sedi-

ment (<.002 mm). As shown in the "Roundness" column, the rock fragments in Layer V are mostly angular and subangular, and the $CaCO_3$ content and pH are moderately high. These are characters of freshly deposited sediments. In contrast, the underlying Layer U shows a sharp decrease in 32-128 mm rocks and a marked increase in clay. Its rounded to subrounded rock fragments and decreased $CaCO_3$ content with a parallel decrease in pH are common indicators of weathering. Additionally, in Layer V shiny snail shells occur together with chalky ones, but in Layer U all of the shells are chalky and weathered. Another example comes from the upper part of Layer S1 where there are similar weathering indicators.

The fourth category is radiometric dating, provided mainly by some 50 radiocarbon dates on charcoal (see Jacobsen and Farrand 1987 for details), and also by indirect dating of the tephra in Layer Q (Vitaliano et al. 1981). The radiocarbon samples were not collected as part of a systematic attempt to date lithologic boundaries, unfortunately, but wherever datable material was encountered during excavation. These dates are arranged according to their normalized height above sea level for each of the trenches (Figure 4). Straight-line curves have been fit by eye to series of dates that seem to be coherent. Changes in slope of the straight-line segments are placed at the logical intersections between two adjacent segments, for example at 4.2 and at 6.6 meters/sea level on the FA curve in Figure 4, or at a level where sedimentological data indicate a weathered horizon, thus an inferred unconformity. Such unconformities are times of zero net sediment accumulation, whether due to non-deposition or erosion, as shown by horizontal wavy lines in Figure 4.

These four lines of input, therefore, led to the recognition of contacts (boundaries) between the lithostratigraphic layers Y2 through P seen on Figure 2. The contacts may be either conformable (no time gap) or unconformable. As stated at the beginning of this paper, the unconformities are either times of erosion (natural or anthropogenic removal) or times of non-deposition, and their interpretation depends on sedimentological data and bio- and ethnostratigraphic information. Weathering (chemical alteration) of the sediment underlying the unconformity may have occurred, and the degree of development of the weathering features (such as shown in Figure 3) is an indication of the relative duration of the time gap and/or intensity of the weathering processes.

The Missing Record

The correlation of the layers from one trench to the other was based on lithologic similarities of the two sequences plus chronometric control by the radio-

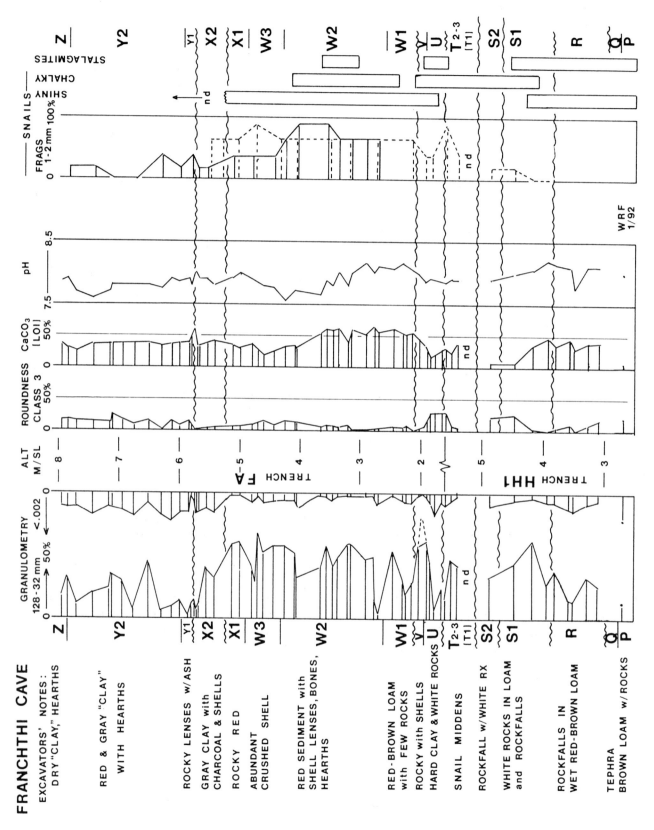

Figure 3. Summary diagram of sedimentological analyses, Franchthi Cave (after Farrand, n.d.).

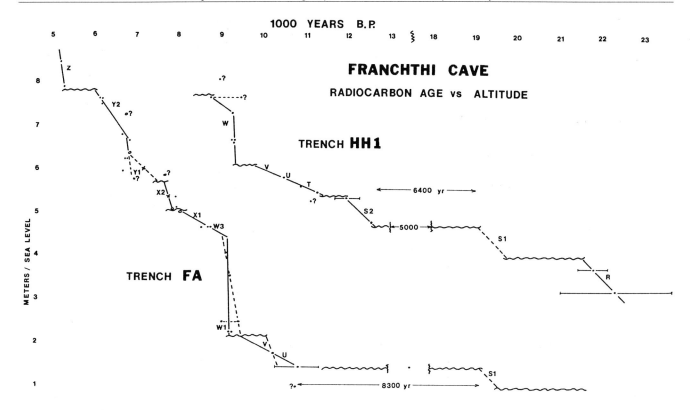

Figure 4. Sedimentation rates for Trenches FA (lower curve) and HH1 (upper curve) based on radiocarbon chronology (after Farrand, n.d.) Wavy horizontal lines are unconformities. Solid dots indicate the position of ^{14}C dates, all of which are on charcoal; a few x's and o's show dates correlated from trenches other than FA and HH1. Alternate interpretations are shown by dashed lines. Note the break in the time scale between 13,000 and 18, 000 B.P. Horizontal error bars (±1 sigma) are shown only for those dates with unusually large standard deviations. Other standard deviations are usually < 150 years. Letters (Y1, X2, X1, W,...) indicate positions of lithostratigraphic units, as in Figure 2.

carbon dates. This correlation led to the discovery that the unconformities in the different trenches were not necessarily of the same duration, meaning that deposition was occurring on some areas of the cave floor while other areas were sites of non-deposition or even erosion. The most conspicuous example finds Layer U lying directly on top of a thin Layer S1 in Trench FA, whereas in Trench HH1 Layers T1, T2, T3, S2, and a much thicker S1 occur in the stratigraphic interval missing in FA.

These unconformities imply that the stratigraphic and cultural sequence in Franchthi is not continuous. Table 1 lists the durations of all the recognized gaps in each trench estimated from the sedimentation rate curve in Figure 4. However, these relations are easier to appreciate when viewed in a plot of lithostrati-

Table 1. Durations of Various Unconformities in Franchthi Cave.

Tr. FA	Unconformity	Tr. HH1
700?	Z/Y2	?
300	Y1/X2	100?
200	X2/X1	500?
300-600	W1/V	500
n.a.	T3/S2	500
8000-8500	U/S1	n.a.
n.a.	S2/S1	6000
ca 1200	S1/R	ca 1000
?	R/Q	?
≥10,700	Total years missing	≥8600

graphic units vs absolute age (Figure 5). This conservative estimate of documented missing time for the total succession—from tephra Q at ca. 30,000 B.P. to the end of the Neolithic at 5000 B.P.—amounts to 42.8 per cent (10,700 years) in FA and 34.4 per cent (8600 years) in HH1.

Since not all gaps are present in both trenches, or have different durations, one can make a conservative estimate of the minimum time that is not represented at all in both trenches. These are the underlined values in the table, totalling 8300 years in the interval 22,300 to 6000 B.P., or 50.9 per cent of that time span (note that this is a shorter time span than that tabulated in Table 1). Moreover, it is not inconceivable that other gaps have gone undetected in these trenches, having left no discernible evidence in the sediments or falling into intervals not controlled by the available radiocarbon dates. On the other hand, some of these gaps might be represented by deposits elsewhere in the cave, which potentially could be revealed in future excavations. To repeat, for emphasis, at least 50 per cent of the time span from 22,300 to 6000 B.P. is not represented in any part of our excavations in Franchthi Cave.

Archaeological Implications

What does all this mean for the interpretation of the cultural sequence? As an example, Figure 6 shows the lithostratigraphy of Trench FAS (i.e., the south half of Trench FA) with all the gaps indicated, along with the stratigraphic zones and phases of several of my colleagues, each column plotted against excavation unit numbers (vertical scale). My point here is not to enter into a discussion of the culture history, but to illustrate the nature of the problem stemming from the discontinuities in the lithostratigraphic sequence.

It can be seen that some of the breaks in ethno- or biostratigraphic zones and phases, some of which are identified as "interphases" or "interzones" by my colleagues, coincide with the lithostratigraphic breaks, and others do not. This is perfectly acceptable, and can lead to the formulation of reasonable explanations for those cases where there is lack of coincidence. For example, some environmental shifts may lead to the deposition of different kinds of sediments, or non-deposition, without any impact on cultural activities. The discrepancies can lead to a re-evaluation of each data set in order to verify that the lack of coincidence is real. In other words, each stratigraphy, litho-, bio-, or ethno-, is initially established independently of the others, and all are interrelated only by means of excavation units (Jacobsen and Farrand 1987: 7). Absence of certain kinds of data from a given excavation unit or

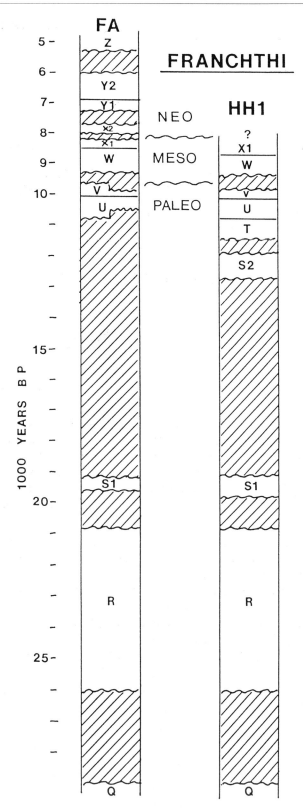

Figure 5. Lithostratigraphic units in Trenches FA and HH1 plotted against an absolute time scale in radiocarbon years, illustrating the time gaps (diagonal ruled lines) in both trenches. Lithostratigraphic units (Z, Y2, Y1,...) as given in Figures 2 and 3.

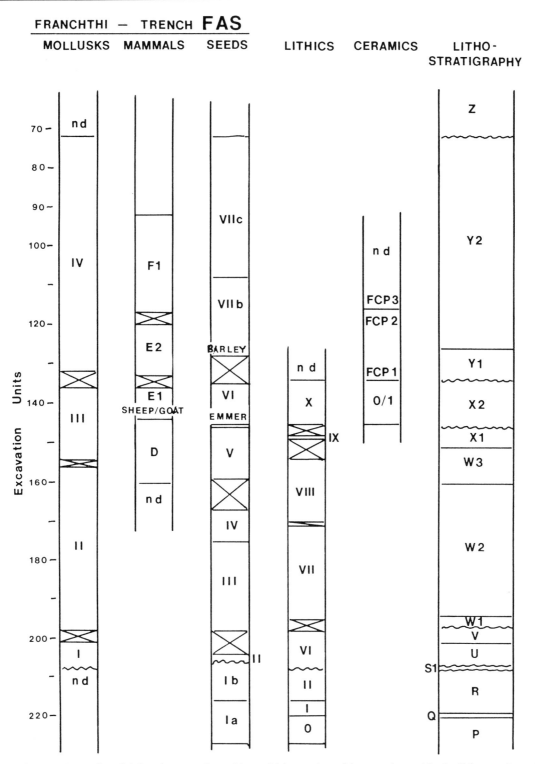

Figure 6. Comparison of multiple ethnostratigraphic and biostratigraphic zonation with the lithostratigraphic sequence for Trench FA-South (FAS) in Franchthi Cave, plotted in relation to excavation units (vertical scale).

ambiguities in the data (crosscutting of strata, unclear relationships of the artifact or fossil assemblages) can lead to initial placements of zone boundaries, in terms of excavation units, that are subject to change when the mutual relationships of all the stratigraphic hierarchies are considered together. Such adjustments may bring some zone boundaries into conjunction or lead us to the conclusion that some changes in sedimentation, cultural activity, or resource exploitation occurred independently of others.

In several cases, the coincidence of lithostrati-graphic gaps and phase or zone breaks is striking. For example, a gap of two to five centuries, in trench FA and HH1, respectively, between Layers X2 and X1 falls exactly at the Mesolithic/Neolithic boundary as recognized by the appearance of emmer wheat (seed zone VI), 90 per cent sheep/goats (faunal zone E1), and Neolithic lithics (phase X) at ca. 8000-8300 B.P. Similarly, the gap between Layers W1 and V, perhaps 300-600 years long, coincides with the Paleolithic/Mesolithic "transition," centered on 9600 B.P. Unfortunately, of course, these gaps do not facilitate answering questions of cultural evolution, continuity, or disruption by outsiders in southern Greece across these critical stages in cultural evolution.

Conclusions

An independent lithostratigraphy with its implications for time gaps, weathering intervals, and sediment accumulation rates is an important construct to be compared with the various ethno- and biostratigraphies erected on the basis of all the different bodies of materials recovered from a site. These multiple stratigraphies can be interrelated by reference to the smallest volumes of sediment (here called "excavation units") removed during the dig. Coincidences and discrepancies between litho-, ethno-, and biostratigraphic units can then be evaluated for their significance in terms of site formation and cultural history.

The detailed lithostratigraphy in Franchthi Cave reveals that at least 50 per cent of the nominal time span of the stratigraphic sequence is completely missing from the excavated portion of the site. In individual trenches as much as 10,700 out of 25,000 years may be missing without breaks or disruptions being obvious during excavation or in the final trench profiles. Such a situation imposes considerable constraints on the interpretation of continuity or disruption in cultural change, and on the rate of that change in any particular site. It leaves open the question of whether a cultural shift following a given time gap was a cultural event or reflects some environmental disruption or both.

Franchthi Cave is a not unique. Most, if not all, deeply stratified sites are likely to have been loci of such stop-and-go sedimentation with inherent limitations for the interpretation of culture and environmental history. I have recorded a similar depositional history at the Abri Pataud (Dordogne, France), where two hiatuses of about 3000 - 4000 years each occur within the interval from 34,000 to 20,000 B.P. (Farrand 1975b: 51), thus accounting for some 7000 years of the 14,000-year span. Campy (1990;

Pons et al. 1989) has discussed such discontinuities in cave and rockshelter sites in three regions of France, showing important hiatuses in all cases, with substantial gaps in the French Alps, shorter but still considerable gaps in the Franche-Comté (east-central France), and numerous but briefer hiatuses in southwestern France. In the latter region, Laville has assembled a great amount of sedimentological data from numerous caves and rockshelters into a climatostratigraphic scheme (Laville et al. 1980). Cold, dry climatic phases alternate with mild, temperate ones, which are identified by various weathering indicators in the sediments, such as those that I described above. A number of "stratigraphic unconformities" are recognized as "episodes of erosion that carried away most of the relevant sediments" (Laville et al. 1980: 138), but Laville does not explicitly address the question of how much time might be missing in his sequences. The gaps are quantifiable only where sufficient chronological control is available, such as the case of the Abri Pataud mentioned above and Franchthi Cave, as discussed in detail in this paper. I have no doubt that the occurrence of substantial hiatuses in deeply stratified sites is the rule, not the exception.

In terms of excavation strategy, the potential existence of unconformities of considerable duration requires careful attention on the part of excavators to any sort of change in the character of the sediment that might be associated with a hiatus. The abrupt occurrence of weathering indicators, angular discordances, or abrupt changes in color or compaction of the sediment should alert the excavator to the possibility of an unconformity. The resident geologist or geoarchaeologist should be consulted immediately, and he or she should examine the sediments in question on the spot, ideally in a field sedimentology laboratory. Potential materials for radiometric dating should be collected just above and just below the possible gap, and dated as quickly as possible. One can also inspect the artifacts and bones above and below the break for sudden shifts in character. If the preliminary examinations indicate the likelihood of an unconformity in a given trench, then one should look for similar indications in any other trenches exposing correlative strata. Then the field director might consider expanding the excavation in one direction or another in the hope that the gap will be filled and the stratigraphic record more complete elsewhere on the site.

Acknowledgments

My sincere appreciation is extended to all my Franchthi colleagues who at various times and places have offered advice, insight, and criticism concerning the lithostratigraphic sequence and chronology as I have assembled it. In particular, I acknowledge the valuable feedback on drafts of this paper that I have received from Tom Jacobsen, Catherine Perlès, and K.

D. Vitelli. I wish to thank also the volume editors who encouraged me to expand my discussion for the benefit of archaeologists less familiar with sedimentology.

References Cited

Campy, M.
 1990 L'Enregistrement du temps et du climat dans les remplissages karstiques: l'apport de la sédimentologie. *Karstologia*, Mémoires no. 2, pp. 11-22.

Farrand, W. R.
 1975a Analysis of a Prehistoric Rockshelter: the Abri Pataud. *Quaternary Research* 5:1-26.
 1975b Analysis of the Abri Pataud sediments. In *Excavation of the Abri Pataud, Les Eyzies (Dordogne)*, edited by H. L. Movius Jr., pp. 27-68. Bulletin 30, American School of Prehistoric Research, Harvard University.
 n.d. *General Geology, Lithostratigraphy, and Sedimentology of Franchthi Cave.* Excavations at Franchthi Cave, Greece, T. W. Jacobsen, general editor. Indiana University Press, Bloomington and Indianapolis.

Fedele, F. G.
 1984 Towards an Analytical Stratigraphy: Stratigraphic Reasoning and Excavation. *Stratigraphica Archaeologica* 1:7-15

Hansen, J. M.
 1978 The Earliest Seed Remains from Greece: Palaeolithic through Neolithic at Franchthi Cave: *Bericht der Deutsches Botanisches Gesellschaft* 91:39-46.
 1991 *The Palaeoethnobotany of Franchthi Cave*, Greece. Excavations at Franchthi Cave, Greece, fasc. 7, T. W. Jacobsen, general editor. Indiana University Press, Bloomington and Indianapolis.

Jacobsen, T. W.
 1976 17,000 Years of Greek Prehistory. *Scientific American* 234:76-87.

Jacobsen, T.W. and W. R. Farrand
 1987 *Franchthi Cave and Paralia: Maps, Plans, and Sections.* Excavations at Franchthi Cave, Greece, fasc. 1, T. W. Jacobsen, general editor. Indiana University Press, Bloomington and Indianapolis

Laville, H., J-P. Rigaud, and J. Sackett
 Rockshelters of the Périgord. Academic Press, New York.

Payne, S.
 1982 Faunal Evidence for Environmental/Climatic Change at Franchthi Cave (Southern Argolid, Greece), 25,000 BP to 5,000 BP - Preliminary Results. (Abstract) British Archaeological Reports International Series 133:133-136.

Perlès, C.
 1987 *Les Industries Lithiques Taillées de Franchthi.* Tome I, *Présentation générale et Industries Paléolithiques.* Excavations at Franchthi Cave, Greece, fasc. 3, T. W. Jacobsen, general editor. Indiana University Press, Bloomington and Indianapolis.
 1991 *Les Industries Lithiques Taillées de Franchthi (Argolide, Grèce).* Tome II. *Les Industries du Mésolithique et du Néolithique Initial.* Excavations at Franchthi Cave, Greece, fasc. 5, T. W. Jacobsen, general editor. Indiana University Press, Bloomington and Indianapolis.
 n.d. *Les Industries Lithiques Taillées de Franchthi.* Tome III. *Le Néolithique.* Excavations at Franchthi Cave, Greece, T. W. Jacobsen, general editor. Indiana University Press, Bloomington and Indianapolis.

Pons, A., M. Campy, and J. Guiot
 1989 The last climatic cycle in France: the diversity of records. *Quaternary International* 3/4: 49-55.

Shackleton, J. C.
 1988 *Marine Molluscan Remains from Franchthi Cave.* Excavations at Franchthi Cave, Greece, fasc. 4, T. W. Jacobsen, general editor. Indiana University Press, Bloomington and Indianapolis.

Shackleton, J.C. and T.H. van Andel
 1986 Prehistoric Environments, Shellfish Availability, and Shellfish Gathering at Franchthi Cave, Southern Argolid, Greece. *Geoarchaeology* 1:127-143.

Stein, J.K.

1987 Deposits for Archaeologists. *Advances in Archaeological Method and Theory*, vol. 11, edited by M. B. Schiffer, pp. 337-395. Academic Press, New York.

1990 Archaeological Stratigraphy. *Archaeological Geology of North America*, edited by N. P. Lasca and J. Donahue, chap. 29, pp. 513-523. Geological Society of America, Centennial Special Volume 4.

Vitaliano, C. J., S. R. Taylor, W. R. Farrand, and T. W. Jacobsen

1981 Tephra Layer in Franchthi Cave, Peleponnesos, Greece. In *Tephra Studies*, edited by S. Self and R. S. J. Sparks, pp. 373-379. Riedel Pub., Amsterdam.

Vitelli, K.D.

1993 *Franchthi Neolithic Pottery*. Volume I. Excavations at Franchthi Cave, Greece, fasc. 8, T. W. Jacobsen, general editor. Indiana University Press, Bloomington and Indianapolis.

7

The Genesis and Alteration of Archaeological Patterns at the Abri Dufaure: An Upper Paleolithic Rockshelter and Slope Site in Southwestern France

Michael D. Petraglia
Smithsonian Institution

Beginning in the mid-1960's archaeologists began to convincingly argue that Paleolithic activities could be interpreted from co-occurring sets of artifacts and spatial distributions of material remains (e.g., Binford and Binford 1966; Freeman and Butzer 1966; Freeman 1973; Binford 1973; Whallon 1973a, 1973b, 1974). Behavioral interpretations inferred from Old World sites were, however, seriously critiqued by Bordes (1975, 1980a, 1980b; Bordes et al. 1972), who argued that daily activities could not often be reconstructed from prehistoric occupation surfaces due to the slow rates of geological burial of materials and the subsequent mixing of materials by postdepositional disturbances. At about the same time that these arguments were being launched in the Old World, archaeologists in North America were beginning to conceive of the prehistoric record as a complex interplay of cultural and natural processes. The archaeological record was viewed to be the byproduct of numerous human events (e.g., maintenance, recycling, artifact loss) and natural agents (geological and biological) (see Schiffer 1972, 1976).

Criticisms about the character and resolution of the prehistoric record impelled archaeologists to construct more sophisticated arguments about the very processes which created vertical deposits and horizontal patterns. As a result, attempts were made to refine notions about the behavioral meaning of intrasite patterns (e.g., Yellen 1977; Binford 1978; Cahen 1980; Kent 1987), stratigraphic sequences (e.g., Binford 1981, 1982; Villa 1977, 1982; Cahen et al. 1979) and natural processes (e.g., Butzer 1982; Wood and Johnson 1978; Schiffer 1983, 1987; Nash and Petraglia 1987).

As Schiffer (1983, 1987) has clearly explained, while research on site formation processes has increased dramatically in recent years, studies on these processes have rarely been incorporated into the recovery, analysis and inference stages of archaeological investigations. In an effort to remedy this situation, this chapter explores the processes responsible for the formation of the archaeological patterns at the Abri Dufaure, an Upper Paleolithic site in southwestern France. The study of Dufaure was performed in an attempt to understand the degree to which the material patterns recovered at the site reflected the interplay of cultural and natural processes. Before attempting elaborate analyses of site structure and human activities at Dufaure, an assessment of the formation of the sites' deposits and material patterns was considered necessary.

Interpretations about the meaning of spatial distributions at Dufaure were based primarily on expectations derived from analysis of hillslope geomorphology (e.g., Young 1960, 1972; Schumm

1967a, 1967b; Carson and Kirkby 1972; Schumm and Mosley 1973; Ritter 1978; Leopold 1982; Selby 1982) and from archaeological studies in rockshelter and slope contexts (e.g., Bordes 1972; Laville et al. 1980; Rick 1976; Fuchs et al. 1977; Butzer 1982; Kornfeld 1982; Frostick and Reid 1983; Schuldenrein 1986; Petraglia and Nash 1987). Although these studies are not reviewed in this chapter, many conclusions about depositional and postdepositional processes were based on findings raised from these studies (see Petraglia 1987 for background).

The site formation study was only one aspect of a larger multidisciplinary project which embraced a number of related paleoanthropological objectives (see Straus et al. 1988). These objectives included achieving an understanding of Dufaure's environmental setting, chronology, subsistence, and activity. Other reports concerning the site formation study appear elsewhere (Straus et al. 1988; Straus n.d.; Petraglia 1987, 1992).

The Abri Dufaure

The Abri Dufaure is located in Les Landes, southwest France (Figure 1). The site lies at the northern edge of the Gave d'Oloron valley, facing south-southwest, 0.75 km from the present river course. The river runs into the Bay of Biscay 40 air km due west of Dufaure. The Abri Dufaure was one of four major rockshelter/slope sites located along the base of the Pastou cliff in Sorde-l'Abbaye. Directly in front of the Pastou sites there was a ford which provided humans with easy access to the south side of the valley and the Basque hillcountry beyond. The Pastou sites are thought to be related to exploitation of seasonal migrations of reindeer. The Abri Duruthy, situated .25 km west of Dufaure, revealed large-scale occupations, and the construction of extensive cobblestone pavements, among the largest structures known from the Paleolithic (Arambourou 1978).

During one week in 1900, the deposits of the small rockshelter at Dufaure were completely dug out

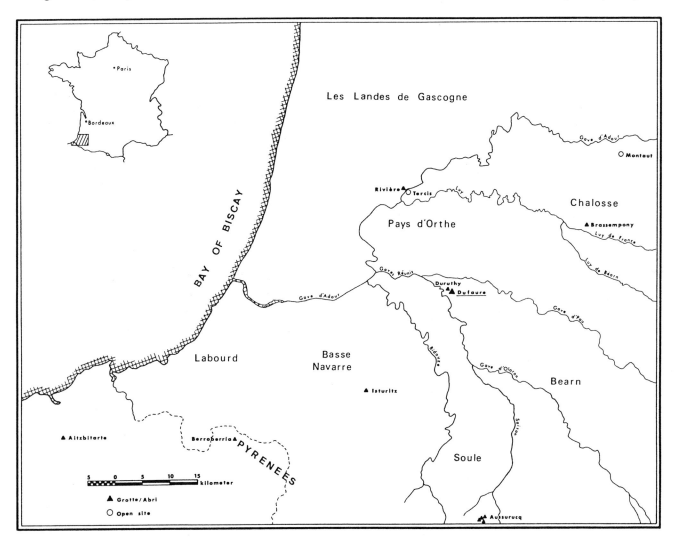

Figure 1. The Abri Dufaure and other Upper Paleolithic sites in the French Basque country and adjacent areas.

under the direction of the Abbé Breuil and P. Dubalen (1901). New excavations at Dufaure were conducted from 1980-1984 by Dr. Lawrence Straus of the University of New Mexico (USA).

The Abri Dufaure consisted of the small rockshelter, the rockshelter border (I row) (a narrow flat area on the top of the talus), the upper slope (J-L rows), the midslope (M-P rows), a steep break in slope

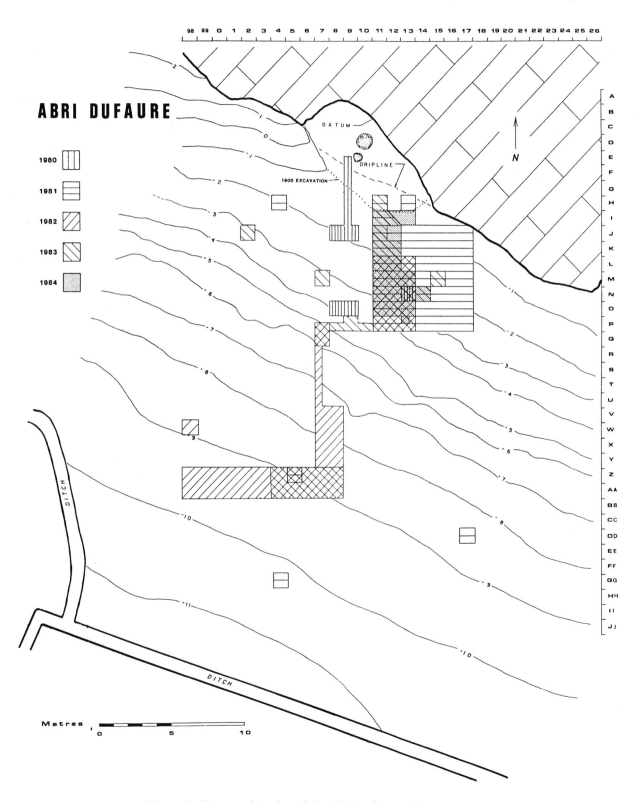

Figure 2. Topographic plan of the Abri Dufaure, with excavation areas.

(Q-S rows), the lower slope (T-Y rows), and the footslope or lower area (Z-GG rows) (Figure 2). There was a 10 meter vertical drop between the top and bottom of the talus, over a distance of 30 horizontal meters from north to south.

Specifically, three main horizontal areas are compared in the following study, together forming the central area: 1) the rockshelter border (row I/11-13), 2) the upper slope (rows J-L/11-13), and 3) the midslope (rows M-P/11-13). Strata 3-5 in the central area contain thick accumulations of cultural material (Figure 3). The "I row" was probably under the former rockshelter overhang, the mass of blocks in Stratum 3 probably representing a collapse and retreat of the overhang. The Stratum 3 deposits consisted of scattered artifacts and triturated faunal remains often in discontinuous lenses and patches. Stratum 4 was particularly significant and was marked by the presence of cobblestone pavements, rich in artifacts and faunal remains (Figure 4). Features within the cobble pavements were rare. Stratum 5 consisted of scattered lithics and faunal remains as well as pavements of sandstone slabs, known as plaquettes. The Stratum 5 deposit was missing atop the bedrock ledge in front of the abri (I row), probably a result of erosion during the earliest period of site occupation. Stratigraphic and spatial evidence suggested that the extreme western and eastern margins of the site were eroded by major solifluction event(s), resulting in dense accumulations of assemblages in Stratum IV of the lower area (Laville n.d.; Petraglia 1987, n.d.a).

The lithic industries from the Abri Dufaure were late Upper Paleolithic in age, and dated to the Magdalenian and Azilian periods. The archaeological deposits were radiocarbon dated mainly by coherent determinations on bone collagen from 9,600 to 14,600 B.P. (Straus and Evin 1989) (Table 1).

Certain key variables, useful for assessing the role of cultural and natural processes, were applied in the Abri Dufaure site formation study. The variables used to examine the site included material distributions (lithics, tools, cobbles, *éboulis*), burning patterns, orientations, inclinations, and lithic patination, breakage and refitting. The goal of the site formation analysis was to interpret the meaning of the intra-site patterns so that appropriate behavioral inferences could be made. Since other contributions of the Abri Dufaure project detail intra-site patterns attributable to human activities, functional analyses are not emphasized here, but are mentioned when pertinent for illustrating certain aspects of site formation (see Straus et al. 1988, Straus n.d., Akoshima n.d., for behavioral interpretations). The following sections present interpretations about the depositional and postdepositional processes.

Depositional Processes

Site Integrity

One of the most important aims of the site formation study was to consider if the central area was a

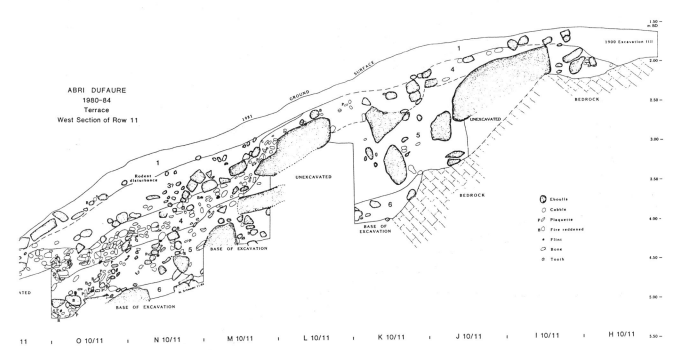

Figure 3. Sagittal profile of the Abri Dufaure's central area stratigraphy.

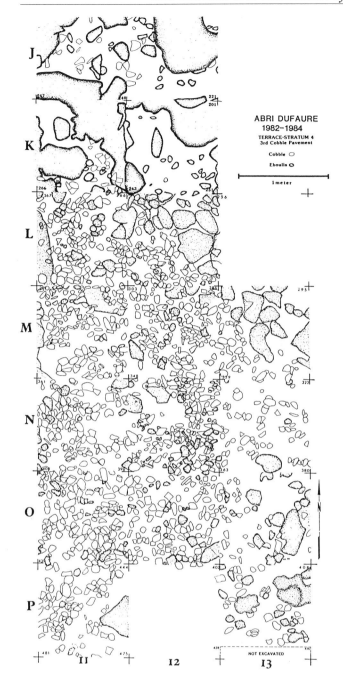

Figure 4. Plan of the third cobble pavement of Stratum 4.

Table 1. Radiocarbon Dates of the Abri Dufaure (after Straus and Evin 1989).

Lab Number	Stratum	Date (B.P.)
Ly-4224	3	9,600 +/-290
AA-2477	3	9,750 +/-110
AA-2478	3	9,810 +/-100
Ly-4223	3	10,310 +/-270
Ly-2666	4	10,910 +/-220
Ly-3181	4	11,750 +/-300
Ly-3245	4	12,030 +/-280
Ly-3182	4	12,260 +/-400
Ly-3591	5	12,690 +/-230
Ly-2923	5	12,990 +/-270
Ly-3582	5	14,570 +/-390
Ly-3583	6	14,020 +/-340
AA-3030	6	14,590 +/-100
AA-3029	6	14,640 +/-230

providing strong evidence for the gradual accretion of the central area deposits.

While there were no 'evident' features, artifact density varied by stratum and site area, suggesting there was the potential for identifying areas of human activity. Field observations suggested that *éboulis* and the dense accumulation of cobbles in Stratum 4 were probably an important factor in site preservation. Investigators have found that natural or cultural features or obstructions on slopes may preserve spatial patterns or prevent downslope movement (e.g., Rick 1976; Fuchs et al. 1977; Butzer 1982; Frostick and Reid 1983; Petraglia and Nash 1987). Artifacts were often pocketed between boulders and were wedged between cobbles and cobble floors. While some proportion of the artifacts may have been moved from their original spots, accumulating between *éboulis* boulders, the field observations suggested that the boulders likely prevented any further downslope movement. Moreover, the construction of thick cobble floors from the rockshelter to the midslope at Dufaure was probably an important factor in site integrity, the cobbles probably limited vertical or downslope movements of materials.

The integrity of artifact patterns in the central area was certainly demonstrated by five distinct concentrations of refittable lithics, which were horizontally confined to areas on the rockshelter border, the upper slope and the midslope. The spatial distribution of patinated lithics was definable by site area and stratum, suggesting that the stone assemblages were not transported or wholly mixed. On the rockshelter border, there was no preferred orientation (Figure 5) and 91% of the objects were less than 45 degrees in

primary deposit. Stratigraphic and spatial evidence was used in an attempt to determine if the central area was in fact a primary deposit, or whether it was eroded or transported by natural processes. An analysis of the lithic size over the central area indicated that there was no selective patterning that could be attributed to natural processes.

In terms of stratigraphic evidence, there were no visual signs of major postdepositional disturbances in the central area. A number of radiocarbon dates were obtained and were stratigraphically coherent,

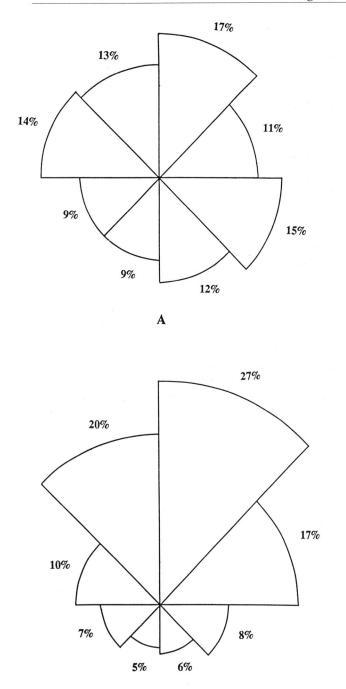

Figure 5. Orientations in Stratum 4 of the rockshelter border (A), the midslope (B).

inclination, suggesting little or no rearrangement by natural processes. In the central area there were clusters of burned material in strata 3-5 (Figures 6-8), providing further support for the integrity of the patterns and deposits.

Based upon the stratigraphic sequence and the material analyses, the central area was considered to be intact, and not transported by natural processes.

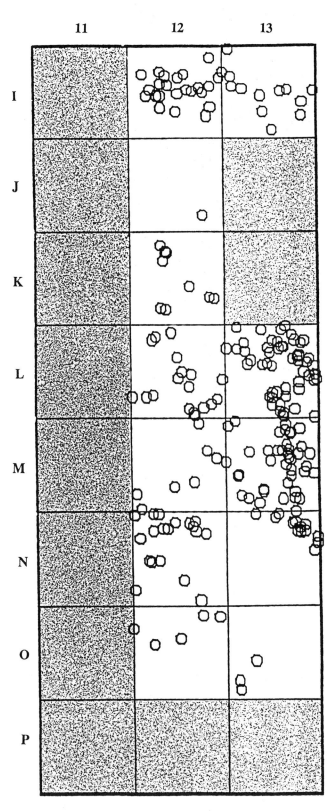

Figure 6. Plan of burned objects in Stratum 3.

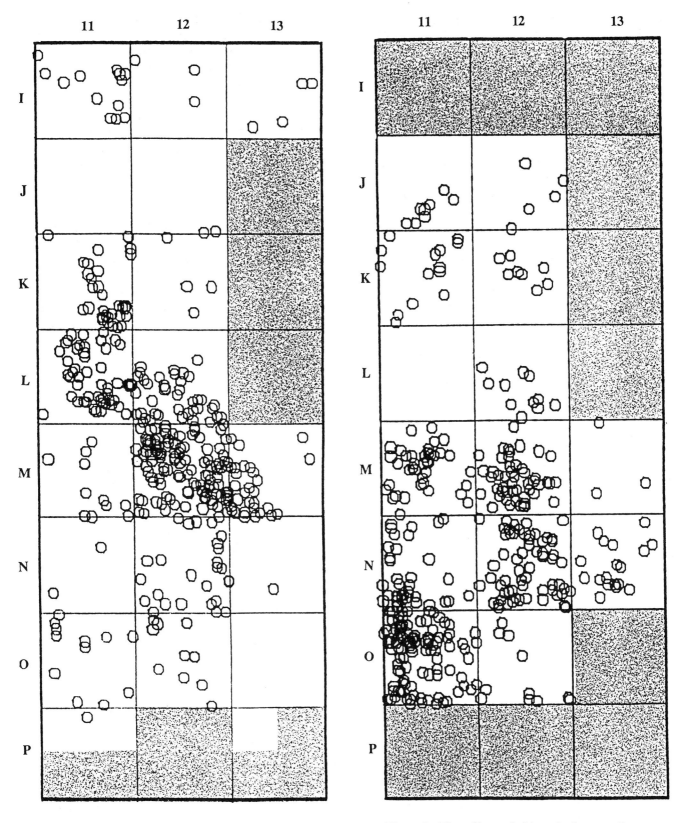

Figure 7. Plan of burned objects in Pavement 4, Stratum 4.

Figure 8. Plan of burned objects in Stratum 5.

While there may have been some rearrangements of material by natural processes, the stratigraphic sequence and the material distributions demonstrate that the central area patterns were essentially manifestations of human behavior.

Stratigraphic Resolution

The coherent set of dates obtained from the Stratum 4 cobble pavements was used to assess the general rate of assemblage burial. Stratum 4 was radiocarbon dated between about 12,200 and 11,000 B.P., thus the half-meter layer of cobbles represented a 1,200 year period. On average, each of the approximately twelve cobble pavements represented about a century of intermittent site use. To estimate the 'grain' of the deposits (Binford 1982), the Abri Dufaure tool density was compared to the cobble pavement sites of the Isle valley in the Dordogne (Gaussen 1980) and to the Abri Duruthy (Arambourou 1978).

The central area at Dufaure contained 111 tools per square in Stratum 4, four times greater than the dense deposits at Solvieux and three times greater than the densest level at Duruthy (Table 2). Compared to Dufaure, the Isle valley sites appear to be sites with limited activity and of high temporal resolution. This was indicated by their small size, low artifact density, definable structure, distinguishable workzones, and relatively shallow stratigraphy in most of the sites. These characteristics likely indicate quicker burial of these floodplain sites. In contrast, the stratigraphic

Table 2. Relative Number of Cobbles and Tools per Meter Square from Upper Paleolithic sites.

Site	Cobbles (per m2)	Tools (per m2)
Isle Valley		
Le Cerisier	50	2
Solvieux	75	31
Guillassou	130	5
Le Mas (Cabane 1)	13	2
Le Mas (Cabane 2)	19	7
Plateau Parrain	--	6
Le Croix-de-Fer	--	1
Abri Duruthy		
Azilian	--	13
Magdalenian VI	--	39
Magdalenian V	--	38
Magdalenian IV	--	44
Magdalenian III	--	24
Abri Dufaure		
Stratum 3	14	15
Stratum 4	294	111
Stratum 5	43	66

resolution at Dufaure was coarse-grained, suggesting some overlaps in occupations. The 1,200 year sequence of the Stratum 4 deposits, and the high density of tools and cobbles, suggested that there was probable re-use and re-construction of unburied or partly buried pavements. While individual pavements at the Abri Dufaure may have been re-used, the presence of interstitial silts between cobbles and the detection of individual episodes of activity also suggested that there were periods of abandonment.

Activity Areas

Given that the central area consisted of primary deposits, material distributions were analyzed to discern potential human activities. As in other cave and rockshelter contexts (Straus 1979, 1990), the physical features of Dufaure (shelter walls and overhang, boulders, the talus slope and its microtopographic variations) were studied to determine if these features served as a framework for structuring the spatial organization of activities (Binford 1982).

The presence of concentrations of burned material over the central area appeared to demonstrate that repeated activity occurred in the same locations. The differences in the dimensions and the contents of the burning concentrations likely signals differences in behavioral activities. In some cases, burning patterns were superimposed, and could not be separated into discrete patterns. While individual patterns could not be deciphered, computer back-plotting showed that the size and location of the fires shifted through time, suggesting changes in the specific types and spatial positioning of activities such as meat roasting and cooking and in the provision of light and heat. Indicative of activity changes, the Stratum 3 burning concentrations mainly consisted of bone and lithics, the Stratum 4 concentrations were dominated by cobbles, and the Stratum 5 concentration mainly consisted of plaquettes (Table 3). These differences suggest a number of cultural functions were responsible for the patterns.

The distribution of refit lithics suggested that the topography at Dufaure was used in a particular way by

Table 3. Number of Burned Items by Material and Stratum.

Material	03	04	05	Total
Cobbles	23	964	113	1100 (42.5%)
Lithics	276	161	23	460 (18%)
Bone	43	32	17	92 (3.5%)
Eboulis	13	513	133	659 (25.5%)
Plaquettes	1	148	123	272 (10.5%)
Total	356	1818	409	2583

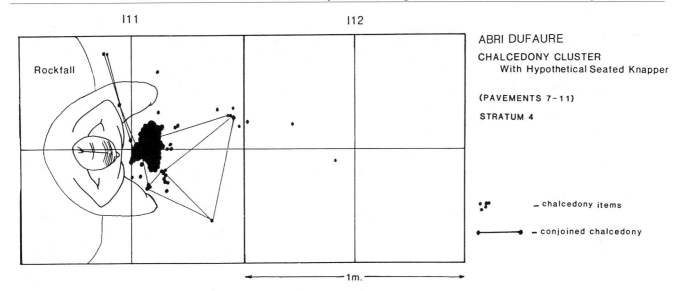

Figure 9. Chalcedony refit cluster with hypothetical seated knapper.

the site inhabitants (Petraglia 1992, n.d.b). On the flat rockshelter border, there were three sets of refit material, one dump and two reduction areas, one of which appeared to be an *in situ* reduction area (Figure 9). The discovery of three sets of refit material on the rockshelter border was unusually high given the small size of this area (1 x 3 m). In contrast, on the uneven and bouldered surface of the ancient dripline zone of the upper slope, there were no concentrations of reduced or intentionally placed materials. On the midslope, a refit set was found deliberately placed adjacent to and underneath large *éboulis* boulders. In addition, there were two crystal quartz concentrations (Squares M 7, N 13) on the midslope. This differentiation in space use was most likely due to intrasite characteristics and topography. The flat area of the rockshelter border was likely sheltered, and a comfortable area to reduce lithic materials. In contrast, the heavily bouldered and wet upper slope and the relatively steep area of the midslope did not serve as comfortable areas for reduction of the stone materials. While the midslope was steep, the large boulders provided places for possible seated reduction and for caching material.

Differences in the spatial distribution of tools by site area suggested variation in intrasite activities. The rockshelter border contained the highest density of tools per square, exceeding the midslope density by 70 tools per square. The higher tool density on the flat, but spatially limited, surface of the rockshelter border was important and testified to the intensified use of this area. While it is beyond the scope of this report to describe specific activity areas, there appears to be some functional differences in tool discard according to site area. For instance, there appear to be differences in the distribution of burins over the central area (Figure 10). The upper slope contains the fewest

number of tools per square. The generally lower number of tools on the upper slope may be due to human avoidance of the wet, heavily bouldered surface of the dripline zone. As there were differences in the horizontal distribution of tools, there were differences in the number of tools according to stratigraphic position, signalling changes in site use through time. The Stratum 3 deposits contained a low number of tools per square, and the deposits of Strata 4 and 5 contained high tool densities. These differences likely signal changes in site use through time.

There were differences in the spatial distribution of cobbles by site area. High mean densities of cobbles were encountered on the rockshelter border (274.77 kg/m3) and on the midslope (253.11 kg/m3), likely demonstrating that the floors were repeatedly re-built over time. The rate of cobble pavement construction on the rockshelter border and the midslope points to the intensity of human activity (whether from primary activity in these areas or from secondary dumping). In contrast, the lowest mean density of cobbles was encountered on the upper slope (209.78 kg/m3), perhaps the result of the wet conditions in the dripline zone and the heavily bouldered surface. In Stratum 3 of the central area, there were low mean densities of cobbles (32.44 kg/m3). Stratum 4 contained a high mean density of cobbles (205.89 kg/m3), while there were low densities of cobbles in Stratum 5 (25.27 kg/m3) (although high densities of plaquettes were encountered). The relatively low densities of cobbles in Strata 3 and 5, the dense accumulation of cobbles in Stratum 4, and the presence of a number of plaquettes in Stratum 5 signals important functional differences in site activities through time.

Based on the foregoing stratigraphic and spatial evidence, the central area deposits were shown to be

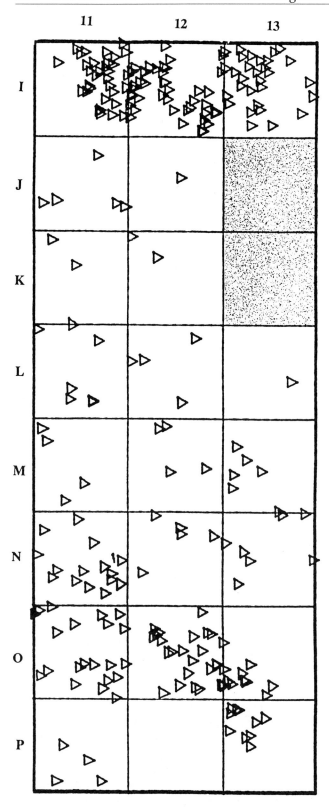

Figure 10. Plan of the burin distribution, Stratum 4.

coherent set of radiocarbon dates suggested that the levels accumulated gradually, however. While the deposits could be characterized as coarse-grained, the use of space was structured through time, and there were instances of well-preserved, short-term activities.

Postdepositional Processes

Although the stratigraphic and spatial evidence implied that the deposits in the central area were intact, containing patterns attributable to human activity, other lines of evidence pointed to some horizontal and vertical movements of materials.

On the midslope, there were preferred alignments of material, thus indicating that pre-burial movements of material may have occurred (Figure 5). This evidence suggested that common slope processes, such as gravity and sheetwash, aligned objects, and led to some horizontal movements.

After burial of the objects and assemblages, the material remains appear to have been subject to vertical movements. Mean lithic weights, lithic size ratios and percentages of debitage types by stratum indicated some selective size sorting. Indicative of post-burial movement of material, smaller lithics were found in greater proportion with increasing stratigraphic depth, mean lithic weights were 9 g in Stratum 3 and 5 g in Stratum 5. In support of this trend, the small trimming flakes increased in proportion from higher to lower strata, while the larger flakes decreased in proportion from higher to lower strata (Figure 11). The refitting evidence supplied evidence for some vertical movements, functionally related objects sometimes passing through pavements and strata. For instance, in one case refittable artifacts were separated by 76 cm. On the upper slope, the heterogeneity of the artifact orientations and the high inclination values corresponded with a dense accumulation of *éboulis*. It is probable that the accumulation of objects around the *éboulis* rockfall resulted in the presence of inclined artifacts. The lack of absolute vertical and horizontal trends in patinated lithics may also indicate that some movements and mixtures of individual artifacts occurred.

In terms of the evidence for vertical mixing, small empty voids were occasionally noted during excavation. Although the agency responsible for these empty spaces was never clear, their presence clearly suggested an avenue for downward or upward movements of small material. The presence of rodent microfauna at Dufaure (Altuna et al. 1991) may suggest some role for these animals to contribute to material patterns. During the excavation of Dufaure, the burrowing activities of small reptiles was

intact and not eroded or transported. The behavioral resolution of the deposits was coarse-grained, representing superimposed cultural patterns. The vertically

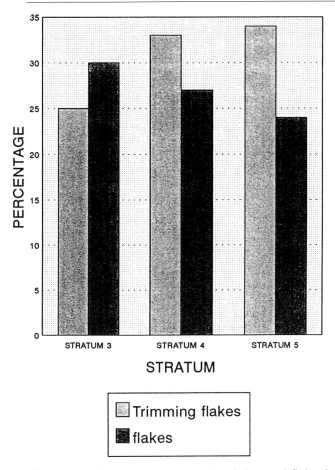

Figure 11. *Percentage of trimming flakes and flakes by stratum.*

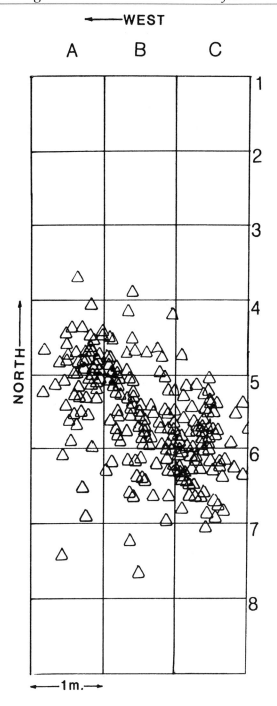

Figure 12. *Simulation of a burning pattern on a slope, original pattern.*

observed. The reptiles could only displace small objects such as lithics and bones, but they did not have the ability to move larger objects such as cobbles.

Support for limited displacement of original cultural patterns was also suggested by the wide scatter of burned material. One of the burning patterns was replicated and horizontal movement simulations were performed (Figure 12). The simulations at 10 to 20 cm intervals did not produce significant spatial changes. However, more substantial spatial changes were noticeable at 30 cm movement intervals (Figure 13). At 1 meter of lateral displacement intervals, the patterns became obliterated (Figure 14). While the original burning pattern at Dufaure may have been more clustered, and thus experienced some degree of lateral displacement of material, the simulations suggest that this disturbance was certainly no greater than 1 meter, where patterns become obliterated. It is therefore likely that the burning patterns at Dufaure were modified, but only to a minor extent.

Patterns of artifact breakage suggested the influence of natural processes on the stone materials and over the site. Artifact breakage was shown to be related to artifact type and stratigraphic depth. Delicate objects such as backed bladelets and bladelets were shown to be broken with greater frequency than more durable objects such as flakes (Figure 15). Artifacts were broken with greater frequency with increasing stratigraphic depth implying that postdepositional processes were responsible for breakages (Figure 16). Sets of individual refits consisted of

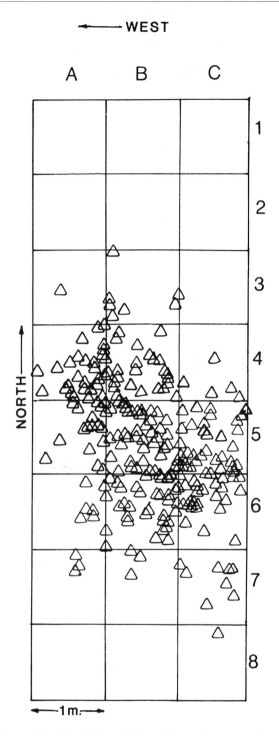

Figure 13. Simulation of a burning pattern on a slope after 30 cm movement per object. Standard deviation=50cm.

broken blades, often snapped in their midsection (Petraglia 1987, 1992). The broken blades were likely fractured in their midsection because of the physical stresses by the overburden.

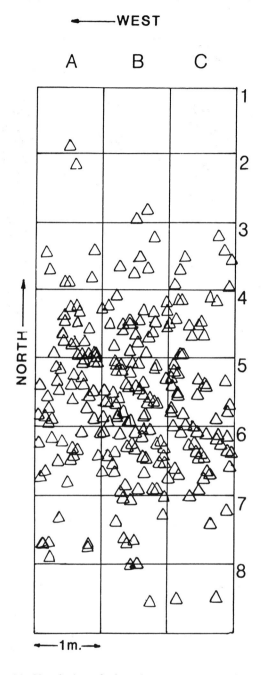

Figure 14. Simulation of a burning pattern on a slope after 1 m movement per object. Standard deviation=1m.

Conclusion

There have been few studies which systematically address formation processes at Paleolithic sites. Before attempting elaborate analyses of site structure and human activities at the Abri Dufaure, it was felt that an assessment had to be made to determine the degree to which the deposits and material patterns

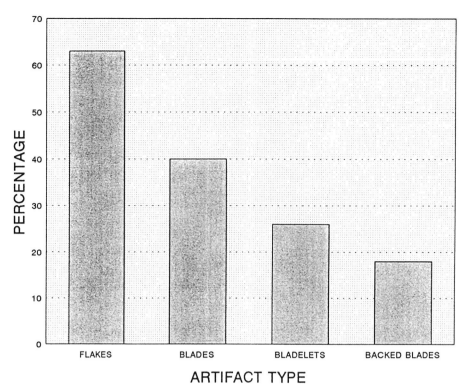

Figure 15. Percentage of whole artifacts by type.

represented the contributions of human and natural agents. The analysis clearly showed that the Abri Dufaure deposits represented a complex interplay between cultural and natural processes. The deposits were characterized as coarse-grained, cultural and natural processes together accounting for the archaeological patterns. Because of the complex interplay of cultural and natural factors, both short- and long-term processes were represented. Given these conditions, this study has provided initial interpretations about the meaning of the spatial patterns at the Abri Dufaure. This study was performed so that other investigators involved with the Abri Dufaure Prehistoric Project could chose appropriate research problems and analytic strategies to make the most prudent, behavioral interpretations. This approach has hopefully ensured a more accurate foundation on which to build credible behavioral inferences from the patterns at Dufaure. In a broader realm, the site formation study has hopefully provided an example of how archaeologists may detect and analyze the processes created by human behavior and the natural environment.

Acknowledgments

Lawrence Straus, the Director of the Abri Dufaure excavations, generously provided all available data, and strongly supported this project from its inception.

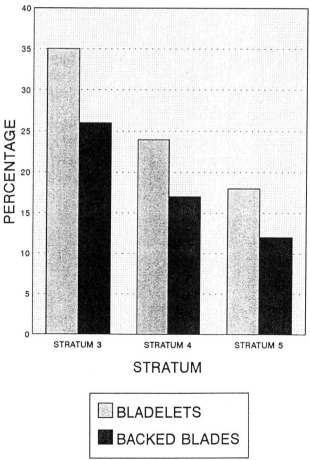

Figure 16. Percentage of whole bladelets and backed blades by stratum.

The late Dr. R. Arambourou, former Director of the Musée D'Arthous, provided the needed laboratory facilities for the refitting project. Mark Stiger of the Western State College of Colorado provided the software for the burning simulations. This study has been supported by two L.S.B. Leakey grants, a National Science Foundation doctoral dissertation improvement grant (BNS86-11418), a National Science Foundation (BNS81-03589) stipend from Lawrence Straus, and grants from the University of New Mexico. This paper was originally formulated while I was a postdoctoral fellow at the National Museum of Natural History, Smithsonian Institution. The current support of the Smithsonian Human Origins Program, directed by Richard Potts, is also gratefully acknowledged.

References Cited

Akoshima, K.

n.d. Analyse des Structures d'Habitat de la Couche 4. In *Les Derniers Chasseurs du Renne Le Long Des Pyrenees: L'Abri Dufaure, Un Gisement Tardiglaciaire en Gascogne*, edited by L.G. Straus, Mémoires de la Société Préhistorique Française, in press.

Altuna, J., A. Eastham, K. Mariezkurrena, A. Spiess, and L. Straus

1991 Magdalenian and Azilian Hunting at the Abri Dufaure, SW France. *Archaeozoologia* 4:87-108.

Arambourou, R.

1978 *Le Gisement Préhistorique de Duruthy*. Mémoires de la Société Préhistorique Française 13, Paris.

Binford, L.R.

1973 Interassemblage Variability—the Mousterian and the 'Functional' Argument. In *The Explanation of Culture Change*, edited by C. Renfrew, pp. 227-254. Duckworth Publishers, London.

1978 *Nunamiut Ethnoarchaeology*. Academic Press, New York.

1981 Behavioral Archaeology and the 'Pompeii Premise'. *Journal of Anthropological Research* 37:195-208.

1982 The Archaeology of Place. *Journal of Anthropological Archaeology* 1:5-31.

Binford, L.R. and S. Binford

1966 A Preliminary Analysis of Functional Variability in the Mousterian of Levallois Facies. In *Recent Studies in Paleoanthropology*, edited by J.D. Clark and F.C. Howell. *American Anthropologist* 68:238-295.

Bordes, F.

1972 *A Tale of Two Caves*. Harper and Row, New York.

1975 Sur la Notion de Sol d'Habitat en Préhistoire Paléolithique. *Bulletin de la Société Préhistorique Française* 72:139-144.

1980a Question de Contemporanéité: l'Illusion des Remontages. *Bulletin de la Société Préhistorique Française* 77:132-133.

1980b Savez-Vous Remonter les Cailloux à la Mode de Chez Nous? *Bulletin de la Société Préhistorique Française* 77:232-234.

Bordes, F., J.P. Rigaud, and D. de Sonneville-Bordes

1972 Des Buts, Problémes et Limites de l'Archéologie Paléolithique. *Quaternaria* 16:15-34.

Breuil, H., and P. Dubalen

1901 Fouilles d'un Abri à Sordes. *Revue de l'Ecole d'Anthropologie de Paris* 8:251-268.

Butzer, K.W.

1982 *Archaeology as Human Ecology*. Cambridge University Press, Cambridge.

Cahen, D.

1980 Question de Contemporanéité: l'Apport des Remontages. *Bulletin de la Société Préhistorique Française* 77:230-232.

Cahen, D., L.H. Keeley, and F.L. Van Noten

1979 Stone Tools, Toolkits and Human Behavior in Prehistory. *Current Anthropology* 20:661-683.

Carson, M.A., and M. Kirkby

1972 *Hillslope Form and Process*. Cambridge University Press, London.

Freeman, L.G.

1973 The Significance of Mammalian Faunas from Paleolithic Occupations in Cantabrian Spain. *American Antiquity* 38:3-44.

Freeman, L.G., and K.W. Butzer

1966 The Acheulian Station of Torralba (Spain): A Progress Report. *Quaternaria* 8:9-21.

Frostick, L., and I. Reid
  1983 Taphonomic Significance of Sub-Aerial Transport of Vertebrate Fossils on Steep Semi-Arid Slopes. *Lethaia* 16:157-164.
Fuchs, C., D. Kaufman, and A. Ronen
  1977 Erosion and Artifact Distribution in Open-Air Epi-Palaeolithic Sites on the Coastal Plain of Israel. *Journal of Field Archaeology* 4:171-179.
Gaussen, J.
  1980 *Le Paléolithique Supérieur de Plein Air en Périgord.* CNRS, Paris, 14.
Kent, S. (editor)
  1987 *Method and Theory for Activity Area Research.* Columbia University Press, New York.
Kornfeld, M.
  1982 Down the Hill Without a Site. *Wyoming Contributions to Archaeology* 3:91-104.
Laville, H.
  n.d. Caractéristiques et Signification des Dépôts. In *Les Derniers Chasseurs du Renne Le Long Des Pyrenees: L'Abri Dufaure, Un Gisement Tardiglaciaire en Gascogne,* edited by L.G. Straus, Mémoires de la Société Préhistorique Française, in press.
Laville, H., J.P. Rigaud, and J. Sackett
  1980 *Rockshelters of the Périgord.* Academic Press, New York.
Leopold, L.B.
  1982 Downslope Movement of Rocks on Red Bluff Hill. In *Fieldtrip Guidebook, American Geomorphological Fieldgroup,* edited by L.B. Leopold, pp. 105-112. Pinedale, Wyoming.
Nash, D.T., and M.D. Petraglia
  1987 *Natural Formation Processes and the Archaeological Record.* BAR International Series, 352, Oxford.
Petraglia, M.D.
  1987 *Site Formation Processes at the Abri Dufaure: a Study of Upper Paleolithic Rockshelter and Hillslope Deposits in Southwestern France.* University Microfilms International, Ann Arbor, Michigan.
  1992 Stone Artifact Refitting and Formation Processes at the Abri Dufaure, an Upper Paleolithic Site in Southwest France. In *Piecing Together the Past: Applications of Refitting Studies in Archaeology,* edited by J.L. Hofman and J.G. Enloe, pp. 163-178. BAR International Series, Oxford, 578.
  n.d.a Processus de Formation du Gisement. In *Les Derniers Chasseurs du Renne Le Long Des Pyrenees: L'Abri Dufaure, Un Gisement Tardiglaciaire en Gascogne,* edited by L.G. Straus, Mémoires de la Société Préhistorique Française, in press.
  n.d.b Remontages. In *Les Derniers Chasseurs du Renne Le Long Des Pyrenees: L'Abri Dufaure, Un Gisement Tardiglaciaire en Gascogne,* edited by L.G. Straus, Mémoires de la Société Préhistorique Française, in press.
Petraglia, M.D., and D.T. Nash
  1987 The Impact of Fluvial Processes on Experimental Sites. In *Natural Formation Processes and the Archaeological Record,* edited by D.T. Nash and M.D. Petraglia, pp. 108-130. BAR International Series, Oxford, 352.
Rick, J.W.
  1976 Downslope Movement and Archaeological Intrasite Spatial Analysis. *American Antiquity* 41:133-144.
Ritter, D.F.
  1978 *Process Geomorphology.* William C. Brown Co. Publishers, Dubuque.
Schiffer, M.B.
  1972 Archaeological Context and Systemic Context. *American Antiquity* 37:156-165.
  1976 *Behavioral Archeology.* Academic Press, New York.
  1983 Toward the Identification of Formation Processes. *American Antiquity* 48:675-706.
  1987 *Formation Processes of the Archaeological Record.* University of New Mexico Press, Albuquerque.
Schuldenrein, J.
  1986 Paleoenvironment, Prehistory, and Accelerated Slope Erosion along the Central Israeli Coastal Plain (Palmahim): A Geoarchaeological Case Study. *Geoarchaeology* 1:61-81.
Schumm, S.A.
  1967a Rates of Surficial Rock Creep on Hillslopes in Western Colorado. *Science* 155:560-561.
  1967b The Development and Evolution of Hillslopes. *Journal of Geological Education* 14:98-104.

Schumm, S.A., and M.P. Mosley (editors)
  1973 *Slope Morphology*. Dowden Hutchinson and Ross, Stroudsburg, Pennsylvania.
Selby, M.J.
  1982 *Hillslope Materials and Processes*. Oxford University Press, Oxford.
Straus, L.G.
  1979 Caves: a Palaeoanthropological Resource. *World Archaeology* 10:331-339.
  1990 Underground Archaeology: Perspectives on Caves and Rockshelters. In *Archaeological Method and Theory*, Volume 2, edited by M.B. Schiffer, pp. 255-304. University of Arizona Press, Tucson.
  n.d. *Les Derniers Chasseurs du Renne Le Long Des Pyrenees: L'Abri Dufaure, Un Gisement Tardiglaciaire en Gascogne*. Mémoires de la Société Préhistorique Française, in press.
Straus, L.G., K. Akoshima, M.D. Petraglia, and M. Séronie-Vivien
  1988 Terminal Pleistocene Adaptations in Pyrenean France: The Nature and Role of the Abri Dufaure Site (Sorde-L'Abbaye, Les Landes). *World Archaeology* 19:328-348.
Straus, L.G., and J. Evin
  1989 Datations par le Radiocarbone des Couches Azilienne et Magdalénienne de l'Abri Dufaure (Sordes-l'Abbaye, Les Landes). *Bulletin de la Société Préhistorique Française* 86:146-155.
Villa, P.
  1977 Sols et Niveaux d'Habitat du Paléolithique Inférieur en Europe et au Proche Orient. *Quaternaria* 19:107-134.
  1982 Conjoinable Pieces and Site Formation Processes. *American Antiquity* 47:276-290.
Whallon, R.
  1973a Spatial Analysis of Occupation Floors I: Application of Dimensional Analysis of Variance. *American Antiquity* 38:266-278.
  1973b Spatial Analysis of Palaeolithic Occupation Areas. In *The Explanation of Culture Change*, edited by C. Renfrew, pp. 115-130. Duckworth, London.
  1974 Spatial Analysis of Occupation Floors II: the Application of the Nearest Neighbor Analysis. *American Antiquity* 39:16-34.
Wood, W.R., and D.L. Johnson
  1978 A Survey of Disturbance Processes in Archaeological Site Formation. In *Advances in Archaeological Method and Theory*, Volume 1, edited by M.B. Schiffer, pp. 315-381. Academic Press, New York.
Yellen, J.E.
  1977 *Archaeological Approaches to the Present*. Academic Press, New York.
Young, A.
  1960 Soil Movement by Denudational Processes on Slopes. *Nature* 188:120-122.
  1972 *Slopes*. Oliver and Boyd, Edinburgh.

8

Site Formation Processes and Behavioral Deposition Episodes: The View from Le Flageolet II

Todd A. Koetje
Indiana University of Pennsylvania

The Paleolithic contains what is surely one of the more intricate archaeological records. The caves and rockshelters that form the basis for our understanding of this time period present particularly difficult challenges to our methods of interpretation. Perhaps surprising to the non-specialist, there are a large number of caves and rockshelters where the deposits are not particularly well understood. This chapter focuses on Le Flageolet II, a site that is interesting from a number of perspectives, not the least of which is the inconsistency between the radiocarbon dates and the industrial attribution. In many ways though, it is fairly typical of late Upper Paleolithic sites. Perhaps most striking is the relatively thick, seemingly undifferentiated deposit found in Layer IX. Most often this type of deposit has been dealt with very superficially, ignored or eliminated from detailed consideration, or treated as the result of a single occupation because of the difficulties involved in defining tractable units. This is in fact the manner in which Le Flageolet II was initially, and is still very commonly approached. I hope to show that these types of deposits can be productively analyzed, and that this process may lead to some useful insight into both the detailed use of the site itself, and its place within a larger regional framework.

Le Flageolet II is a rockshelter containing late Magdalenian deposits in the Périgord region of southern France. The shelter overlooks the Dordogne River Valley from the northern cliffs, and is the product of a geologic fault crossing the valley from the northeast (Figure 1). Le Flageolet I, the companion site, is relatively better known and contains primarily Aurignacian deposits (Simek 1984a, 1984b, 1987; Simek and Larick 1983; Simek at al. 1985). Deposition at Le Flageolet II was affected drastically by a major erosion event during the Later Würm, some 16,000 years ago, and probably corresponding to the period formerly considered to be the Würm III/IV interstade (Laville 1970, 1977, 1988; Laville et al. 1980). At this time a spring opened just above the shelter, and scoured the protected area now known as Flageolet II down to bedrock. This allowed subsequent occupation by Magdalenian peoples to begin at or near the bedrock, and created the great discontinuity in deposits between the areas designated I and II (Figure 2). Subsequent deposits in Le Flageolet II seem to have originated primarily from outside of the shelter, and to have, from the beginning, contained at least small numbers of artifacts (Laville 1970, 1977).

Formal excavations at Le Flageolet II were initiated in 1968 by a team from the University of Bordeaux, headed by Dr. Jean-Philippe Rigaud, and continued until 1976 (Rigaud 1970, 1977, 1982). Twelve stratigraphic layers were defined in an excavated area of ca. 10 x 4 x 2 meters. Layers I-VIII, and X-XII are rela-

113

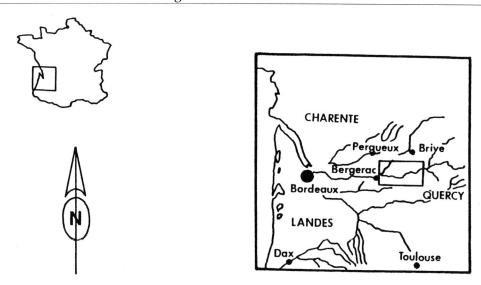

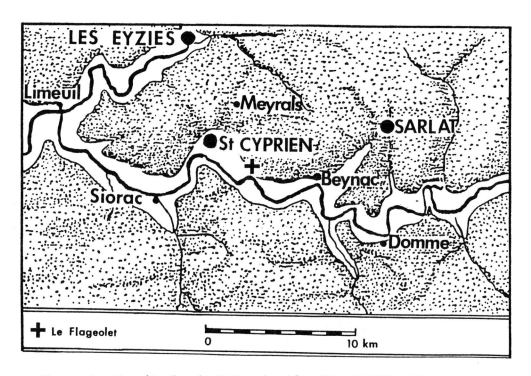

Figure 1. Location of Le Flageolet II. Reproduced from Rigaud (1982), with permission.

tively thin (ca. 10–20 cm), contained very few artifacts, and an extremely small number of diagnostic tools (in all cases less than 100). These layers are attributed to the Magdalenian by the excavators. Layer IX, in contrast is up to 60 cm thick, and contains some 12,000 artifacts, with approximately 800 classifiable tools (Figure 3). On the basis of the Bordian lithic tool types found in Layer IX, it has been attributed to the Magdalenian VI phase (Rigaud 1970, 1977, 1982). In

general, Layer IX appears to be a relatively typical Upper Magdalenian deposit. It is thick, rich in artifacts, and the sediment shows substantial organic staining and much evidence of burning. Radiocarbon dates from Layer IX, however, place it several thousand years earlier than other assemblages in the region with the same typological attribution. The dates are similar in range to those from other sites attributed to the Magdalenian III and IV phases. Two

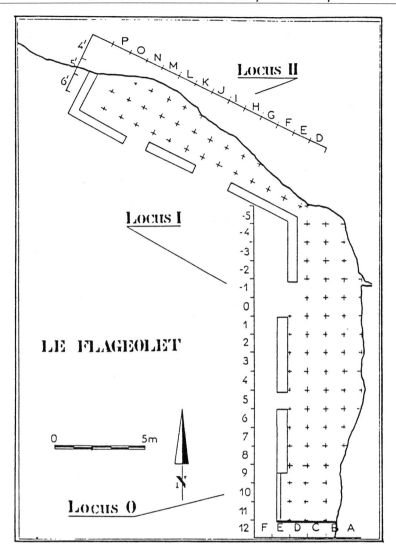

Figure 2. Plan map of Le Flageolet II. Reproduced from Rigaud (1982), with permission.

radiocarbon dates from precisely located objects (both bones) are available from Layer IX. The stratigraphically uppermost date is from just below the bottom of the pavement, near the top of the layer, while the lowermost date is from nearly 60 cm lower, near the bottom of Layer IX, and its boundary with Layer X. At 14110 ± 690 B.P. (Ly 917) and 15250 ± 320 B.P. (Ly 918) respectively, they span approximately 1000 yrs (Rigaud 1982: 399-410) although at 2 standard errors there is substantial overlap (Figure 4).

The Layer IX fauna is dominated by cold adapted species (Delpech 1970, 1977), which, when considered in the chronostratigraphic scheme for the region (Laville et al. 1980: 334), is supportive of the early radiocarbon dates. Pollen data also support this early placement (Paquereau 1970). Clearly, the assemblage is anomalous in that several diagnostic types from the late Magdalenian occur with a microblade based industry, but early dates and fauna.

Natural Formation Processes

Sediment seems to have accumulated in Le Flageolet II through three basic processes. Roof and wall exfoliation can reasonably account for much of the larger sediment, and limestone gravels and slabs (*éboulis*). Most of the remaining sediment can be accounted for via low velocity wind and water transport, and generalized mass wasting of the surrounding slope. With some minor exceptions, such as the talus slope outside of the sheltered area and the northern end of the shelter where it meets the slope face, on a site wide scale these materials seem to have been deposited in more-or-less horizontal layers. There is little or no good evidence for subsequent, substantial sediment disturbance as the result of natural processes. There are no preserved rodent burrows, water channels, slumps, etc. that disturb large areas. At least two large boulders occur in Le

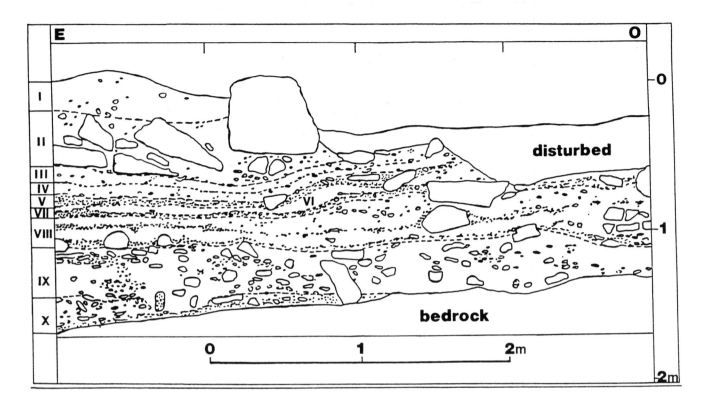

Figure 3. Stratigraphic section of Le Flageolet II. Reproduced from Rigaud (1982), with permission.

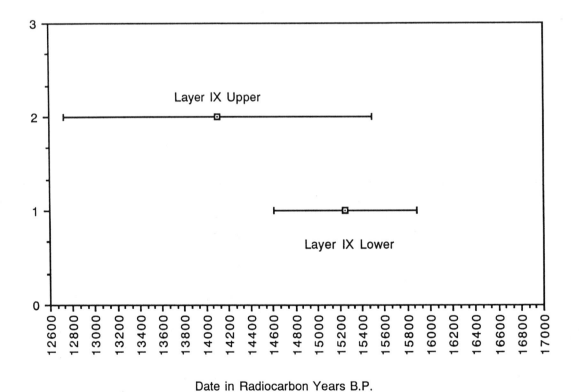

Date in Radiocarbon Years B.P.

Figure 4. Le Flageolet II, Layer IX radiocarbon dates, with 2 standard errors.

Flageolet II, raising the possibility of disturbance via major rock falls. But while their effect on the sediments that immediately underlie them is obvious, there is no good evidence to suggest that either had a major effect on the overall sediment bedding process. It seems reasonable to conclude that, at least in general, the natural processes that brought and kept sediment at Le Flageolet II are generally understood, and that there were no major postdepositional disturbances attributable to natural processes.

Cultural Formation Processes

Behavioral formation processes on the other hand, can be seen to have played a more substantial role, both in the original deposition and subsequent modification of the sediments at Le Flageolet II. This can be most dramatically seen in Layer IX, where the sediments are extremely rich in organic debris and burned material. Also very evident in Layer IX are large numbers of quartzite river cobbles that have frequently been burned or heated, and broken. In the upper portion of this layer, these cobbles, in combination with large, limestone *éboulis,* make up a distinct pavement covering most of the excavated area. This pavement occurs in a single distinct layer some 5–6 cm thick, and although its topography is somewhat irregular, particularly towards the ends of the sheltered area, it is roughly horizontal and conforms well to the sediment layers above and below it. Similar pavements occur in many other sites dating from the Magdalenian period throughout Northern and Western Europe, particularly in southern Germany and the Isle River Valley in SW France (Gaussen 1980).

It is reasonably clear, then, that substantial amounts of material have been brought in and dumped or deposited casually as the result of abandonment or clean-up activities, but that large amounts of material have also been deposited in distinctly, and intentionally patterned arrangements.

Within Layer IX at least, there is some evidence that can be taken to imply increasing occupational intensity, or at least changes in the nature of the occupations, perhaps from shorter to longer term (Koetje 1987b, 1991a). Three well defined features are found in Layer IX, including the pavement, in the upper portion of the level, and two hearths, one near the middle of the layer, and another near its bottom. This suggests that the earlier occupations of the site were less intense, perhaps shorter term uses of the area. The labor involved in constructing a pavement largely from cobble sized rocks that had to be either carried up from the river floodplain or mined out of the existing deposits, argues for a more substantial,

perhaps longer term use of the site in the upper portion of Layer IX. If this type of shift in the use of the site was actually occurring, it is also reasonable to expect substantial shifts in the assemblages associated with these features. The exact nature of expected changes in Magdalenian assemblages as the result of shifts in the intensity or duration of occupation has yet to be worked out. Surprisingly little is known, in any detailed sense, of Magdalenian subsistence-settlement patterns, or their changes through time in any particular region. This may be particularly true of SW France, where most effort has been focused on understanding individual cave and rockshelter sites, and relatively little focused on how they may have functioned together as part of a larger system. Studies that address these issues, such as White's (1985), Gordon's (1987), and Le Tensorer's (1981) have been few and far between. It would seem reasonable to expect an increase in formal tools or their production as occupational intensity or duration increased. Changes in use and discard rates could also be expected.

Pavement construction also raises the possibility that there may have been a substantial amount of excavation, or at least some serious surface disturbance during the occupation or occupations doing the construction. It is not currently possible to detail how much sediment might have been removed or disturbed during this operation. The pavement topography, however, is not very distinct from that of either the under or overlying sediments. This suggests that very little excavation or leveling may have been involved in this case. With few exceptions, such as Le Cerisier (Gaussen 1980), this is consistent with most of the known Magdalenian pavements, which seem to be largely composed of cobbles set on or into an existing surface. The existence of two relatively intact hearths below the pavement level also suggests that excavation or disturbance for pavement construction was, at least, not vertically extensive.

The majority of the postdepositional cultural formation processes affecting the sediment in Layer IX probably relate most clearly to a human occupation of the contemporary surfaces. Thus, processes such as trampling, and limited excavation for hearth construction, etc. can be expected. The effects of such processes, although well documented, do not often appear to form distinctly recognizable patterns in the archaeological record (Schiffer 1983, 1987; Wood and Johnson 1978). Most experimental studies of trampling, for example, do not show clearly patterned evidence of vertical sorting by weight, size or volume, nor do they show patterned horizontal orientation in such a manner as to allow easy recognition in the archaeological record (Cahen and Moeyersons 1977; Gifford 1978; Gifford and Behrensmeyer 1977; Gifford et al. 1985; Villa and Courtin 1983). These studies do tend to show that trampled artifacts have a high incidence of vertical, or at least out of horizontal orientation.

Detailed strike and dip measurements were not taken during the excavation of Le Flageolet II, although obviously 'off horizontal' objects were noted. Analysis of the field notes shows that these objects were very rare, amounting to some .01% of the total. Although this cannot be considered conclusive data, given a reasonably rigorous excavation crew it certainly suggests that the overwhelming majority of the objects found were more-or-less horizontally oriented. This is inconsistent with the notion that extensive trampling was occurring. Thus while trampling and similar types of formation processes evidently occurred, they cannot be demonstrated from the detailed artifact patterning found at Le Flageolet II.

Experimental trampling studies have also shown that, depending upon the size of an object, vertical movement of up to 20 cm can be expected in an unconsolidated matrix such as loose, dry sand (Gifford et al. 1985; Villa and Courtin 1983; Siiriainen 1977). Given the much more compact sediment and the presence of cobbles and large *éboulis* slabs, it seems reasonable to suggest that the range of vertical movement expected at Le Flageolet II would be much less than this. Although none of these factors have been analyzed quantitatively, additional evidence suggesting that vertical movement within Layer IX as the result of postdepositional factors was minor or insignificant includes: A) the large number of complete, fragile, bone and lithic artifacts, B) the essentially horizontal strike and dip of most flat *éboulis*, C) the 'fresh', relatively undamaged macroscopic appearance of most flint edges, D) the 'fresh', relatively undamaged appearance of samples of flint tools and debitage that have been examined under high and low power microscopy, and, E) the well defined boundary between Layers IX and X.

It often seems easiest to think about postdepositional disturbance of this kind in terms of energy input into the sediment. It takes energy input above some threshold value to cause a given degree of movement in different types of sediment under different conditions of temperature, humidity, etc., but any energy input will have some effect, however small and localized. At this point in time, artifact movement from trampling has not been conclusively demonstrated in coarse grained, mixed, or consolidated sediment, and is difficult to infer in the absence of large numbers of vertically oriented objects. It is clear, however, that trampling is an energy input, and the same energy that may move sediment and arti-

facts, could also break fragile objects, destroy the fine edges of freshly struck flakes and blades, disrupt features, and blend, disrupt, or prevent the creation of distinct sediment boundaries. These characteristics of a site and its assemblages may be even more sensitive indicators of disturbance than artifact movement, because they may respond to or record much lower energy impacts.

If there had been a substantial amount of sediment churning due to any type of significant energy input after deposition, one would not expect to find the characteristics noted above. It seems reasonable then, to assume that postdepositional vertical movement within Layer IX was minimal, and probably below the threshold of current archaeological visibility. This is not to say that it did not happen, since at some level it certainly did happen, but simply that we cannot monitor its extent or nature at this time.

Hearth and Pavement Focused Levels

Layer IX at Le Flageolet II can be viewed as a single deposit representing at least three distinct occupational episodes. Recently, quantitative methods have been developed that enable a single, relatively thick archaeological layer to be reliably broken up into a number of horizontally oriented sub-levels, which can often be attributed to distinct depositional events. These methods require that several relatively simple assumptions be made about the original layer. These include: 1) the deposits are essentially horizontal, 2) sub-units within the larger layer are also essentially horizontal, and, 3) there has been little or no heterogeneous postdepositional vertical movement of sediment. The details of this process have been presented several times elsewhere, so only a brief outline is presented here. The full method is discussed in Koetje (1989, 1990, 1991a, 1991b). In essence, analytic levels can be "created" or "recovered" through a 2 step process. The first step involves transforming the 3 dimensional coordinates marking an object's position in space into an "equal variance space" to eliminate the inherently distinct scales of measurement used in measuring vertical and horizontal coordinates. The second step involves transforming the resulting space again, and then clustering the new coordinates using a technique that preserves most metric properties of the new analytic space. The results are sets of objects that are assigned to the same sub-levels when mapped back into the original coordinate system. Experimentally, these techniques can recover pre-existing sub-level structure with error rates in assigning individual objects to their correct sub-level of between 0 and 10%, depending on the initial set of parameters used.

Much of the evidence cited above can be used to suggest that Layer IX meets the general requirements necessary for using this method. When applied to Layer IX, the results are sets of objects belonging to three distinct "analytical levels" corresponding closely to the vertical positions of the two hearths and the pavement. Once these analytical levels have been isolated, their contents become available for more detailed analysis. The fauna represented, for example, does not change significantly. Each level is dominated by Reindeer *(Rangifer sp.)*, as is the site as a whole (Delpech 1970, 1977). Oddly though, there is a significant correlation between the weight (but not size) of the faunal material and its depth in Layer IX. Heavier bones tend to be lower in the layer than lighter ones. Examining and comparing the assemblages associated with each of these levels throws an interesting light on the site and its place within the larger regional system.

Figure 5 shows a histogram of the lithic tool classes represented in each layer. Table 1 shows the definition of each class, both in terms of the formal, Bordian types represented, and in more prosaic terms. Each class is meant to represent a general functional category, rather than a specific morphological type. Looking at the tools in this manner, allows us to avoid

being locked into the traditionally defined types and their associated temporal phases, and instead consider groups of functionally similar types.

Initial inspection of the raw histogram data suggest considerable differences in the three tool assemblages (Figure 5). However, when the raw data are standardized so that sheer magnitude has less of an effect, the similarity in class distribution between the levels is rather remarkable (Figures 6 and 7). This interpretation is supported by the high degree of correlation between the tool class counts for each level, and the high Rank Correlation Homogeneity measure (Table 2). Table 3 presents additional support for the essential similarity of these levels, in the form of the independent K' measure of homogeneity (Koetje 1987a). This index measures diversity by taking into account both evenness and richness, and is calculated both for individual levels and for all levels combined. Global homogeneity for these levels is high at 0.882, and the individual levels each have a relatively high K value, showing clearly that one level is not overwhelming the others.

Because these tool classes are composed of functionally similar objects, so far as we can determine this, the similarity in proportions suggests a basic similarity in the activities that took place at the site during three distinct occupations.

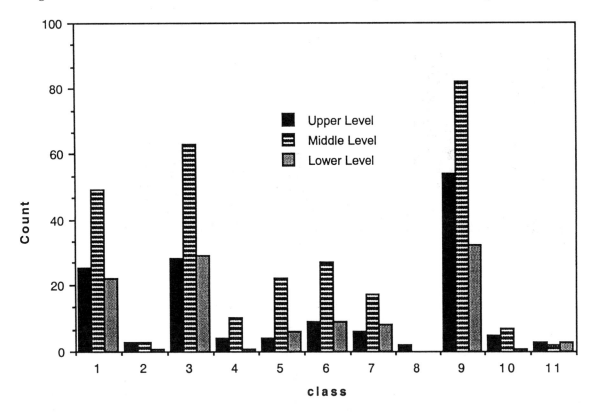

Figure 5. Le Flageolet II, Layer IX Raw Counts by Tool Class and Level.

Table 1. Tool Class Definitions for the Le Flageolet II Analyses.*

Class	Types	Contents
1	1-18	Grattoirs
2	20-29	Percoirs/Becs
3	19,30-46	Burins
4	50,51,54,55,56,65,66, 68-70,92,96-102	Points
5	53,57-60	Truncated Elements
6	61,62,74-76,105	Miscellaneous Retouched Pieces
7	72,73	Notches
8	77-82	Microliths
9	84-88	Backed Bladelets
10	83,90,91,93-95	Bladelets
11	63,64,103,104	Heavily Retouched Blades

*Tool type numbers follow the Type du Paleolithique Supérieur (1972) from Le Tensorer (1981).

Table 2. Spearman Rank Order Correlation Coefficients for the Tool Counts (by Class) for the Three Analytically Defined Levels from Layer IX at Le Flageolet II.

	LEV1	LEV2	LEV3
LEV1	1.000		
LEV2	0.945	1.000	
LEV3	0.908	0.927	1.000

N= 11, p<= .05 for all cases.
Simek's (1984a) Rank Correlation Homogeneity (RCH) = 1.0

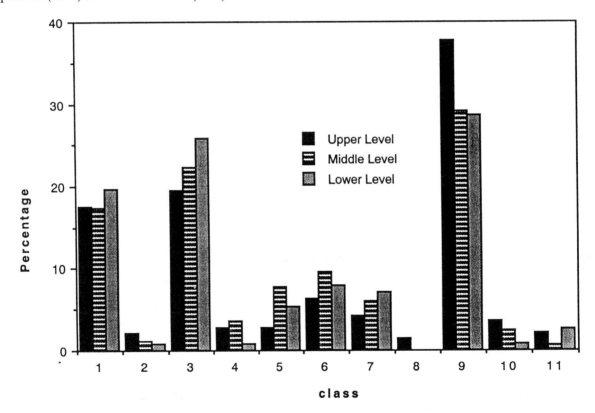

Figure 6. Le Flageolet II, Layer IX tool class percentage by level.

Discussion

The contents of the analytically defined levels suggest a very different interpretation of changes in the use of the site through time than do the 'architectural' remains. Elsewhere, I have argued that shifts from single hearth dominated levels to a level in

which a pavement was constructed signaled a shift in site use, and perhaps a shift in the site's role within a regional subsistence system (Koetje 1991a, 1989). I argued that pavement construction may have been indicative of an increase in the 'intensity' of site use. There seem to be several logical possibilities for the

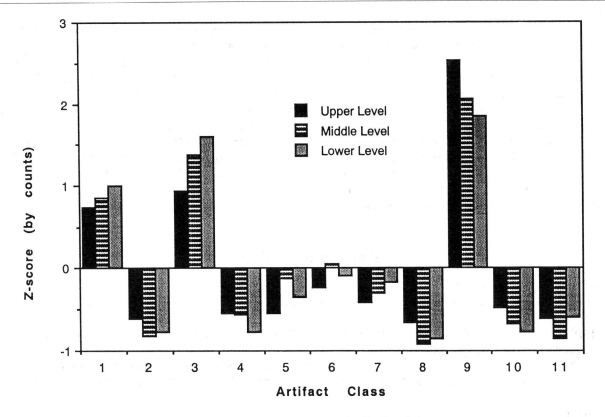

Figure 7. Le Flageolet II, Layer IX standardized tool class counts.

Table 3. K and K' values (Koetje 1987, 1989) for the Class Counts of 3 Analytic Levels from Le Flageolet II. Both K and K' vary from a maximum homogeneity of 1 to a minimum of 0. K' is a proportionally weighted average of the K values across a series of groups.

	K	K'
Level 1	.857	
Level 2	.896	
Level 3	.877	
Global		.882

nature of these shifts, all more-or-less difficult to distinguish from one another. A shift from shorter to longer length single occupations, and a shift from less to more frequent shorter occupations, may well produce similar patterns and so would be difficult to distinguish. Similarly, a stable occupation pattern, but a shift in the number of inhabitants, may also appear similar in the archaeological record, again causing difficulty in distinguishing the precise cause. These types of shifts, however, are reasonable explanations for the new and substantial energy investments involved in pavement construction. These shifts would be expected to be accompanied by changes in the tool and faunal assemblages. It is also reasonable

to think that, in general, these expected changes in the assemblages would be changes in tool category proportions, rather than simply more or fewer in the same proportions.

However, these kinds of changes are not occurring in Layer IX. Instead, tool category proportions are similar if not identical when magnitude is controlled. Similarly, there is no clear change in the faunal assemblages between the three analytical levels. It is also interesting to note that if one measures "intensity" of occupation by the sheer number of tools, the more intense occupation was not that involving the pavement, but instead, the middle, or second hearth occupation.

Perhaps, however, we can now interpret the Magdalenian use of Le Flageolet II in an entirely different manner. If the site's functions on the level of the regional subsistence system remained constant throughout the Layer IX period, as suggested by the tool and faunal assemblages, then perhaps shifts at the level of the site itself, in terms of intensity, etc. are unimportant. Perhaps pavement construction does not, in this case, signal an increase in occupational intensity, but instead simply a way to stabilize a habitation surface in the face of the increasingly warm, moist climate evident in the uppermost portions of Layer IX (Laville 1970, 1977). If this is the case, the site clearly plays an important enough role in the subsistence system, that despite the increasing difficulty of occupation, efforts were made to moderate its physical unsuitability. This suggests a group of people that are very closely tied to the use of specific locations on the landscape, perhaps through extensive territoriality, symbolic systems, or 'logistical' necessity when exploiting specific resources. This last, in particular, seems like a very strong possibility. Particularly during the Magdalenian, as suggested by White (1985), sites in the region are often located near fords, which are commonly created where geologic faults cross the river valleys. Le Flageolet II owes its existence to a fault that crosses the Dordogne Valley just below the shelter.

Thus, far from being evidence for shifts in the nature of subsistence systems across a region, pavement construction in previously occupied sites, might be indicative of the conservative nature of resource and landscape use during Magdalenian times. Despite a changing climate, and the necessary time and energy expenditures to maintain the location's habitability, the same fixed point on the landscape was occupied repetitively.

References Cited

Cahen, D., and J. Moeyersons
   1977 Subsurface Movement of Stone Artifacts and Their Importance for Prehistory. *Nature* 266:812-815.
Delpech, F.
   1970 L'Abri Magdalénien du Flageolet II (Bezenac, Dordogne)— Paleontologie. *Bulletin de la Société Préhistorique Française* 67:475-488
   1977 Les Faunes de la Fin des Temps Glaciares dans le Sud-Ouest de la France. In *La Fin Des Temps Glaciares en Europe,* edited by D. de Sonneville-Bordes, pp. 169-176. Centre National de Recherche Scientifique, Paris.
Gaussen, J.
   1980 *Le Paleolithique Supérieur de Plein Air en Périgord.* XIVe supplément à Gallia Préhistoire. Centre National de Recherche Scientifique: Paris.
Gifford, D.P.
   1978 Natural Processes Affecting Cultural Materials In *Explorations in Ethnoarchaeology,* edited by R.A. Gould, pp. 77-101. University of New Mexico Press, Albuquerque.
Gifford, D.P., and A.K. Behrensmeyer
   1977 Observed Formation and Burial of a Recent Human Occupation Site in Kenya. *Quaternary Research* 8:245-266.
Gifford, D.P., Damrosch, D.B., Damrosch, D.R., Pryor, J., and R.L. Thompson
   1985 The Third Dimension in Site Structure: An Experiment in Trampling and Vertical Dispersion. *American Antiquity* 50:803-821.
Gordon, B.
   1987 *Of Men and Reindeer in the Paleolithic.* BAR International Series, 421, Oxford.
Koetje, T.A.
   1987a *Spatial Patterns in Magdalenian Open Air Sites from the Isle Valley, Southwestern France.* BAR International Series, 346, Oxford.
   1987b Pavement Features from the European Upper Paleolithic. Paper presented at the 52nd annual meeting of the Society for American Archaeology, Toronto.
   1989 *Approaches to the Investigation of Intrasite Spatial Patterning in Three Dimensions.* Unpublished Ph.D. dissertation, Department of Anthropology, University of Tennessee, Knoxville.
   1990 A Simulation Approach to Recovering Archaeologically Meaningful Levels. *Journal of Quantitative Anthropology* 2: 257-280.
   1991a Dealing With Three Dimensional Site Structure: An Example Using Simulated Archaeological Levels, and the Magdalenian Site of le Flageolet II (Dordogne, France). *Journal of Field Archaeology* 18:187-198.
   1991b Quantification, Simulation, and Three Dimensional Modelling: Archaeological Applications. In *Archaeology in the Information Age,* edited by S. Reilly and S. Rahtz. Unwin-Hyman, London.
Laville, H.
   1970 L'Abri Magdalénien du Flageolet II (Bezenac, Dordogne)— êtude Geologique. *Bulletin de la Société Préhistorique Française* 67:475-488.

1977 Chronostratigraphie des Depots de la Fin du Wurm en Périgord. In *La Fin Des Temps Glaciares en Europe*, edited by D. de Sonneville-Bordes, pp. 529-547. Centre National de Recherche Scientifique, Paris.

1988 Recent Developments on the Chronostratigraphy of the Paleolithic in the Perigord. In *Upper Pleistocene Prehistory of Western Eurasia*, edited by H.L. Dibble, and A. Montet-White, pp. 147-161. University of Pennsylvania Museum, Philadelphia.

Laville, H., J.-Ph. Rigaud, and J. Sackett
1980 *Rockshelters of the Périgord: Geological Stratigraphy and Archaeological Succession.* Academic Press: New York.

Paquereau, M-M.
1970 Étude Palynologique du Gisement du Flageolet II (Dordogne). *Bulletin de la Société Préhistorique Française* 67:489-493.

Rigaud, J.-Ph.
1970 Étude Préliminaire des Industries Magdalénien de l'Abri Flageolet II, (Commune de Bezenac, Dordogne). *Bulletin de la Société Préhistorique Française* 67:456-474

1977 A Propos des Industries Madaléniennes du Flageolet. In *La Fin Des Temps Glaciares en Europe*, edited by D. de Sonneville-Bordes, pp. 467-469. Centre National de Recherche Scientifique: Paris.

1982 *Le Paleolithique en Périgord: Les Données du Sud-Ouest Sarladais et leur Implications.* These de Doctorat d'Etat des Sciences Naturelles. Université de Bordeaux I.

Schiffer, M.B.
1983 Toward the Identification of Formation Processes. *American Antiquity* 48:675-706.

1987 *Formation Processes of the Archaeological Record.* University of New Mexico Press: Albuquerque.

Siirianen, A.
1977 Pieces in Vertical Movement: A Model for Rockshelter Archaeology. *Proceedings of the Prehistoric Society* 43:349-353.

Simek, J.F.
1984a *A K-Means Approach to the Analysis of Spatial Structure in Upper Paleolithic Habitation Sites.* BAR International Series 228, Oxford.

1984b Integrating Pattern and Context in Spatial Archaeology. *Journal of Archaeological Science* 11:405-419.

1987 Spatial Order and Behavioral Change in the French Paleolithic. *Antiquity* 61:231-242.

Simek, J.F., and R. Larick
1983 Recognition of Multiple Spatial Patterning: A Case Study from the French Upper Paleolithic. *Journal of Archaeological Science* 10:165-178.

Simek, J., Ammerman, A., and K. Kintigh
1985 Explorations in Heuristic Spatial Analysis: Analyzing the Structure of Material Accumulations Over Space. *PACT* 11:229

Le Tensorer, J.-M.
1981 *Le Paleolithique de l'Agenais.* Cahiers Du Quaternaire # 3. Centre National de Recherche Scientifique, Paris.

Villa, P., and J. Courtin
1983 The Interpretation of Stratified Sites: A View from Underground. *Journal of Archaeological Science* 10:267.

White, R.K.
1985 *Upper Paleolithic Land Use in the Perigord.* BAR International Series # 279, Oxford.

Wood, W.R., and D.L. Johnson
1978 A Survey of Disturbance Processes in Archaeological Site Formation. In *Advances in Archaeological Method and Theory*, Vol. 1, edited by M.B. Schiffer, pp. 315-381. Academic Press, New York.

9

Distinguishing Stone Artifacts from Naturefacts created by Rockfall Processes

David T. Nash
University of New Mexico

During the late 19th and early 20th centuries, archaeologists were confronted with a causal ambiguity resulting from a perceived similarity between the form and pattern of "rudimentary", man-made stone tools and flaking debris and stone specimens fractured and modified by a variety of noncultural processes. In an attempt to resolve this ambiguity, investigators initiated a number of studies most appropriately characterized as "middle-range" research (see Grayson 1986). As defined by Binford (1981:21-30), middle-range research emphasizes the study of agents and processes in the contemporary world, where criteria of recognition can be obtained by directly linking cause to effect. Once such recognition criteria have been defined, the processes responsible for creating similar or identical patterning in the archaeological record may be inferred with a greater degree of accuracy.

In the context of the late 19th and early 20th century artifact debates, researchers attempted to establish or refute a set of diagnostic attributes by which stone flaked by human hands could be distinguished from stone flaked by non-human agencies. During this initial period of investigation, a number of flake and core/retouched piece attributes were defined as diagnostic of human lithic tool production (e.g., de Mortillet 1885; Moir 1912; Rutot 1904; Schwartz and Beevor 1909). These attributes included, but were not restricted to, the presence of striking platforms, bulbs of force, ripple lines, fissures, bulbar scars, and acute platform angles on flakes and the presence of multiple flake scars, bifacial or multidirectional flaking, sequential retouch, acute edge angles, replication of morphological forms, and use-wear on cores/retouched pieces. Today, these attributes are still recognized as symptomatic of human stone tool production (e.g., Crabtree 1972; Oakley 1959; Patterson 1983; Toth 1991). However, during these early controversies, a number of researchers were able to effectively demonstrate that these attributes were not exclusive to human stone working and instead could also be identified from assemblages of stone fractured by a variety of noncultural processes, including glaciation, wave action, high velocity water movement, soil movements, temperature variations, tectonic movements, solifluction, and trampling (e.g., Arcelin 1885; Barnes 1939; Boule 1905; Breuil 1910; Pei 1936; Warren 1905, 1914). Thus, rather than resolving this initial ambiguity, these studies seemed to magnify the problem. This condition led Breuil (1910:406) to conclude that the criteria required to distinguish the effects of rudimentary intentional stone working from the effects of nature had not been found and probably did not exist. Ultimately, many ancient sites containing such stone specimens were largely dismissed as natural when the claims for an artifactual origin of the lithic specimens could not be verified and when it was demonstrated that the geologic age of the deposits in which they occurred predated hominid occupation.

Recently, controversies over the validity of collections of flaked stone recovered from proposed early man sites in the Old and New Worlds (e.g., the sites of Calico Hills, Pikimachay, Monte Verde, Pedra Furada, Texas Street, Ulalinka, Diring Yuriakh, Riwat, and Saint Elbe) are a clear indication that this fundamental problem of distinguishing simple stone artifacts from "naturefacts" (specimens possessing naturally produced attributes which resemble or are identical to cultural attributes) has never been adequately resolved. Structured similarly to the earlier artifact/naturefact controversies, these new debates have stemmed from a general failure of researchers to demonstrate that a proposed interpretation for the origin of patterning observed in a lithic assemblage has a higher probability of being accurate, than alternative explanations for the same phenomena. Since there is presently no definitive "litmus test" for distinguishing between lithic materials fractured by humans and those fractured by certain natural processes (Toth 1991:56), other than in a probabilistic sense, this evaluation must be based upon an accurate identification of the natural processes acting on materials at a particular site context and a knowledge of the types and ranges of alterations that can be produced by these processes, acting alone or in combination.

At present, it is extremely difficult to establish and effectively evaluate a series of alternative hypotheses regarding the origin of flaked specimens and their attributes. In order for such an evaluation to be rigorous and objective, researchers must possess reliable qualitative and quantitative information on the types and ranges of alterations to fractured stone that could be expected in a variety of geomorphic contexts (Schnurrenberger and Bryan 1985). Unfortunately, this information is currently lacking for a number of natural processes which are capable of flaking stone. One of the processes in which researchers have relatively little knowledge of, and as a consequence is often neglected during the evaluation of alternative hypotheses, is how stone is altered by episodes of rockfall. This chapter attempts to partially alleviate this shortcoming, by describing the results of an experiment simulating patterns of lithic fracture produced by rockfall processes.

Rockfall Processes at Caves and Rockshelters

One of the potential causes of natural rock fracture which might mimic culturally produced artifacts, are the modifications produced by natural rockfall. For the purposes of this discussion, rockfall is defined here as simply the free falling of stone through the action of gravity. The ability of episodes of rockfall to produce naturefacts was discussed by Clark (1958). While working in the Batoka Gorge, Zambia, Clark collected a sample of 23 simple flakes and 15 split and fractured pebbles. Based on the recovery context of these specimens and the absence of evidence of fluvial modifications (i.e., the development of incipient cones and abrasion), Clark attributed the observed flaking and splitting exhibited by these specimens to direct percussion resulting from rocks falling down the sides of the gorge and impacting wedged pebbles (Clark 1958:70-72). These specimens were similar in form and technical attributes to split and fractured pebbles discovered in Uganda and defined as the Kafuan Industry of the Lower Paleolithic (Van Riet Lowe 1952). It was Clark's contention that the Kafuan industry was noncultural and was probably produced by similar rockfall processes.

Although Clark's conclusions seemed plausible based on a knowledge of lithic fracture mechanics and his observations on the geologic context of the sites, they remained unverified by middle-range studies documenting the relationship between rockfall processes and patterns of lithic fracture. Nevertheless, his conclusions did highlight the need for a detailed documentation of the types of fracture caused by rockfall in a variety of environmental settings. Rockfall is often a prominent, active process at a number of contexts, including caves and rockshelters, cliffs, rocky bluffs, and plunge basins at the base of seasonal waterfalls. Because rockfall is often the single most dominant process during the development and degradation of caves and rockshelters and evidence of human activities is actively sought at these contexts, the relevance of rockfall processes to the production of lithic naturefacts will be restricted here to caves and rockshelters.

Archaeologists working at caves and rockshelters often encounter deposits dominated volumetrically by coarse detritus produced during the mechanical and chemical weathering of the surrounding bedrock. The ability of this detritus to reflect the local climatic conditions under which it was detached and subsequently modified has been investigated in considerable detail for some regions (e.g., Laville et al. 1980). However, despite its typically enormous volumetric contribution to cave and rockshelter infillings, relatively little research has been devoted to investigating how this coarse detritus and episodes of rockfall may modify lithic and faunal materials occurring at these contexts and how it may influence archaeologically recovered spatial distributions.

During the development, gradual enlargement, and subsequent degradation of caves and rockshelters, spalls (*éboulis*) are detached from the walls and ceiling of the feature. Although spalls can be produced and modified by a number of different mechanisms (including cryoclastism, hydration, thermoclastic weathering, chemical weathering, and earthquakes), cryoclastism or frost-weathering is regarded by many researchers as the primary mechanism in the production of *éboulis* and the formation of rockshelters (but cf. Collcutt 1979; Farrand 1985). Rock fragments produced during the exfoliation of shelter walls and ceilings will vary in size and shape, depending in part upon lithology and ambient climatic conditions. Spalls which are produced by primary frost-weathering tend to have polyhedric shapes and possess sharp edges and angles (see Laville et al. 1980:56:Figure 3.6). Possessing these attributes, and often exhibiting multiple flake scars from previously spall detachments, some clasts may on occasion resemble the form and pattern of simple or embryonic cores and tools. But, because such fracture results from internal stresses, these specimens can generally be distinguished from true artifacts produced by percussion by the absence of negative dorsal bulbs and defined striking platforms.

Depending on the rates and types of bedrock weathering and sedimentary infilling, in conjunction with the spatial constraints imposed by shelter morphology, once deposited on the floor of a shelter, it is likely that before spalls become buried by sediments and/or additional spalls, they will receive multiple impacts from subsequent rockfall. If this spall material possesses conchoidal properties and if clast geometry and the direction and amount of force imparted by episodes of rockfall favors percussion fracture, then it is reasonable to expect that specimens will occur which possess many or all of the attributes that characterize humanly induced percussion fracture. In addition, the problem of distinguishing artifacts from naturally flaked stone in these contexts may be further complicated by the possibility that due to the characteristics of the naturally fractured stone (i.e., hardness and sharp edges), humans would have selected these specimens for immediate use with little or no further modification (see Dillehay 1989 for a discussion of the analytic and interpretive difficulties resulting from this type of ambiguity at the open-air site of Monte Verde).

At the majority of cave and rockshelter sites investigated to date, the ability to distinguish lithic artifacts from naturally weathered and flaked *éboulis* presents no major interpretive difficulties. This is true because most limestones in which these shelters are commonly formed do not possess the material qualities for controlled fracture (i.e., being elastic, homogeneous, isotropic, and fine-grained). Consequently, this mate-

rial was generally not selected by hominids for tool manufacture and use and fortuitously fractured specimens generally do not possess attributes in common with cultural flaking. However, the same argument can not be made for shelters formed in certain silicified limestones, basalts, quartzites, sandstones, dolomites, and welded tuffs, or contexts containing secondarily deposited veins of cryptocrystalline materials (i.e., flints, cherts, and jaspers) or flakeable materials transported to the site context by noncultural processes. If hominids exploited these contexts, it is logical to anticipate that these materials would have been opportunistically and or expediently exploited for tool production and use and that episodes of rockfall could independently produce specimens resembling this human toolmaking behavior.

In recent years, excavations at a number of caves and rockshelters have yielded lithic assemblages, that are derived from either the local bedrock in which the shelters were formed or from materials transported to the site by noncultural processes, which have been interpreted as evidence of cultural modification and/or use. Examples of these sites include Makapansgat Cave (Maguire 1980), Pedra Furada (Guidon and Arnaud 1991), Pikimachay Cave (MacNeish et al. 1980), Belle Roche Cave (Cordy 1980), Pendejo Cave (MacNeish 1991: personal communication), Nelson Bay Cave (Klein 1972), and Friesenhahn Cave (Sellards 1952). Because many of these sites are argued to contain evidence of human occupation older than previously demonstrated for a region, critics have been reluctant to accept such claims, arguing that some or all of these specimens could have been produced by natural forces, especially rockfall (e.g., Butzer 1973; Dincauze 1984; Krieger 1964; Lynch 1990; Payen 1982; Roebroeks and Stapert 1986; Toth 1991). The studies required to effectively eliminate one of these competing hypotheses have unfortunately not been carried out in a comprehensive and objective manner. In order to achieve this, researchers need to obtain qualitative and quantitative information on the traits and patterns of materials modified by rockfall processes through a middle-range approach (either experimental or where a specific cause can be implicated based on detailed contextual evidence—see Villa and Mahieu 1991:28). The experiments described below attempt to remedy this situation by developing criteria for the identification of naturefacts produced by rockfall processes.

Experimental Procedures

In order to evaluate the hypothesis that rockfall can produce modifications to stone specimens similar or identical to those produced during human percussion flaking, an experiment simulating rockfall processes was conducted. The immediate goal of this experiment was to document the ranges, dimensions, and spatial patterning of alterations to lithic specimens that might be produced during impact by rockfall. It was hoped that the results of these experiments would provide some general criteria to aid in distinguishing stone artifacts from naturefacts found in cave/rockshelter contexts.

First, eighteen 50 cm x 50 cm grid squares were constructed. Each grid square had a substrate of 10 cm of unconsolidated medium-fine sand. In nine of these squares, 50 to 60 clasts of welded tuff and jasper were laid out in multiple, overlapping layers. In the remaining nine squares, 20 to 25 welded tuff and jasper clasts were laid out in single, non-overlapping layers. In each of the squares, the number of clasts of jasper and welded tuff were approximately equal. These two sets of grid squares served as models of two types of strata often encountered at caves and rockshelters: a coarse-textured deposit of stony *éboulis* with little interstitial matrix (*éboulis sec*) and a medium/fine-textured deposit of stony *éboulis* incorporated in a matrix of fine interstitial sediment.

The clasts utilized in this experiment were collected from a random generated sample of *éboulis* located on the surface of the archaeological/paleontological site of Haystack Cave. Haystack Cave is a small tube-shaped feature located in southwestern Colorado. Excavations were conducted here by the author to investigate the validity and nature of a possible pre-Clovis occupation at the site and to elucidate the cause and effect relationships of specific formation processes in a cave environment (Nash 1987:114). The cavity occurs in a welded tuff bedrock and contains secondarily deposited veins of jasper. Both of these materials can be flaked by percussion and exhibit conchoidal to sub-conchoidal fracture. Based on modern observations on the effects of freeze-thaw cycles within the cave over a three year period, the surface sample of *éboulis* is believed to have a predominantly cryoclastic origin (although other forms of mechanical and chemical weathering were observed). These clasts exhibit varying degrees of angularity and secondary weathering and possess size ranges from 3 cm to 20 cm in maximum length and 5 g to 3 kg in weight. Each of the clasts utilized in this experiment were weighed, measured, and examined for the presence of any attributes which might indicate cultural modification. Any clast possessing these attributes was excluded from the experiment.

Next, three pairs of welded tuff clasts were selected for use as the experimental rockfall specimens or "percussors". The percussors in each of the three pairs had weights of 300 g, 650 g, and 1 kg each and represent the higher weight ranges of the Haystack Cave surface *éboulis*. Although not identical, the percussors in each pair were as similar as possible in geometry and size dimensions. Each clast was polyhedric and sub-angular. In order to simulate rockfall processes, each percussor was held directly above a grid square and dropped from three different heights: 1.5 m, 2.5 m, and 3.5 m. Each percussor was dropped until 200 impacts had occurred in each grid square. Table 1 summarizes this experimental design.

Table 1. Experimental Design. "A" Labelled Grid Squares Consist of Mutiple, Overlapping Layers of Welded Tuff and Jasper Clasts. "B" Labelled Grid Squares Consist of Single, Non-Overlapping Layers of Welded Tuff and Jasper Clasts.

Grid Square Designations	Percussor Weight	Freefall Distance
A1a, B1a	300 g	1.5 m
A1b, B1b	300 g	2.5 m
A1c, B1c	300 g	3.5 m
A2a, B2a	650 g	1.5 m
A2b, B2b	650 g	2.5 m
A2c, B2c	650 g	3.5 m
A3a, B3a	1 kg	1.5 m
A3b, B3b	1 kg	2.5 m
A3c, B3c	1 kg	3.5 m

After each grid square had received 200 impacts, all debris and modified specimens greater than 2 mm in maximum dimension were collected. This material was sorted into flakes, angular or shatter debris, and "cores/retouched" pieces. For this analysis, a flake was defined as a specimen having a length or width at least three times its maximum thickness (Patterson et al. 1987:94). All flakes and retouched pieces were subjected to detailed analyses to determine whether the typical attributes of controlled flaking, as defined by a number of researchers in recent years (e.g., Patterson 1983; Patterson et al. 1987; Toth 1991), were present or absent. In addition to size and weight measurements, the following attributes were recorded: bulb of force: present, absent; ripple lines: present, absent; bulbar scars: present, absent; radial lines: present, absent; striking platform: intact, crushed, absent; striking platform angle: measured in degrees; facet platform: present, absent; cortex on platform: present, absent; platform thickness and width measurements; number of dorsal face facets; flake type: primary, secondary, interior; flake termination: feather, step, hinge; and flake portion: complete, proximal, midsection, distal.

Experimental Results

Table 2 presents a summary of the type and frequency of debris produced during the rockfall simulations. Of the 3600 impacts occurring between the percussors and surface clasts, 2116 (59%) resulted in fracture initiations. As might be anticipated, as the weight of the percussor and freefall distance increased, so too did the number of fracture episodes. Also in each of the "A" grid squares containing overlapping layers of clasts, a greater number of fracture episodes occurred relative to the "B" grid squares of corresponding percussor weight and freefall distance. This is accounted for by the observation that when a rock is supported on another clast and struck, force is induced by both the percussor and the anvil clast and the elastic limit of the material is exceeded with a much higher frequency than if the anvil clast is absent. But, even a percussor with a weight of 300 g and a freefall distance of 1.5 m produced enough force to initiate fractures to clasts supported on unconsolidated sediment on 15% of the impacts.

The 2116 fracture episodes produced 4756 pieces of angular debris and 236 flakes with a maximum dimension greater than 2 mm. A 1 kg sample of substrate was collected from grid square A2b and screened through a standard soil sieve with a mesh size of 0.125 mm. This screening resulted in the recovery of 98 pieces of microdebitage as defined by

Fladmark (1982). Although not included in this analysis, the small residues produced during these experiments probably numbers in the thousands. In the absence of distinct micromorphological traces of human activity, the micromorphological techniques illustrated in the following section of this volume would appear to have great potential as an aid in assessing the relative contribution of rockfall processes to the modification of coarse-sized *éboulis*.

The large number of angular debris produced during this experiment appears to be generally related to the mechanical properties of the welded tuff and jasper clasts utilized in the experiment and to the location of the point of contact between the percussor and the impacted clast. The jasper utilized was highly silicified and quite brittle and required little force to initiate a fracture. When placed under stress, this material tends to break prematurely and snap, step, and hinge fractures are common. The welded tuff on the other hand is coarse-grained and much more resistant to stress than the jasper. Table 3 separates the type of debris produced by material type. In addition, many of the clasts utilized contained flaws, cracks, inclusions, and crystal pockets. When force was applied to such specimens, they almost always shattered into multiple pieces of angular debris. For these reasons, it is hypothesized that the higher percentage of impacts that resulted in fracture initiations and the

Table 2. Frequency and Type of Debris Produced by Rockfall Experiments.

Grid Squares	Impacts	Fracture Episodes	Angular Debris	Flakes
A1a	200	46 (23%)	95	1
A1b	200	84 (42%)	202	7
A1c	200	138 (69%)	263	11
A2a	200	99 (49.5%)	215	6
A2b	200	138 (69%)	307	17
A2c	200	157 (78.5%)	421	25
A3a	200	116 (58%)	269	16
A3b	200	160 (80%)	428	24
A3c	200	191 (95.5%)	615	29
B1a	200	30 (15%)	47	1
B1b	200	67 (33.5%)	88	5
B1c	200	127 (63.5%)	172	9
B2a	200	75 (37.5%)	131	4
B2b	200	112 (56%)	207	12
B2c	200	141 (70.5%)	264	20
B3a	200	102 (51%)	215	11
B3b	200	148 (74%)	397	18
B3c	200	185 (92.5%)	450	20
TOTAL	3600	2116 (59%)	4756	236

Table 3. Frequency and Type of Debris Produced by Material Type.

Material Type	Angular Debris	Flakes
Welded Tuff	387 (8%)	43 (18%)
Jasper	4,369 (92%)	193 (82%)
Total	4,756	236

resulting angular debris produced is slightly inflated due to the specific mechanical properties of the materials utilized during the experiment.

In addition, when a clast was impacted away from its margins and toward the center of the piece and a fracture was initiated, these impacts tended to create lateral snap fractures across the body and angular debris was produced. Due to the enormous differences in the surface area between the margins and the body of the clast and the non-directed application of force, fractures created by rockfall are much more likely to result from contacts made to the body of a clast and to result in a preponderance of angular debris.

However, when a percussor struck a clast near a margin possessing an acute striking platform angle (and occasionally an obtuse striking platform angle), a flake was often detached. During these experiments, a total of 236 flakes was produced. Figure 1 illustrates a sample of these flakes. Table 4 summarizes the major flake attributes of these specimens. The flakes examined had a size range of 3 mm to 8 cm in maximum dimension. The majority of these specimens possessed

bulbs of force (75%; 52% with prominent bulbs), intact, unfaceted platforms (68%), bulbar scars (28%), ripple lines (64%), and acute platform angles (84%). Taken together, these figures compare well with similar technical analyses of known flake artifact assemblages or assemblages produced during knapping experiments, while contrasting with assemblages produced by natural processes other than rockfall (e.g., Patterson et al. 1987; Peacock 1991). Attributes which appear to deviate from known cultural assemblages included a high percentage of specimens with hinge or step fractures (75%), a low percentage of flakes possessing two or more flake scars on the dorsal face (36%), a low percentage of flakes possessing dorsal flake scars parallel to the medial axis (28%), and a low flake length/platform thickness ratio ($\bar{x}$=2:1).

Most of these features can be attributed to the material quality summarized above and the manner in which force was applied. By simulating rockfall processes, percussion was initiated by a straight line impact. Unless a surface spall was inclined, the angle of the applied force was directed perpendicular to the core. This direction of force application often created an insufficient energy transfer and fractures subsequently occurred transversely to the edge of the clast. These fractures tended to produce short flakes relative to platform size and a high incidence of step and hinge terminations as flakes were sheared off. Additional variables which influenced the form of this assemblage

Table 4. Flake Attributes.

Attributes	Welded Tuff Flakes (n=43)	Jasper Flakes (n=193)	Total (n=236)
Force Bulbs	37 (86%)	141 (73%)	178 (75%)
Prominent	29 (78%)	93 (66%)	122 (69%)
Diffuse	8 (22%)	48 (34%)	56 (31%)
Bulbar Scars	26 (60%)	41 (21%)	67 (28%)
Ripple Lines	25 (58%)	127 (66%)	152 (64%)
Platform Intact	35 (81%)	125 (65%)	160 (68%)
Acute Platform Angle	39 (91%)	158 (82%)	197 (83%)
More Than One Flake Scar on Dorsal Surface	12 (28%)	73 (38%)	85 (36%)
Dorsal Scars Parallel to Medial Axis	17 (40%)	48 (25%)	65 (28%)
Flake Termination: Hinge/Step	18 (42%)	159 (82%)	177 (75%)

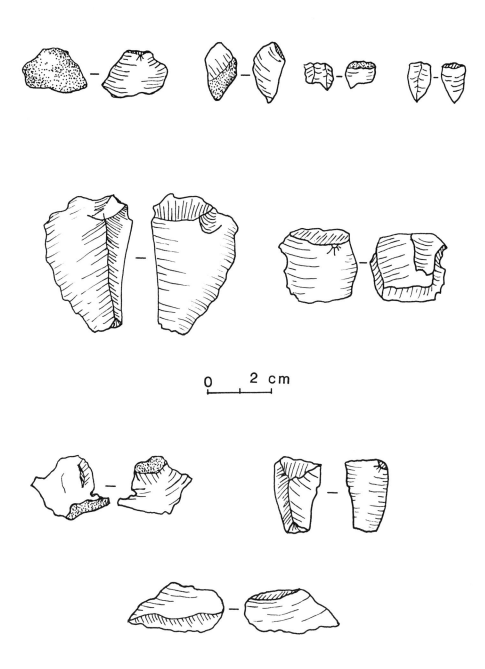

Figure 1. Flakes produced during rockfall experiment.

include the short interval of contact between percussor and impacted clast, the size of the contact area, the manner in which a clast was supported and free to move with impact, and the specific morphology of a clast prior to impact. The majority of flakes produced during these experiments had a maximum dimension between 1 cm and 4 cm (Figure 2).

A total of 39 specimens was produced which exhibited attributes of cores and retouched pieces. Thirty of these specimens resembled retouched pieces and nine specimens resembled man-made cores. For the retouched flakes, edge microflaking was largely variable in size and placement. A sample of these specimens is illustrated in Figure 3. Because the impacted specimens were rarely overturned, unifacial retouch was a much more common occurrence than bifacial retouch. Twenty-one of the flakes possessed unifacial edge retouch (a total of 14 of the 21 cases displayed more than three scars). On 15 of these unifacially retouched pieces, the edge damage

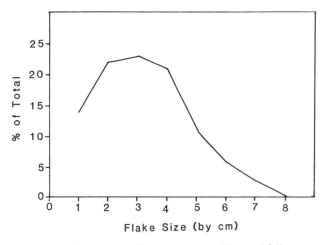

Figure 2. *Flake size distribution produced by rockfall experiment.*

consisted of short, steep, and uneven non-overlapping facets occurring in a random manner. These characteristics are typical of natural and fortuitous edge damage (e.g., Luedtke 1986; Mallouf 1982; Miller 1982; Patterson 1983; Tringham et al. 1974). On the other hand, eight specimens were characterized by long, uniform parallel flake scars, a characteristic of human retouch (Patterson 1983:303). Nine specimens exhibited bifacial edge retouch. For three of these specimens, the microflaking produced flake scars of uniform placement, shape, and size, and localized along one edge. Because the pattern of applied force was relatively consistently repeated, it is not surprising that some specimens were produced exhibiting sequential flaking.

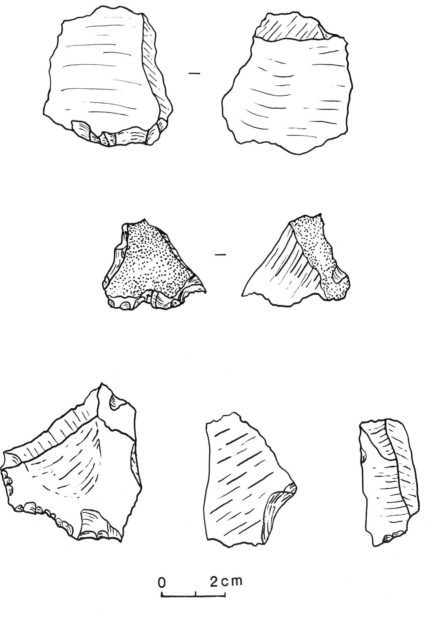

0   2 cm

Figure 3. *Retouched pieces produced during rockfall experiment.*

Clasts which had two or more flake scars, excluding microflaking, and those scars which were present on the specimens from prior spall detachments, were classified as cores. Nine clasts had multiple flake scars resulting from the simulated rockfall. Three of the clasts had two flakes removed, three had three flakes removed, two had four flakes removed, and one had five flakes removed. There are four examples where more than one flake was removed from a single platform. Flake scars exhibit points of percussion, negative bulbs, and ripple lines. Flaking on these specimens is generally multidirectional and edge angles are acute. Corresponding to the flakes removed, flake scars are relatively short and wide. With the exception of the small size of the flake scars, all of these attributes taken together are highly characteristic of a cultural percussion struck core (Patterson 1983:304).

Discussion

It is a common conception among many lithic technologists, that percussion flaking in nature is a rare occurrence and if it does occur, only a small number of flaked specimens will be produced and these will exhibit random patterns (e.g., Carter 1980; Patterson 1983). Patterson (1983:299) has stated that "There are no demonstrated examples now available where nature has produced concentrations of percussion flakes of significant sizes...". The experiment described above demonstrates that, at least at some contexts, episodes of rockfall can not only fracture rock in a percussive manner, but that the resulting specimens may possess the same attributes which characterize patterns of human manufacture (especially, a high percentage of prominent force bulbs, ripple lines, bulbar scars, and the presence of cores/retouched pieces with sequential retouch). If the flakes, cores, and retouched pieces created here were encountered during excavations, a researcher could, by identifying the typical man-made lithic attributes that are present in quantitatively significant amounts within this subset, demonstrate the likelihood of human manufacture compared to the larger subset of angular debris or unmodified clasts. However, if the materials were analyzed as a single population, it would become apparent that these specimens represent a gradation in the full range of rockfall modification. Furthermore, a knowledge of the type and range of modifications that can be produced by rockfall would demonstrate that these specimens are not anomalous to the depositional environment. Conversely, the same results might be obtained if a true artifact assemblage of small size was created from these materials.

Confronted with this type of ambiguity, Schnurrenberger and Bryan (1985:139-143) have constructed a general research design for evaluating problematic sites which is adopted here. First, at cave and rockshelter contexts where ambiguity may be anticipated, a systematic program of data retrieval must be employed. In these contexts, it is crucial to collect not only those specimens which appear to be culturally modified, but at a minimum, a representative sample of all lithic specimens (both fractured and unfractured) from both within and between strata. The three-dimensional provenience of these specimens should be systematically recorded, as well as inclination and orientation measurements. Since the attributes produced during percussion fracture are heavily dependent on the quality and form of the material, it is also important that samples be collected for both flintknapping and rockfall experiments in order to document the basic physical properties of a given material type. Ideally, one would like to collect altered specimens of the same material type from a context characterized by the same rockfall parameters as the site in question and where man can be eliminated from the taphonomic equation. However, for caves and rockshelters such a situation is rare. This leaves the researcher with recourse to experimental studies and detailed comparisons of materials within and between strata.

Next, it is imperative that contextual studies be conducted which permit an accurate reconstruction of the ranges and distributions of energy in space and time. This reconstruction should be supported by interdisciplinary analyses (e.g., sedimentology, geomorphology, chemistry). If supported by sound middle-range research, this information can be used to predict the type, frequency, and distribution of altered specimens at a site in question.

Finally, a technical analysis of the significant attributes exhibited by these specimens must be recorded and quantified using objective technical criteria. These attributes include the spacing, size, and shape of flake scars.

These three components should allow the researcher to test a goodness of fit between the types and ranges of alterations documented from an excavated assemblage with those that are products of known natural alteration or with predicted ranges of attribute states based on a knowledge of a site's formation processes. If it can be demonstrated that the attributes and spatial distributions exhibited by the specimens in question are anomalous to the depositional environment, then the hypothesis of a cultural origin is strengthened. But, if it can be shown that these alterations are not anomalous, but instead represent gradations, then a cultural origin must be viewed with suspicion. Unfortunately, the knowledge required to accurately predict the noncultural attributes and distributions for a variety of contexts and noncultural formation processes is currently not available.

The results of the rockfall experiment reported here, permit at least an initial prediction of the types and ranges of alterations that might result from rockfall processes in a cave/rockshelter context. Figure 4 presents a simplified model of the predicted relative frequency and spatial distribution of naturefacts produced in a rockshelter setting using the critical parameters of direction, amount, frequency, and pattern of applied force. In this model, it is predicted that the frequency of naturefacts and associated angular debris produced by rockfall will increase with the size and frequency of rockfall and the distance of free fall. Strata containing a preponderance of large rockfall blocks should contain a greater number of

flakes, than those strata characterized by smaller sized clasts. Also, the frequency of flakes should increase in the areas characterized by a higher frequency of spalls (the mouth of the shelter and near the walls, where spalls from both ceiling and walls are likely to overlap). This model could be complicated further by including differences in clast geometry (frost slaps versus angular clasts). It is predicted that in this context there should be a wide range of flake size classes, both obtuse- and acute-angled flake removals, abrupt terminations, and edge and ridge microflaking. It should also be expected that refits are spatially constrained (although during the experiments described above, a number of detached flakes traveled outside the experimental grid squares). Based on shelter morphology and variations in bedrock lithology, these parameters are expected to vary synchronically and diachronically.

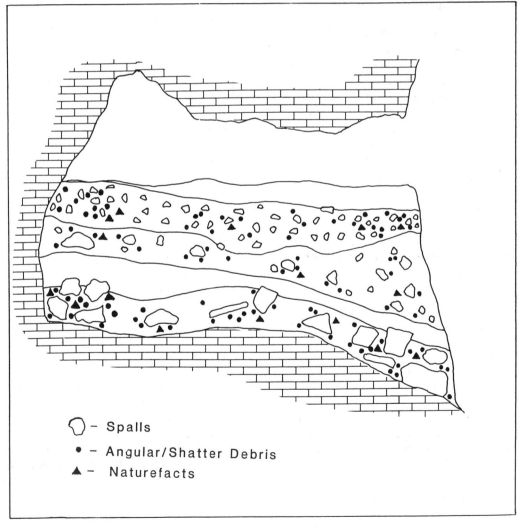

- 🗍 – **Spalls**
- • – **Angular/Shatter Debris**
- ▲ – **Naturefacts**

Figure 4. Hypothetical formation model of the frequency and spatial distribution of naturefacts and angular/shatter debris produced by rockfall processes in a cave/rockshelter context.

Conclusions

Controversies over the artifactual status of flaked stone have been entrenched in archaeology since the late 19th century and have proven highly resilient to successful resolution. Much of the inconclusiveness associated with these debates results from a disparity of knowledge between how people manufacture and use stone implements and how stones are altered by a wide variety of natural processes (Schnurrenberger and Bryan 1985). In the absence of qualitative and quantitative data on the many different attributes that might characterize stone fractured by a range of natural processes, it has proven difficult to develop and evaluate alternative hypotheses regarding the origin of simply flaked lithic assemblages. As a result, researchers have tended to evaluate these assemblages either subjectively or by a set of attributes believed to be diagnostic regardless of context. This study stresses that criteria for distinguishing artifacts from naturefacts must be flexible with regard to context. Criteria that are appropriate for distinguishing artifacts from naturefacts at one context, may not be appropriate for another. This is true both between different depositional environments and within similar depositional environments.

This study clearly establishes that episodes of rockfall can, through high energy dynamic loading, detach flakes by percussion fracture and that specimens created from such impacts may exhibit many or all of the attributes of intentional percussion flaking. Because potentially thousands of impacts can occur to clasts situated on the floors of caves and rockshelters, numerous naturefacts may be produced. Depending on shelter morphology, in conjunction with variability of spalling within a shelter (i.e., a higher frequency of spalling near the walls and mouth of the feature), naturefacts produced by rockfall may exhibit a nonrandom spatial distribution. Several criteria were suggested as possible aids in distinguishing artifacts from naturefacts in these contexts. These include: a high incidence of angular debris spatially associated with flakes, a high proportion of flakes with step or hinge terminations, and a high proportion of flakes with a low flake length/platform ratio. However, these features are not exclusive to stone fractured by rockfall processes. Because the force available in most rockfall contexts is sufficient to induce fracture, these experiments indicated that the proportion between the number of impacts by rockfall and the number of flakes produced is relatively constant regardless of percussor weight and free fall distance (unless weight and distance are quite small), and is probably more a function of clast geometry and the location of contact. But, fracture initiations seem to increase with increases in the weight of rockfall specimens and the distances fallen, resulting in a higher frequency of flakes and cores/retouched pieces. Also a substrate of *éboulis* increases the frequency of fracture initiations and the amount of debris produced. These distinctions should shed light on the relationships between the frequency and location of ambiguous lithic specimens, shelter morphology, and types of bedrock weathering. Furthermore, the ability to separate these specimens from the occurrence of true cultural assemblages produced from the same raw material at these contexts will remain a formidable task.

There remains an obvious need for better controlled, replicative experiments of the sort reported here, utilizing different force parameters, different lithic materials, and varying material form (i.e., pebbles and cobbles). If rockfall processes can produce similar alterations to stone clasts as those produced by man, then it is probable that these same processes can also produce modifications to bones which resemble hominid modifications (see Oliver 1989). This is an avenue of research which may have significant taphonomic implications. Finally, there is a need for a greater understanding of the conditions under which hominids produced and utilized expedient technologies. It is hoped that this chapter will serve as an impetus for similar studies to be conducted in the near future, when ambiguity created by a similarity in the form and pattern between artifacts and naturefacts has been demonstrated or is anticipated.

Acknowledgments

The experiments here were conducted with the assistance of David Shaeffer and George Stewart. George also provided many valuable insights from his vast flintknapping experience and knowledge of lithic fracture mechanics. Research at Haystack Cave was partially supported by grants from the L.S.B. Leakey Foundation, the National Science Foundation (BNS8601945), and Colorado State University.

References Cited

Arcelin, A.
1885 Silex Tertiaires. *Materiaux pour l'Histoire Primitive et Naturelle de l'Homme* 19:193-204.

Barnes, A. S.
1939 The Difference between Natural and Human Flaking in Prehistoric Flint Implements. *American Anthropologist* 41:99-112.

Binford, L. R.
1981 *Bones: Ancient Men and Modern Myths*. Academic Press, New York.

Boule, M.
1905 L'Origine des Éolithes. *L'Anthropologie* 16:257-267.

Breuil, H.
1910 Sur la Présence d'Éoliths à la base de l'Eocène Parisien. *L'Anthropologie* 21:385-408.

Butzer, K.
1973 Geology of Nelson Bay Cave, Robberg, South Africa. *South African Archaeological Bulletin* 28:97-110.

Carter, G. F.
1980 *Earlier Than You Think*. Texas A. M. University Press, College Station.

Clark, J. D.
1958 The Natural Fracture of Pebbles from the Batoka Gorge, Northern Rhodesia, and its Bearing on the Kafuan Industries of Africa. *Proceedings of the Prehistoric Society* 24:64-77.

Collcutt, S. N.
1979 The Analysis of Quaternary Cave Sediments. *World Archaeology* 10:290-301.

Cordy, J-M.
1980 Le Paléokarst de la Belle Roche (Sprimont, Liège): Premier Gisement Paléontologique et Archéologique de Pléistocene Moyen en Belgique. *Comptes Rendus de l'Académie des Sciences, Paris* 219 D:749-752.

Crabtree, D. E.
1972 *An Introduction to Flintworking*. Occasional Papers of the Idaho State University Museum 28, Pocatello.

de Mortillet, G.
1885 Silex tertiares intentionnellement taillés. *Materiaux pour l'Histoire Primitive et Naturelle de l'Homme* 19:252-263.

Dillehay, T. D.
1989 *Paleoenvironment and Site Context. Monte Verde: A Late Pleistocene Settlement in Chile*, vol. I. Smithsonian Institution Press, Washington D. C.

Dincauze, D. F.
1984 An Archaeo-logical Evaluation of the Case for Pre-Clovis Occupations. In *Advances in World Archaeology*, vol. 3, edited by F. Wendorf and A. Close, pp. 275-323. Academic Press, New York.

Farrand, W. R.
1985 Rockshelter and Cave Sediments. In *Archaeological Sediments in Context*, edited by J. K. Stein and W. R. Farrand, pp. 21-39. Center for the Study of Early Man, Institute of Quaternary Studies, University of Maine, Orono.

Fladmark, K. R.
1982 Microdebitage Analysis: Initial Considerations. *Journal of Archaeological Science* 9:205-220.

Grayson, D. K.
1986 Eoliths, Archaeological Ambiguity, and the Generation of "Middle-Range" Research. In *American Archaeology Past and Future*, edited by D. J. Meltzer, D. D. Fowler, and J. A. Sabloff, pp. 77-133. Smithsonian Institution Press, Washington D. C.

Guidon, N., and B. Arnaud
1991 The Chronology of the New World: Two Faces of One Reality. *World Archaeology* 23:167-178.

Klein, R. G.
1972 Preliminary Report of the 1970 Excavations at Nelson Bay Cave (Plettenberg Bay, South Africa). *Paleoecology of Africa* 6:177-208.

Kreiger, A. D.
　1964　Early Man in the New World. In *Prehistoric Man in the New World*, edited by J. D. Jennings and E. Norbeck, pp. 23-81. University of Chicago Press, Chicago.

Laville, H., J-P. Rigaud, and J. Sackett
　1980　*Rockshelters of the Périgord*. Academic Press, New York.

Luedtke, B. E.
　1986　An Experiment in Natural Fracture. *Lithic Technology* 15:55-60.

Lynch, T. F.
　1990　Glacial-Age Man in South America? A Critical Review. *American Antiquity* 55:12-36.

MacNeish, R. S., A. Nelken-Turner, R. K. Vierra, and C. J. Phagan
　1980　*Prehistory of the Ayacucho Basin, Peru*, Vol. 3, Nonceramic Artifacts . University of Michigan Press, Ann Arbor.

Maguire, B.
　1980　Further Observations on the Nature and Provenience of the Lithic Artifacts from the Makapansgat Limeworks. *Paleontology African* 23:127.

Mallouf, R. J.
　1982　An Analysis of Plow-Damaged Chert Artifacts: The Brookeen Creek Cache (41HI86), Hill County, Texas. *Journal of Field Archaeology* 9:79-98.

Miller, R.
　1982　Pseudo-Tools Created by Livestock from Halawa, Syria. *Journal of Field Archaeology* 9:281-283.

Moir, J. R.
　1912　The Natural Fracture of Flint and its Bearing upon Rudimentary Flint Implements. *Proceedings of the Prehistoric Society of East Anglia* 1(2):171-185.

Nash, D. T.
　1987　Archaeological Investigations at Haystack Cave, Central Colorado. *Current Research in the Pleistocene* 4:114-116.

Oakley, K. P.
　1959　*Man the Tool-Maker* . University of Chicago Press, Chicago.

Oliver, J. S.
　1989　Analogues and Site Context: Bone Damages from Shield Trap Cave (24CB91), Carbon County, Montana, U. S. A. In *Bone Modification*, edited by R. Bonnichsen and M. Sorg, pp. 73-98. Center for the Study of the First Americans, Orono, Maine.

Patterson, L. W.
　1983　Criteria for Determining the Attributes of Man-Made Lithics. *Journal of Field Archaeology* 10:297-307.

Patterson, L. W., L. V. Hoffman, R. M. Higginbotham, and R. Simpson
　1987　Analysis of Lithic Flakes at the Calico Site, California. *Journal of Field Archaeology* 14:91-106.

Payen, L. A.
　1982　*The Pre-Clovis of North America: Temporal and Artifactual Evidence*. Ph. D. dissertation, University of California Riverside. University Microfilms, Ann Arbor.

Peacock, E.
　1991　Distinguishing between Artifacts and Geofacts: A Test Case from Eastern England. *Journal of Field Archaeology* 18:345- 361.

Pei, W. C.
　1936　Le Role des Phénomènes Naturels dans l'Éclatement et le Faconnement des Roches Dures Utilisées par l'Homme Préhistorique. *Revue de Géographie Physique et de Géologie Dynamique* 9:349-423.

Roebroeks, W. and D. Stapert
　1986　On the "Lower Paleolithic" Site of La Belle Roche: An Alternative Interpretation. *Current Anthropology* 27:369-371.

Rutot, A.
　1904　Sur la Cause de l'Éclatement Naturel de Silex. *Mémoires de la Société d'Anthropologie de Bruxelles* 1904(1).

Schnurrenberger, D., and A. L. Bryan
    1985   A Contribution to the Naturefact/Artifact Controversy. In *Stone Tool Analysis* , edited by M. G.
        Plew, J. C. Woods, and M. G. Pavesic, pp. 133-159. University of New Mexico Press, Albuquerque.
Schwartz, A. S., and H. R. Beevor
    1909   The Dawn of Human Invention. An Experimental and Comparative Study of Eoliths. *Memoirs
        and Proceedings of the Manchester Literary and Philosophical Society* 53(8):1-34.
Sellards, E. H.
    1952   *Early Man in America: A Study in Prehistory*. University of Texas Press, Austin.
Toth, N.
    1991   The Material Record. In *The First Americans: Search and Research*, edited by T. D. Dillehay and D.
        J. Meltzer, pp. 53-76. CRC Press, Boca Raton.
Tringham, R.D., G. Cooper, G. Odell, B. Voytek, and A. Whitman
    1974 Experiments in the Formation of Edge Damage: A New Approach to Lithic Analysis. *Journal of
        Field Archaeology* 1:171-196.
Van Riet Lowe, C.
    1952   *The Pleistocene Geology and Prehistory of Uganda, Part 2. Prehistory*. Memoirs of the Geological
        Survey of Uganda, 6.
Villa, P. and E. Mahieu
    1991   Breakage Patterns of Human Long Bones. *Journal of Human Evolution* 21:27-48.
Warren, S. H.
    1905   On the Origin of "Eolithic" Flints by Natural Causes,   Especially by the Foundering of Drifts.
        Journal of the Royal Anthropological Institute of Great Britain and Ireland 35:337-364.
    1914   The Experimental Investigation of Flint Fracture and its Application to Problems of Human
        Implements. *Journal of the Royal Anthropological Institute of Great Britain and Ireland* 44:412-450.

Section III

The Microscopic Scale

In the first two sections of this volume we presented a number of studies that dealt with formation processes from the standpoint of the region or the site. The studies in this section concentrate on observations performed at the millimeter scale and smaller. Traditionally, this avenue of archaeological research has been either not considered or simply ignored. In recent years, archaeologists have begun to examine how microartifacts, and the study of small-scale items in various contexts, may elucidate the role of various cultural and natural processes.

The first chapter in this section, by Arlene Miller Rosen, represents an application of the study of microartifacts (anthropogenic materials <5 mm in diameter) from Israeli tells. This study indicates that much valuable and elusive data can be gathered by this technique. Differences in abundance of materials recovered in the smallest of sieves furnish virtually invisible means for documenting differences in activity areas through space and through time.

The other two chapters in this section make use of the micromorphological technique. Micromorphology is the study of sediments and soils using petrographic thin sections. Although micromorphology has been used in soil science for over fifty years, its utilization in archaeology has been limited and essentially dates to the late 1970s. The technique's strength lies in its ability to document and unravel the sequence of depositional and postdepositional events and processes that are recorded in the undisturbed sample.

Thierry Gé and colleagues attempt to codify how living floors in various kinds of sites may be preserved, drawing examples from a broad range of sites. In the final chapter, Paul Goldberg and Ian Whitbread describe an ethnoarchaeological study designed to examine the spatial arrangement of a Bedouin camp, and document how various activity areas appear under the microscope.

In most of the initial micromorphological studies involving archaeological contexts, emphasis focused on geogenic and pedogenic processes. Although not ignored, anthropogenic processes received little attention, simply because there were scarcely any precedents or previous study guides. Although there was some borrowing from the pedological literature (e.g., biological activity of soil fauna), there were few modern-day micromorphological analogues or comparative data which could be used to interpret anthropogenic features observed in the thin section. The two micromorphology chapters attempt to provide such comparative data, placing particular emphasis on the living floor.

The studies in this section are meant to portray some of the directions in which micro-scale studies are moving, and to show that observations at this scale have large scale implications that can be tied to changes in soils and landscapes and former human activities. These studies represent only the beginning of what can be learned from this area of research.

10

Microartifacts as a Reflection of Cultural Factors in Site Formation

Arlene Miller Rosen
Ben Gurion University

The sediment matrices of archaeological sites have the potential to yield abundant information on site formation processes and past human societies (see for example, Hassan 1976; Rapp 1975; Rosen 1989; Schiffer 1987; Stein 1987). In order to cull such information from sediments, geoarchaeologists borrow techniques from sedimentology, such as analyses of sedimentary structures, composition, and sorting. With these methods at hand and anthropological questions guiding the sample selection and interpretation, we can approach archaeological problems such as activity area analysis, determining the intensity and continuity of occupation, and rates of site abandonment. The value of archaeological sediment analysis is perhaps most obvious for prehistoric hunter/gatherer or pastoral sites which contain relatively few artifact remains, but this paper will attempt to demonstrate that it is also true for tells (complex stratified urban mounds) where the matrix is composed almost exclusively of sediment transported by people (Rosen 1986).

Questions pertaining to the social implications of activity areas and the cultural aspects of site formation are rarely addressed in the archaeology of Levantine tells. A partial explanation for this may be that contrary to common conception, the floors of structures in these urban sites generally produce few primary *in situ* artifact remains. These artifacts were commonly disposed of in midden areas or carried away upon abandonment of the site. Therefore it is difficult to define the function of rooms within a given structure using traditional archaeological methods, and often the purpose of the building itself is in question. Artifacts are sometimes found in place in the rare cases where abandonment was rapid due to the impending destruction of the town by invaders. However, even in these instances, the artifacts reflect activities of the last moments in the life of a town under siege which may not be typical of daily activities.

The study of the microartifact component of the sediment matrix is especially useful in addressing some of these problems. Microartifacts are defined here as artifacts and other culturally derived material (such as bones, seeds, shells, etc.) which range in size from 2 cm–0.25 mm. In archaeologically *in situ* deposits they are informative about activity areas. Because of their small size, they are generally not carried or swept away from the site of the initial activity. Furthermore, as fine sediment builds up on an occupation surface during the time of its use, the microartifacts remain as a record of room use throughout the duration of the room's occupation (Hull 1987; Metcalfe and Heath 1990; Rosen 1989, 1991; Simms and Heath 1990). In disturbed deposits microartifacts furnish clues about the origin of the sediment and processes of deposition by their composition, grain-size distribution, and degree of preservation (Dunnell and Stein 1989; Stein and Teltser 1989).

When analyzing microartifacts it is important to take into account the spatial, temporal and cultural context of the particular archaeological unit (floor, midden, construction fill) that one is dealing with (Butzer 1982). Physical location within the site topography influences the kind of refuse deposited. For example, low places and depressions serve as traps for refuse deposition and runoff. The site-wide cultural context is equally important, and therefore, the study of activities on a particular archaeological surface should be compared with those on floors of other structures in the same stratigraphic horizon. Another consideration is the archaeological unit within its immediate sedimentary surroundings, as for example a floor within a section displaying a series of floors and collapsed brick. The "sedimentary" structures of this section such as graded bedding, laminae, or massive structure are important for understanding the pre- and post-depositional history of the floor being analyzed.

Finally, at the smallest scale of analysis are the microartifacts themselves and their proportional relationship to each other as well as to the natural mineral sediment. The study of the proportional relationships between microartifact types, such as charcoal versus bone, provides us with a unique archaeological opportunity to standardize and directly compare two very different kinds of remains. For example, in a domestic residence, food preparation can sometimes be identified by the positive correlation between the percentages of charcoal and bone in the microartifacts, whereas an industrial activity generally produces no correlation between the two. Another example is the occurrence of a relatively high percentage of sherds in the smaller fractions compared to the non-artifactual mineral components in the same fraction, a phenomenon which could indicate a high degree of traffic and trampling (Rosen 1989, 1991).

It is also useful to look at such factors as grain-size distribution. The percentage distribution of charcoal grain-size fractions is related to the degree of disturbance and mixing in an archaeological deposit. The non-disturbed deposits often display a smooth, continuous distribution of size-fraction percentages which increase with decreasing charcoal size, as opposed to disturbed deposits which exhibit a non-continuous distribution. This factor can help differentiate between *in situ* floor sediment, and secondarily deposited wall collapse, or midden fill in an abandoned room (Rosen 1989).

Sediment Context, Microartifacts, and Site Formation

The excavators of tells are usually faced with the task of moving massive quantities of sediment in order to uncover the architectural foundations and artifacts of interest to their archaeological problems. This task is usually carried out rapidly, with little attention paid to the matrix materials of brick collapse, construction fills and midden debris. However, this fill can be an important source of information on the processes of site formation, which can be obtained by careful examination in the field and laboratory.

Two problems of site formation were addressed in this study using microartifact analyses at two different tell sites in central Israel, Tel Halif and Tel Miqne. The approach to the two problems contrast in that one is a vertical diachronic study of site formation processes that took place stratigraphically with the abandonment and reoccupation of a site, and the other is a synchronic study of differences in the floor deposits of elite versus commoner houses that were occupied during the same period.

Tel Halif

The site of the diachronic study was Tel Halif (or Lahav), a large tell located in the low foothill region of south central Israel. The site contains remains of occupation from the Chalcolithic (ca. 4500 B.C.) through the modern Arab periods, with intermittent intervals of abandonment (Seger et al. 1990). This study concentrated on a three and a half meter thick ashy deposit (Locus 8036) marking the beginning of the Early Bronze Age III (EB III) levels dating to 2500 B.C. Knowledge of the origin and mode of deposition of the ash was important for understanding the possible violent demise of the EB III town at Tel Halif. Three likely origins for the fill are 1) primary construction material, 2) a midden dump deposit, or 3) debris washed in after a major destruction of the site by fire.

Field examination of the structure and lithology of this fill indicated that it was characterized by two depositional phases (Figure 1). The lowermost, represented by Unit 2, appears to have been deposited rapidly. It lacked internal sedimentary structure and was more stony and less compact than the overlying Unit 1. Unit 1 consisted of sediments containing intermittent subunits of laminated sediments which washed in at intervals with winter rains. It also included several non-continuous short-term occupation floors characterized by compacted surfaces and flat-lying sherds, suggesting that the site was visited

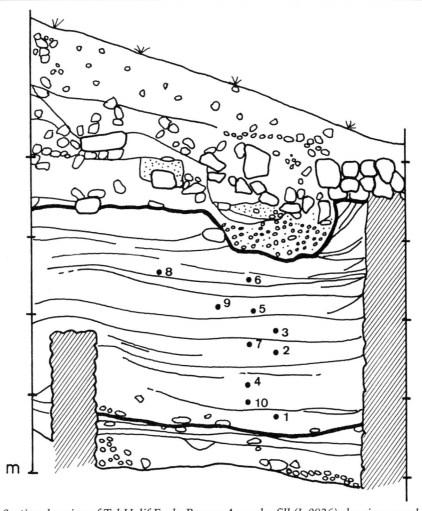

Figure 1. Section drawing of Tel Halif Early Bronze Age ashy fill (L.8036) showing sample locations.

periodically by temporary residents after its general abandonment.

Ten samples of about 150-550g of sediment each were collected for microartifact analysis from Units 1 and 2. These were dried and weighed, and the clay, silt, and fine sands were removed by washing the sediment through a 0.25 mm sieve. The remaining fraction was dried and then passed through a set of nested sieves (sizes 5.00, 2.00, 1.00, 0.50, and 0.25 mm). Each size fraction was examined through a stereo binocular microscope and the volume percentages of artifacts, bone, charcoal, and minerals were determined with the aid of a visual percentage chart (Bullock et al. 1985: Fig. 24).

The results of the sieving and analysis of microartifacts from these two units provide us with information on the origins and differing depositional modes of Units 1 and 2. The three samples from Unit 2 (H-1, H-10, H-4) have high percentages of sherds in the >5.00 mm fraction (Figure 2), and poor sorting resulting from a greater amount of coarse material in the >5.00 mm

fraction. This indicates that the matrix of this unit was transported a short distance and rapidly deposited with little time for water sorting of particle sizes.

The presence of burnt (potlided) and unburnt flint, and both burnt and unburnt large-bone fragments (Figure 3) suggests that there were several sources of archaeological sediments, some which were burned before redeposition and others which were not burned. It is significant to note that in midden deposits I have observed from other tells, large bone fragments and flint chips discarded in the course of normal occupation are usually unburnt (Rosen 1991). In the case of the bone, the cooked meat with the bone is probably removed from the fire before the bone is burnt. Therefore, the large component of burnt bone in all of these samples is unusual and perhaps may be attributed to fires which took place before abandonment of the site. In contrast, the small mammal bone is unburnt and probably intrusive.

In Unit 1, sample H-5 comes from finely laminated water-laid sediments which are a sign of a more

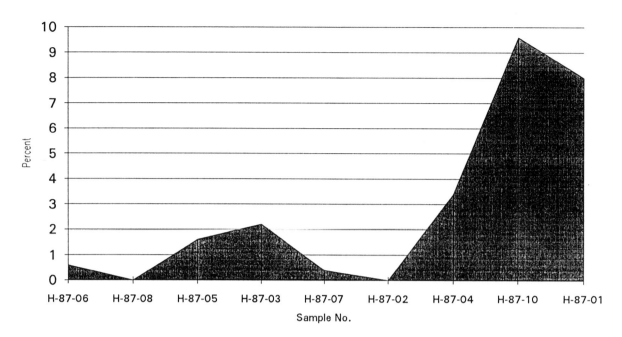

Figure 2. Volume percentage of sherds by size fraction (Tel Halif).

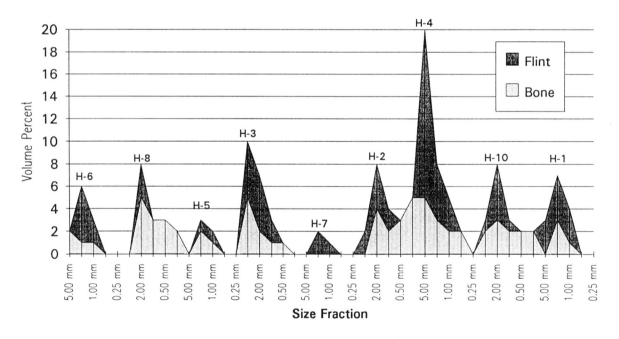

Figure 3. Volume percent of bone and flint by size fraction (Tel Halif).

sustained period of low-energy deposition than the deposits of Unit 2. The smooth percentage curve of the stone in sample H-5 (Figure 4) is a sign of good sorting associated with sediment transported by a relatively steady flow of water. Sample H-8 comes from a short-term ephemeral occupation surface which is defined by flat-lying sherds and more compacted sediment. It contains unburnt large-mammal bone fragments which are probably *in situ* remains of occupation, since they differ from the burnt-bone frag-

ments of the lower unit. Another quite distinctive characteristic present throughout the deposits is a very high proportion of carbonized grain in the charcoal along with high percentages (up to 10%) of large phytoliths from straw and cereal glumes. This perhaps suggests that one source of the sediment for this ashy deposit was a granary.

Of the three possibilities for the origin of this ashy fill, a) construction material, b) midden deposit, and c) destruction debris, the latter is the most likely. The

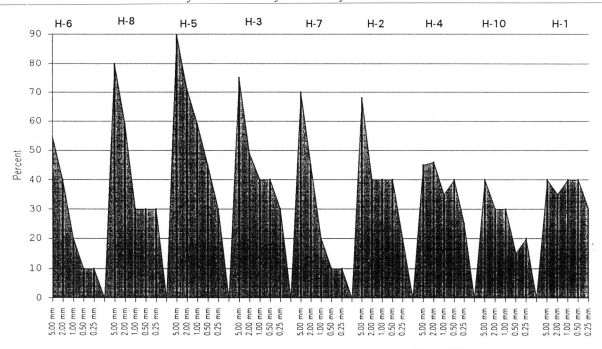

Figure 4. Volume percent of stone by size fraction (Tel Halif).

water-laid deposits, slow deposition rate, and intermittent occupation surfaces of Unit 1 rule out the possibility of a primary deposit of construction fill. The high percentage of burned material in Unit 2 is inconsistent with an interpretation of a reworked construction fill. Furthermore, the colluvial nature of Unit 2, and common occurrences of burnt flint and bones are not typical of midden deposits observed at other tell sites. The third possibility of reworked destruction debris (possibly including a grain storage facility near the sampling location) seems to fit the evidence more closely.

The above results suggest that shortly after the destruction or burning event, Unit 2 was deposited rapidly, perhaps with the first winter rains which washed massive amounts of loose debris into nearby depressions behind the city wall. With time, the source of destruction debris would have become more compacted and less easily transported by water. Thus, the rest of the area began to fill more slowly, giving rise to the laminated sediments. The floors indicate that there were intervals in which people temporarily utilized exposed surfaces.

Tel Miqne

Tel Miqne is located in central Israel, at the border between the low foothills of the Judean Hills known as the Shephela region, and the broad coastal plain. The site contains city levels from the Late Bronze Age (1500 B.C.) through the Iron Age II (8th century B.C.). One of the most extensive phases of urban develop-

ment was in the Iron I Philistine period (11th century B.C.) in which the site was Ekron, one of the five Philistine capital cities (Gitin and Dothan 1987). Results of microartifact analyses from Tel Miqne demonstrate the horizontal or synchronic perspective of microartifact analysis at a large city site. Here, microartifacts from floors were analyzed in order to determine if activities differed in the courtyards of the wealthy elite versus the common residents of the city (see Figure 5). The elite building was distinguished by traditional criteria such as massive architecture and unusual cultic vessels.

In both the common (Locus I.NE.4) and elite (Locus IV.NW.24021) structures, the mud floors of the courtyards were coated with thin lenses of white surface material, extending over most of the breadth of the floor. Microscopic examination of this material showed that it consisted of a smear of phytoliths. This type of floor appears at many sites in the country, and is almost always associated with Philistine courtyards. This suggests a unique floor preparation technique, perhaps a result of coating the surface with animal dung.

A comparison of microartifacts from the elite and commoner courtyards shows that in both locations there are remains of domestic activities associated with food preparation. This is indicated by the relatively high percentages of bone and charcoal, as well as the presence of seeds in addition to wood in the charcoal component (Figures 6 and 7). Both structures, therefore, probably served as residences in spite of the presence of cultic vessels in the elite building.

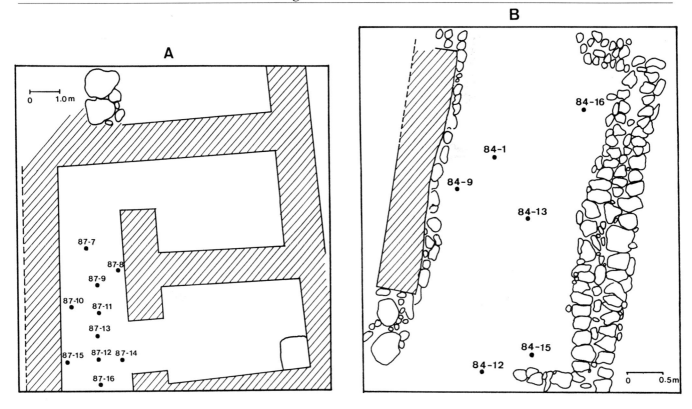

Figure 5. Plans of Iron I Elite (A) and Commoner (B) Courtyards at Tel Miqne showing sample locations.

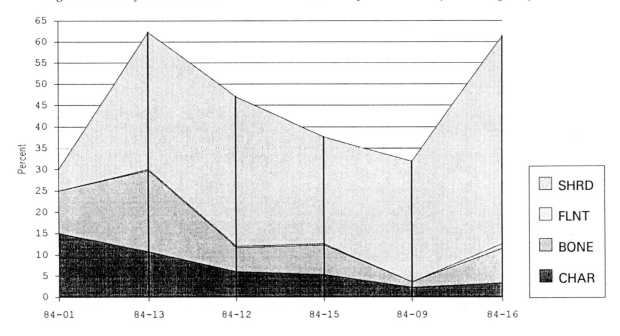

Figure 6. Major microartifact categories from the courtyard of a commoner residence (L.I.NE.4), Miqne.

Although both courtyards were used for ordinary domestic activities, there were some quantitative and qualitative differences setting the two locations apart. In the courtyard of the elite structure, eggshell was found in the coarse sand-sized fraction of the food remains. The surface morphology and thickness of the shell is comparable to that of chicken eggs. This concurs with finds of bird bones from a large ground bird in the same context (B. Hesse, personal communication 1987). Eggshell and bird bones such as these are

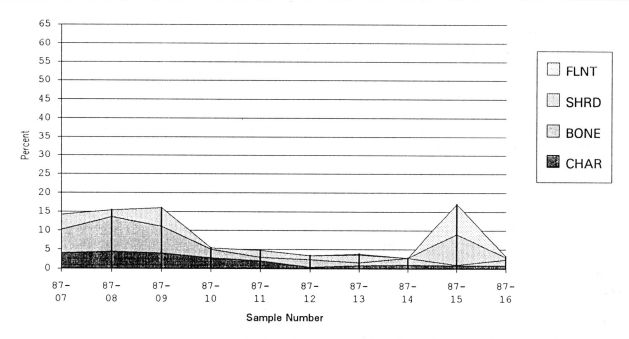

Figure 7. Major microartifact categories from the courtyard of an elite residence (L.IV.NW.24021), Miqne.

unknown from other contexts at the site. It is therefore likely that these bird remains represent a source of food available only to the wealthier segment of the society.

Another difference between these two courtyards is a high percentage of sand-sized sherds in the commoner courtyard, as compared to a much lower percentage in the elite courtyard (see Figures 6 and 7). If sherd breakage can be taken to represent the degree of trampling on these surfaces (Kirkby and Kirkby 1976:237-238), then this may be an indication of limited access to the elite courtyard, and therefore less trampling leading to fewer small sherds.

Rooms adjoining the courtyard were only excavated in the elite structure, but again there were microartifacts not found in other contexts at the site. In one side room of the elite structure, the fine sediment fraction contained a high percentage of tail bones from small mammals. These could be the remains of furs on the room floor (B. Hesse, personal communication 1987). This room also had a high percentage of phytoliths, possibly from reed mats. The co-occurrence of mats and furs would suggest a sleeping area.

In another room adjacent to the courtyard, there were sand-sized particles of weathered ferrous minerals, and a translucent substance resembling amber. These materials were also unique to this context and perhaps resulted from products or resources with high value.

Conclusions

Tells are large and complex sites which are known to yield vast quantities of archaeological material including mountains of potsherds, hills of flint and hummocks of bones and seeds. However, even given this rich inventory of traditional archaeological finds, microartifact analysis can contribute a fine-tuned perspective of daily-life activities during the phase of site occupation as well as small-scale indicators of site formation processes during and after site abandonment that is unattainable from the larger remains. The microartifacts that are routinely embedded in slowly accumulating floor layers during occupation of a room are an *in situ* record of room use through time. Excavations that routinely employ microartifact analysis of all room floors have the potential to compare activity areas within a given structure, building functions within specific sectors at a site, and social and functional variations between different city sectors.

At Tel Miqne, the microartifacts from Philistine levels complimented other finds to reveal some of the differences between the residences of two social classes at this site. Ideally, a broader study of microartifacts could determine a great deal about the daily life within other households as well. This example of lateral differences at Miqne, and the Halif example of vertical temporal changes immediately after a city destruction are only small studies from sites that are as large and complex as the societies of their former residents. However, no matter what the goals or scope of site formation studies at tells, their ultimate value will lie in the success with which they integrate sedimentary and social contexts at the site through time and space.

Acknowledgments

I would like to thank Trude Dothan and Seymour Gitin for access to the samples from Tel Miqne, and Joe Seger, for the samples from Tel Halif. Thanks are also due to Michael Schiffer and the editors of this volume for their most helpful editorial comments. Some of the analyses were conducted with the help of a National Endowment for the Humanities Fellowship at the Albright Institute of Archaeological Research, Jerusalem. This paper was written while the author was a Sir Charles Clore Post-Doctoral Fellow at the Weizmann Institute of Science, Rehovot, Israel.

References

Bullock, P., N. Fedoroff, A. Jungerius, G. Stoops, and T. Tursina
   1985 *Handbook for Soil Thin Section Description.* Waine Research, Wolverhampton, England.
Butzer, K. W.
   1982 *Archaeology as Human Ecology.* Cambridge University Press, London.
Dunnell, R. C., and J. K. Stein
   1989 Theoretical Issues in the Interpretation of Microartifacts. *Geoarchaeology* 4:31-42.
Gitin, S., and T. Dothan
   1987 The Rise and Fall of Ekron of the Philistines: Recent Excavations at an Urban Border Site. *Biblical Archaeologist* 50:197-222.
Hassan, F. A.
   1978 Sediments in Archaeology: Methods and Implications for Palaeoenvironmental and Cultural Analysis. *Journal of Field Archaeology* 5:197-213.
Hull, K. L.
   1987 Identification of Cultural Site Formation Processes through Microdebitage Analysis. *American Antiquity* 52:772-783.
Kirkby, A., and M. J. Kirkby
   1976 Geomorphic Processes and the Surface Survey of Archaeological Sites in Semi-Arid Areas. In *Geoarchaeology: Earth Science and the Past*, edited by D. A. Davidson, and M. L. Shackley, pp. 229-253. Duckworth, London.
Metcalfe, D., and K. M. Heath
   1990 Microrefuse and Site Structure: The Hearths and Floors of the Heartbreak Hotel. *American Antiquity* 55:781-796.
Rapp, G., Jr.
   1975 The Archaeological Field Staff: The Geologist. *Journal of Field Archaeology* 2:229-237.
Rosen, A. M.
   1986 *Cities of Clay: The Geoarchaeology of Tells.* University of Chicago Press, Chicago.
   1989 Ancient Town and City Sites: A View from the Microscope. *American Antiquity* 54:564-578.
   1991 Microartifacts and the Study of Ancient Societies. *Biblical Archaeologist* 54:97-103.
Schiffer, M. B.
   1987 *Formation Processes of the Archaeological Record.* University of New Mexico Press, Albuquerque.
Seger, J. D., B. Baum, O. Borowski, D. P. Cole, H. Forshey, E. Futato, P. F. Jacobs, M. Laustrup, P. Seger, and M. Zeder
   1990 The Bronze Age Settlement at Tell Halif: Phase II Excavations, 1983-1987. *Bulletin of the American Schools of Oriental Research, Supplement* 26:1-32.
Simms, S. R., and K. M. Heath
   1990 Site Structure of the Orbit Inn: An Application of Ethnoarchaeology. *American Antiquity* 55:797-813.
Stein, J. K.
   1987 Deposits for Archaeologists. *Advances in Archaeological Method and Theory* 11. Edited by M.B. Schiffer, pp. 337-395. Academic Press, New York.
Stein, J. K., and P. A. Teltser
   1989 Size Distributions of Artifact Classes: Combining Macro- and Micro-Fractions. *Geoarchaeology* 4:1-30.

11

Sedimentary Formation Processes of Occupation Surfaces

Thierry Gé
Marie-Agnès Courty
Centre National de la
Recherche Scientifique

Wendy Matthews
University of Cambridge

Julia Wattez
Centre National de la
Recherche Scientifique

One of the basic goals of archaeology is to define human activities through the study of material traces which occur in depositional units. Study of human behavior can be achieved by using a variety of methodological approaches, including examination of spatial patterns. Reconstruction of prehistoric activities requires an accurate interpretation of spatial distributions and the resolution of occupation surfaces. Reconstruction of behavioral activities can only be achieved through the recognition of cultural and natural formation processes (Schiffer 1976, 1987; Butzer 1982). Archaeological investigations must therefore be oriented toward the identification of the relationship between the sedimentary matrix and artifactual distributions within archaeological units. Occupation surfaces are considered to be the most favorable unit for achieving paleoethnographic reconstructions. Although reconstruction of past behavioral activities is desirable, identification of occupation surfaces is still a problem and has been widely debated among French archaeologists (e.g., Leroi-Gourhan and Brèzillon 1966, 1972; Bordes et al. 1972; Bordes 1975; David et al. 1973; Villa 1976; Rigaud 1979, 1982; Courtin and Villa 1982; Audouze and Perlès, in press).

At the Upper Paleolithic site of Pincevent, occupation surfaces have been defined on the basis of thin depositional units separated by a layer of sterile alluvial loam (David et al. 1973). In this flood plain context, artifacts abandoned after each occupation were presumed to be rapidly buried by alluvial deposits without significant reworking. The spatial distribution of artifacts has thus been considered to represent an instantaneous picture of prehistoric camping activities after each phase of abandonment.

However, the relationships between the artifacts and the sedimentary matrix could not be clearly defined due to the homogeneity of the sediments. Accurate field observations have shown, however, that the occupation surfaces could be locally defined by specific sedimentary characteristics and by human impacts such as discoloration of the sediments due to ochre, and the presence of charcoal particles, ashes and microartifacts (David et al. 1973). Because these sedimentary features could not be traced on widely exposed surfaces, occupation surfaces were defined during the excavation by surfaces on which artifacts were lying (David et al. 1973). These authors, however, clearly stated that the occupation surface could correspond to three dimensional units. Each archaeological unit has been described as an occupation surface which can be subdivided into three of the following parts (David et al. 1973; Leroi-Gourhan 1978):

1) the topmost-surface, which is a layer a few centimeters to a few millimeters thick, consisting of microartifacts and particles derived from the underlying occupation floor which are embedded in a loamy matrix;

2) the artifactual surface, which is the original occupation surface, or a surface defined by the excavation units but presumed to be referable to prehistoric occupation (e.g., a surface modified by trampling, human induced accumulation of particles, a paved surface, or traces of a surface originally consisting of biodegradable constituents);

3) the under-surface, which consist of disturbances related to the occupation (e.g., artifacts that have been integrated into the lower surface by trampling or by bioturbation).

Recognition of occupation surfaces has been considered to be more difficult in other archaeological contexts, such as in caves and rockshelters, where the rate of natural sedimentation is slow, and where human disturbance can be more prevalent (Bordes 1975). According to Bordes, the identification of specific traces of spatial organization is often limited because successive occupations are superimposed on each other. Determination of the rate and nature of sedimentation, either natural or human induced, and evaluation of postdepositional alteration have been presented as essential for defining the spatio-temporal framework of human activities (Bordes et al. 1972). Moreover, it is difficult to trace occupation surfaces solely by sedimentary attributes because of human impacts, such as transformations induced by trampling, and because of postdepositional disturbances induced by natural agents. Consequently, Bordes (1975) proposed a definition of occupation surfaces which is similar to the one defined by A. Leroi-Gourhan (in David et al. 1973): "An occupation surface is a recognizable surface on which Upper Paleolithic Man was living during a time interval short enough for allowing the determination of human activities on the basis of distribution of the artifacts." Villa (1976) later specified that during continuous occupation of surfaces, physical modifications will be induced by human activities, such as accumulation of artifacts or by trampling. Villa concluded that an occupation surface could be recognized to be anthropogenic accumulations, defined by artifact distributions.

A diachronic perspective on the meaning of occupation surfaces was discussed by Rigaud (1979), who emphasized the spatio-temporal framework of occupations. In this perspective, the occupation surface can only be defined when the relative contemporaneity of all the artifacts has been demonstrated and when it has been proven that the location of these artifacts was not subsequently modified by natural agents. Audouze and Perlès (in press) support this point of view by insisting on the preservation of spatial and temporal relationships among artifacts. They thus define an occupation surface to be the result of cumulative human processes that have taken place within a short time interval. In this perspective, sedimentary characteristics can be taken into consideration for evaluating the degree of preservation of the spatio-temporal framework of occupation surfaces and especially for identifying the subsequent impact of natural agents (e.g., water, soil movements, fauna, taphonomic processes) on the distribution of artifacts.

This review shows that archaeologists are aware of the necessity to evaluate the interactions of cultural and natural processes in the formation of an archaeological unit for characterizing occupation surfaces. These processes have been discussed in order to recognize the sedimentary effects of human actions (accumulation and physical transformations), and for determining the role of natural processes in the preservation of the pertinent spatio-temporal relationships among artifacts. Moreover, the recent development of geoarchaeology has strongly emphasized the importance of recognizing specific sedimentary signatures induced by natural or human agencies (Renfrew 1976; Schiffer 1976, 1987; Butzer 1982). This implies an accurate characterization of the nature of all the sedimentary constituents at different scales of observation, including studies of sedimentary petrography or soil micromorphology. Micromorphological study of thin sections has been developed to characterize archaeological sediments (Courty et al. 1989). These investigations have been devoted to the identification of anthropogenic materials. The objective of this chapter is to investigate how micromorphological analysis can help to define occupation surfaces induced by human activities.

Concept of Sedimentary Contextual Analysis

Sedimentary contextual analyses are based on the microscopic study of thin sections of undisturbed archaeological sediments and whose original fabric is preserved (Courty et al. 1989). Complementary investigations are simultaneously performed to obtain quantified data of some sedimentary parameters (e.g., mechanical particle size analysis) or to document in greater detail the nature of some constituents (e.g., study of microartifacts, X-ray analysis of silt and clay fraction, S.E.M. observations and EDAX micro-analyses, chemical analyses). Micromorphological characterization of archaeological sediments is one aspect of the geoarchaeological approach which has already been widely discussed (Renfrew 1976; Schiffer 1976, 1987; Butzer 1982; Stein and Farrand 1985). Microscopic observations are aimed at understanding the relationships of all constituents in each archaeological unit through the interpretation of specific fabrics which are diagnostic of the different sedimentary mechanisms involved in their formation.

Using concepts similar to those of soil science, an occupation surface can be defined as the interactive zone between the atmosphere and the bio-lithosphere which is affected not only by human agencies but also by other factors, external and internal. Human actions can be subdivided into four types of elementary processes: accumulation, depletion, redistribution and transformation. The nature of the factors which control these different mechanisms can be identified by referring to general principles of sedimentary formation processes. Universality of the sedimentary signatures recognized is founded on the comparison of a large diversity of contexts in order to discriminate the influence of local factors (natural and cultural) on their morphological variability. This comparison enables compilation of a data bank in which constituents and their arrangement may be related to sedimentary forming processes and to controlling agencies. This reference data set can then be used for analyzing both the interactions between the different elementary mechanisms (e.g., superimposition, integration, obliteration) in order to reconstruct their evolutionary sequence. This sequence is delimited within a spatio-temporal framework which includes a succession of phases; each of these phases relates to a specific group of sedimentary signatures which have been formed simultaneously under well defined environmental conditions. In archaeological contexts, the sequence integrates two types of phases: (a) phases of occupation characterized by sedimentary signatures induced both by human agencies and by natural factors, and (b) phases of "non occupation" which comprise sedimentary signatures only induced by natural agencies. The effects of natural processes are in many cases so considerable that they can strongly alter the specific sedimentary signatures induced by human activities. To the contrary, the effects of human activities at the sedimentary scale can be more easily recognized in sites where anthropogenic processes were dominant. Archaeological sites selected for the present study have thus been classified according to their degree of human impact, which is defined by the relative role of human agencies against natural ones on the formation of sedimentary units (Table 1).

Archaeological tells from arid and semi-arid regions (e.g., Pre-Neolithic, Neolithic and Protohistoric villages, Protohistoric urban sites) offer optimal condi-

Table 1. Schematic Classification of the Different Sites Studied.

Type of Archaeological site	Human Impact	Natural Processes
Tells*	+ + + +	(+)
Neolithic caves	+ + + +	+ + + to (+)
Paleolithic caves**	+ +	+ + + +
Open air sites with well defined habitations**	+ +	+ +
Open air sites with poorly defined habitations**	(+)	+ + + +

* : arid and semi-arid conditions
** : temperate and periglacial conditions
(+) to (++++) : relative scale of the involved processes

tions for studying anthropogenic sedimentary fabrics, because they are both characterized by well defined archaeological structures (e.g., habitations of various types, courtyards, lanes, streets) and are only weakly affected by natural processes. The recognition of human induced transformations of an occupation surface also implies an accurate characterization of the original fabric of the surface, often difficult to achieve for sites formed of natural sedimentary materials. The common occurrence in Protohistoric tells of constructed occupation surfaces, which have a well defined fabric, make the identification of human sedimentary signatures easier. Constructed occupation surfaces therefore consist of similar sedimentary signatures showing a low degree of human impact.

This discussion permits comparison of the role of natural conditions in the preservation of anthropogenic sedimentary fabrics in a number of archaeological cases. Sampling strategies have been adapted for each site listed in Table 2. They relate to various constraints determined by the excavation (e.g., density of artifacts, extension of the excavated zones) and the occurrence of well defined archaeological structures (e.g., fire places, areas of dumping, trampling).

Results

Constructed Floors of Tells

Constructed floors are intentionally made occupation surfaces prepared from sedimentary materials. They are most often located in habitation rooms and clearly identified during excavation (Plate 1). Two sedimentary units are generally distinguished: (1) a

Table 2. Occurrence of the Three Types of Sedimentary Micro-structured Facies in the different Archaeological Sites Studied.

Archaeological Sites	Structured Micro-Facies	Residual Micro-Facies	Relict Micro-Facies
Gatas, Bronze Age open air site	X		
Pendimoun, cave stratum 19 Middle Neolithic		X	
Arene Candide, cave Early Neolithic layers	X		
Bavans, Central shelter Mesolithic, layer 7			X
Fontbrégoua, cave layer 63, Epipaleolithic			X
Verberie, open air Upper Paleolithic		X	
Pincevent, open air Upper Paleolithic	X		
Etiolles, open air Upper Paleolithic	X		
Combe-Saunières, cave Upper Paleolithic, layer IVc	X		
Vaufrey cave, layer IV Middle Paleolithic	X		
Vaufrey cave, layer VIII Middle Paleolithic			X
Cave XVI, layer C Middle Paleolithic	X		
Cave XVI, layer OA Upper Paleolithic			X
Baume Bonne, cave Middle Paleolithic			X
Le Lazaret, cave Early Paleolithic	X		

This table emphasizes that the occurrence of human induced micro-structure depends on the cultural context.

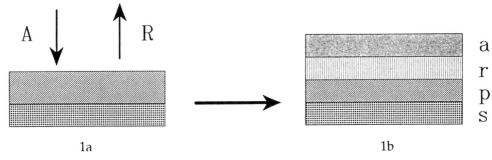

1a   1b

Figure 1. Schematic representation of the formation of an occupation surface from a constructed surface. (a) - Initial state of the constructed surface; A: actions (accumulation, redistribution, physical transformations); R: reactions (Physical transformations). (b) - The final state found in archaeological sites; a: active zone; r: reactive zone; p: passive zone. The thickness of each layer varies between a few mm to a few cm.

coherent unit, and (2) a less coherent unit that contains artifacts. They are respectively interpreted as the constructed floor, and a unit resulting from human activities. Micromorphological study reveals that the microstratigraphy consists in fact of three distinct units. The relationships between the different units and their structural properties are always similar in the various cases studied (Figure 1). The variability observed relates only to the thickness of the different units (a few millimeters to a few centimeters each) and to the nature of anthropogenic constituents.

The Passive Zone

The lowermost unit shows common structural characteristics of sedimentary materials pugged by human actions (Courty et al. 1989). This consists of homogeneity of the ground mass, random distribution of the coarse fraction (which may include anthropogenic constituents), large sized tubular voids lined with phytoliths (when straw was added to the mud), or large elongated cavities and vesicles indicative of intentionally deposited or prepared materials (Plate 2). When the unit is less than 1 cm in thickness, most of the large voids exhibit a sub-horizontal orientation. When the unit is thicker, the sub-horizontal orientation of the voids becomes gradually more expressed towards the top. Effects of pedological processes are in most cases restricted to large voids which may be partially filled by insect excrements or by salt crystallization.

These characteristics indicate that the pugged materials suffered minor transformations subsequent to preparation. Human trampling resulted only in weak modification of the original void pattern whereas no anthropogenic constituents were added to the floor after it was prepared. Considering structural changes in the occupation surface induced by human activities, the lowermost unit is thus a "passive zone".

The Reactive Zone

The micromorphological analysis of constructed floors reveal the occurrence of a distinct transition unit between the two units that were identified during excavation. The reactive zone consists of similar sedimentary materials compared to the lower one, although the abundance of subrounded anthropogenic constituents is commonly higher. The main difference in the microfabric consists of densely packed subangular to subrounded aggregates of various sizes (a few millimeters and less), whereas the microstructure is dominantly fissural with a subhorizontal orientation of the voids. The composition and the microstructure of the aggregates are identical to the materials of the lowermost passive unit.

Moreover, in many cases, a gradual transition can be observed between the compact materials of the passive unit and the aggregated middle one (photo 3). Pedological alterations are similar to those of the passive zone.

All these observations provide clear evidence for interpreting the middle unit as resulting from structural modifications of the constructed surface due to trampling. These can be subdivided into three simultaneous mechanisms: (1) disaggregation, (2) compaction and (3) incorporation of anthropogenic constituents (Plate 4), which is limited in comparison to processes (1) and (2). The middle unit can thus be described as the "reactive zone". Its thickness varies according to the physical properties of the constructed surfaces and in a lesser degree, to intensity of human activity. A full range of types can be observed between: (1) a very thin reactive zone (a few μm thick) when the constructed floor is made of very resistant materials (strong cementation between the constituents), and (2) a thick reactive zone formed at the expense of the passive zone when the constructed floor was made of weakly coherent materials.

The Active Zone

The uppermost unit consists of densely packed subrounded to rounded, well sorted (average 200 μm) micro-aggregates which are finely mixed with abundant anthropogenic constituents (e.g., bones, charcoal, shells, coprolites, phytoliths, ceramic fragments, mortar). A large morphological variability of the microfabric has been observed between two distinct types: (1) random distribution of the aggregates and weakly developed sub-horizontal fissural porosity, and (2) laminated microfabric with a well developed sub-horizontal fissural porosity. The fissural microstructure is generally better expressed and continuous in the upper part of the unit. One mineralogical type of aggregates is represented by sedimentary materials identical to the reactive and the passive zones. Other aggregates are of various mineralogical compositions, in most cases similar to anthropogenic (e.g., unbaked bricks) or natural (e.g., surface soils) sedimentary materials present in close surroundings.

The limit between the reactive zone and the overlying unit is generally clear and often expressed by abundant, horizontally elongated cavities. One distinct type of uppermost unit is represented by: (1) the existence of a sharp boundary, and (2) the occurrence of specific features at this boundary (ferruginous impregnation or well sorted and rounded micro-aggregates or fine vesicles). In this case, there is generally a reduced incorporation of anthropogenic constituents into the reactive zone. In

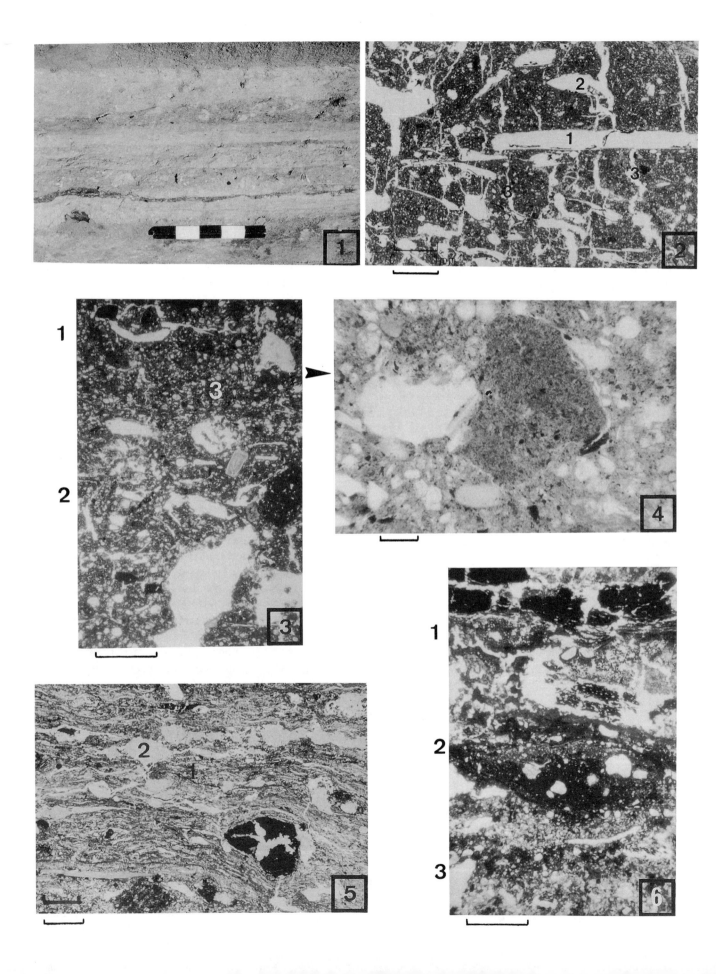

many cases, the layering is not only expressed by the horizontal fissures and by the arrangement of the aggregates, but also by the occurrence of articulated lenses of phytoliths. A considerable variability is observed in the nature and in the abundance of anthropogenic constituents among the different cases studied. Pedological features similar to those in the reactive and the passive zones are present, in addition to the occasional occurrence in the cavities of silty clay textural features.

These various characteristics indicate that the upper unit is essentially formed by the addition of anthropogenic constituents which may have been brought from close surroundings by human trampling or which may have been locally produced by human activities. The distinction between these two mechanisms and the identification of human activities is deduced from the nature of anthropogenic constituents which thus provide reliable data for functional interpretation. For example, the abundance of ash remains and domestic refuse may have been produced by fire related activities in the preparation of food. The aggregation and the compaction are the result of human trampling of the surface (photo 3). These mechanical modifications have induced a fine mixing of sedimentary materials derived from the underlying

constructed floors with anthropogenic constituents brought and produced by human activities.

The uppermost unit can thus be defined as the "active zone" formed by the simultaneous actions of three elementary mechanisms: disaggregation, compaction and addition of sedimentary materials. Very often, there is a limited addition of anthropogenic constituents in the active zone. In this case, two situations have to be considered. Either human activities performed on the living floor were not highly productive from a sedimentary point of view, or the incorporation of anthropogenic residues produced by the activities was limited because the occupation surface was protected by a cover. The latter situation can be identified by the occurrence of a sharp transition between the reactive zone and the upper unit and by the absence of materials derived from the constructed surface in the active zone. The existence of a cover is in this case the only interpretation that can explain why mechanical disturbances induced by human trampling had limited effects on the underlying constructed floor. The specific features found at the sharp boundary provide additional information concerning the type of cover. For example, the coexistence of articulated lenses of phytoliths, probably from lenses of decayed matting, and micro-aggregates suggest that the cover was made of

---

Photo 1. Abu Salabikh (Southern Mesopotamia; excavated by N. Postgate). Main mound, area E, central complex, Early Dynastic III period. Regular succession of constructed floors in the R39 reception room.

Photo 2. Abu Salabikh (Southern Mesopotamia). 5G65 house, R3 reception room. Passive zone of a plaster floor made of orange silty clay with addition of vegetal temper. Absence of disaggregation or accumulated debris is explained by the presence of a green plaster floor on the top that has preserved the orange plaster floor from modification of its characteristics by human activities at the surface. Sub-horizontal planar voids are relicts of vegetal temper (1), vughs and chambers relate to the preparation of the mud floor (2), fine vertical cracks are produced by trampling at the floor surface (3). Plane polarized light (PPL), length of the frame: 1 mm.

Photo 3. Netiv Hagdud (Jordan Valley; excavated by O. Bar Yosef), Pre-Ceramic Neolithic site. The reactive unit (2) of the house floor is formed of finely prepared, grey, pure, calcitic mud, characterized by minor biological disturbances (ch: channels) and presence of debris (d) incorporated by human trampling at the surface. The surficial active zone (1) consists of densely compacted, yellowish brown, calcareous, silty clay with abundant rounded fragments of fine textured silty clay rich in fine charcoal (3 and photo 4). The dense

fabric of the active layer suggests the accumulation of human related debris took place under a surface cover with a very fine mesh. PPL, length of the frame: 1 mm.

Photo 4. Netiv Hagdud (Jordan Valley). Higher magnification of the active zone of photo 3 showing a very dense micro-fabric and very fine integration related to human trampling of silty clay aggregates with very small charcoal that may have been formed by occasional washing of the activity surface. PPL, length of the frame: 100 μm.

Photo 5. Abu Salabikh (Southern Mesopotamia). Example of an active zone formed below a surface cover. Silty clay deposits with a dense fine undulating fibrous, organic rich micro-fabric (1), perhaps a relic of matting, mixed with abundant aggregates of dense, fine grained salts (2). PPL, length of the frame: 1 mm.

Photo 6. Kok Panom Di (Thailand), Bronze Age site. Non constructed floor formed below a wooden board cover (1). The active/reactive zone (2) consists of a thin, irregularly layered, dense silty clay unit derived from the accumulation and compaction of debris through the wooden board cover. The passive unit (3) consists of dense lenses of silty clay and fine sands rich in organic debris that are compacted, trampled materials. PPL, length of the frame: 1 mm.

organic materials (e.g., a reed mat) which was acting as a kind of "sieve" for human debris accumulated at the surface (photo 3). The size of the micro-aggregates is directly related to the mesh size of the covering material. The particular fabric characterized by a micro-lamination and by the regular succession of micro-aggregates and silica or organic remains indicates a progressive accretion of the active zone produced by maintenance activity (continual clearing and resurfacing of mats). The occurrence of textural features in the cavities may also show that the surface was washed at that time (Plate 4).

In other circumstances, absence of anthropogenic constituents in the reactive zone in addition to ferruginous impregnation and dense compaction of the superficial part of the reactive zone provide evidence to suggest that the surface was covered by an impervious material. This impervious material reduced the effects of mechanical disturbances and retained moisture below the cover.

In spite of morphological variability (relating to the physical properties of the constructed floors, to human activities and to the existence of covering materials) occupation surfaces formed on constructed materials can thus be defined by one specific type of micro-stratigraphic sequence (Figures 2a and 2b). The sedimentary signatures identified in the three distinct zones are diagnostic of the various mechanisms induced by human activities: accumulation of sedimentary materials, disaggregation, homogenization and compaction. These are universal processes, the effects of which can theoretically be identified on any kind of material. Micromorphological comparison of the successive constructed floors which form the stratigraphic sequence provides important information about functioning of spaces and rhythms of maintenance activity (Figure 3).

Non-Constructed Occupation Surfaces of Tells

These differ from constructed floors in the fact that the materials forming the occupation surface were not intentionally manufactured. They most generally consist of swept or dumped debris or of construction materials collapsed from perishable buildings. They are usually well recognized in the field by the occurrence of two distinct units overlying the debris or the collapsed fill. The lowermost one appears in many cases as a thin compact layer while the upper one has a weak cohesion. Moreover, the two units can often be distinguished by differences in color and in composition. In the sites studied, non constructed occupation surfaces were observed either within the same stratigraphic sequences as the constructed ones, or in other areas where constructed floors may have been absent such as streets, open courtyards and plazas.

Micromorphological analysis reveals that there is a very close resemblance between the micro-stratigraphic sequence of constructed floors and non-constructed occupation surfaces. The latter are always formed of three distinct units which can be respectively assigned to the passive, the reactive and the active zones previously defined (Figure 4). The lowermost unit, however, presents a clearly different microfabric from the passive zone of constructed floors characterized by a dense packing of aggregates. A similar aggregated structure is generally observed in the underlying layer (debris or collapsed fill) which only differs from the passive zone by a more open fabric and by the absence of subhorizontal fissures, while the mineralogical composition of the two units is the same. Active zones showing a regular micro-laminated fabric have often been observed in microstratigraphic sequences studied from rooms, whereas open courtyards and streets have most generally a micro-aggregated, homogenized fabric.

The fabric of the lowermost unit has in this case a dual origin. The aggregated microstructure relates to the mode of deposition of the materials as shown by the resemblance to the underlying layer, whereas the compaction results from structural transformations induced by trampling. The existence of these modifications indicates that the debris/dumped/collapsed fill layer had a less mechanical resistance to compressional forces than the manufactured materials of the

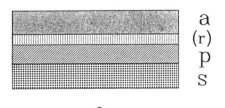

a
(r)
p
s

2a

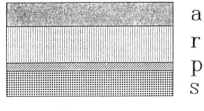

a
r
p
s

2b

Figure 2. Morphological variability of constructed occupation surfaces according to the physical characteristics of the constructed surface. (a) - weakly reactive materials. (b) - strongly reactive materials.

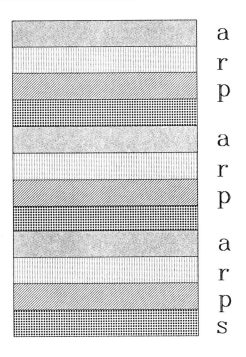

Figure 3. Schematic representation of a microstratigraphic sequence from archaeological tells showing the alternation of occupation surfaces made from constructed materials and debris/dumped fills.

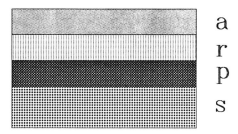

Figure 4. Schematic representation of the formation of an occupation surface from a non-constructed floor in archaeological tells.

constructed floors. The term passive cannot thus be used in this case from a mechanical point of view, although it remains correct regarding the addition of anthropogenic constituents by activities at the occupation surface. We, however, suggest the use of the term "passive" in order to adopt a standardized descriptive terminology.

In a few examples, the existence of a regular laminated fabric (Plate 5) or a dense fine fabric (Plate 6) of the active zones of some non-constructed occupation surfaces indicates that they may have been covered in a similar manner to constructed floors.

Identification of Sedimentary Fabrics in Occupation Surfaces in Other Contexts

The great diversity of facies observed at microscopic scales can be subdivided into four main types from the point of view of human mechanical modifications (Table 2). They are respectively defined as structured, residual, relict, and natural micro-facies, based on the degree of preservation of human induced transformations.

Structured Micro-Facies

This is characterized by fabrics identical to those previously described from constructed and non-constructed occupation surfaces of tells that relate to structural modifications induced by human activities at the occupation surface (Plates 7, 8, 9, 10). A wide variability is observed in the intensity of structural modifications of the ground materials among the different cases studied. These modifications are limited when the underlying deposits consist of sediments or soils which are well cemented or well structured, such as fine dense loam or silty clay compacted soils. In these cases, the compressional forces induced by human actions were insufficient to significantly modify the original fabric derived from former natural processes. The lowermost unit of the structured micro-facies observed can thus be relegated to the passive zone of constructed floors. On the other hand, more important structural modification defined by a compaction and by the development of a sub-horizontal fissural microstructure are observed when the ground materials have a weak cohesion and are characterized by loosely packed grains or aggregates. In these cases, the lowermost unit resembles more closely the "passive" zone of the non constructed floors.

In a few cases, no anthropogenic components were found to have been incorporated by human activities at the ground surface. A sharp contact was observed between the reactive and the active zones associated with the occurrence of specific features, such as ferruginous impregnation of a dense fine layer or laminae of micro-aggregates (Plates 6, 7, 8). These features are similar to those of occupation surfaces from tells which were interpreted to have been protected by a ground cover during the phase of activity. A laminated fabric of the active zone has also been observed in a few cases together with the occurrence of densely packed micro-aggregates and organic remains (e.g., articulated lenses of phytoliths in a middle Neolithic layer of Arene Candide, or burnt animal hair on an occupation surface of Pincevent). These organic relicts provide evidence for recognizing the type of covering materials used on the ground.

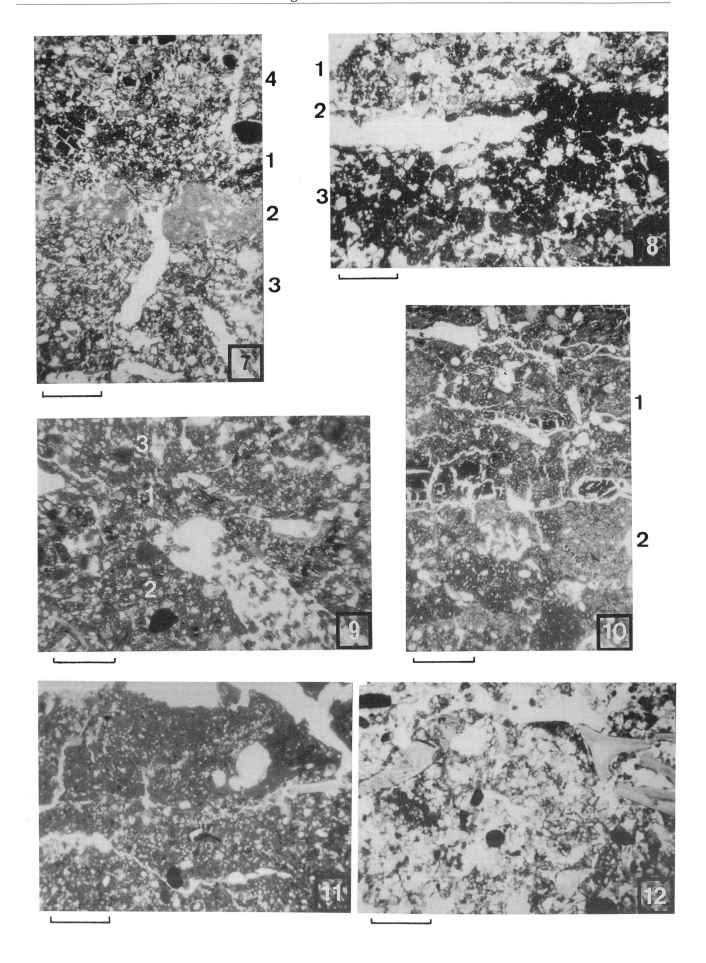

In all the cases studied, features related to pedological processes are always more marked in the three distinct units than in occupation surfaces from tells. These features are of various origin: fine channel porosity due to biological activity (photos 7, 8, 9, 10), local mixing of the units created by bioturbation, textural features created by the percolation of water with a suspended charge through the floor or secondary cementation by calcium carbonate caused by solute transfers. These pedological transformations are, however, always limited and did not significantly alter the structural fabric produced by human activities.

This structured micro-facies can be considered to represent the typical sedimentary fabric of an occupation surface. An accurate study of the anthropogenic constituents of the active zone and of their lateral variability through largely exposed surfaces can help to define the nature of human activities performed at the living surface, their spatial organization and their evolution through time. From a micromorphological point of view, the recognition in the active zone of only homogeneous sedimentary fabric can be considered to correspond to a "monophased occupation surface". To the contrary, "polyphased occupation surfaces" (Figures 5a and 5b) are identified when clear changes of the use of activity area are observed through the active zone by several types of anthropic sedimentary fabrics, without any interruption caused by natural deposition.

These structured micro-facies are generally covered by a layer of sterile sediments (e.g., flood deposits in the case of Pincevent or Etiolles, Plates 9, 10) or by dumped anthropogenic debris characterized by a typical aggregated open microstructure. Good preservation of the fabric of the active zone indicates that the

Photo 7. Pigeon cave at Taforalt (Morocco; excavated by Abbé Roche and J.-P. Raynal), late Paleolithic layer. Structured micro-facies characterized by a passive lower unit (3) formed of densely compacted, dark brown, silty clay sands with high biological activity, a reactive/active unit (2) formed of very dense, yellowish brown, silty clay probably accumulated below a surface cover and a dark brown, micro-aggregated active unit (3). The uppermost part of the active unit (4) presents an open micro-aggregated microstructure that relates to dispersion and disaggregation by human trampling at a non-covered surface. PPL, length of the frame: 1 mm.

Photo 8. Vaufrey cave (South-western France; excavated by J.-Ph. Rigaud), layer IV, Middle Paleolithic. Structured micro-facies formed by human trampling at a ground surface covered by a humic horizon. The passive unit (3) is formed of silty clay, organic rich aggregates, finely mixed with quartzitic sands; the reactive unit (2) presents a very dense, organic rich, silty clay micro-fabric; the active unit (1) consists of loosely packed quartzitic sands, organic aggregates and human debris. The sharp contact and the elongated channels between the passive and the active unit suggest the ground surface was originally protected by a ground cover that explains absence of disaggregation or accumulated debris into the reactive zone. PPL, length of the frame: 1 mm.

Photo 9. Etiolles open air site (Paris Basin, Seine Valley; excavated by Y. Taborin, M. Olive and N. Pigeot), late Magdalenian. Weakly expressed, structured micro-facies showing a calcareous sandy loam passive unit of alluvial origin (2) and a thin, dense, active unit (1) with ferruginous impregnation and very fine charred particles. The sharp contact between the reactive and the active unit suggests the

surface was protected by a ground cover during the phase of activity. The top most unit (3) results from a subsequent accumulation of alluvial loam, weakly reworked by biological activity. PPL, length of the frame: 1 mm.

Photo 10. Pincevent open site (Paris Basin, Seine Valley; excavated by Prof. A. Leroi-Gourhan and his team), late Magdalenian. Well developed, structured micro-facies showing a reactive unit (2) formed of densely packed, calcareous loam micro-aggregates with charred residues and a thick active unit (1) formed of compacted, layered, human debris finely mixed with dark brown calcareous loam incorporated by human trampling during the activity at the ground surface. PPL, length of the frame: 1 mm.

Photo 11. Shelter of Bavans (Eastern France, Doubs Valley; excavated by G. Aimé), Mesolithic. Residual structured microfacies formed of a dense active zone (1) compacted by human trampling and of a sandy loam reactive zone (2) deposited by water. Floods and biological activity are responsible for the partial disaggregation of the activity surface that is identified by randomly distributed fragments. PPL, length of the frame: 1 mm.

Photo 12. Verberie open air site (Northern France, Paris Basin, Oise Valley; excavated by F. Audouze), late Magdalenian. Relictual structured micro-facies strongly reworked by biological activity and flooding. Human activities are identified in the thin section by local accumulation of finely fragmented bone fragments, charred residues and minor evidence of trampling. The relictual structured micro-facies only is preserved below large sized bones and flint accumulation where they have suffered less postdepositional disturbances. PPL, length of the frame: 1 mm.

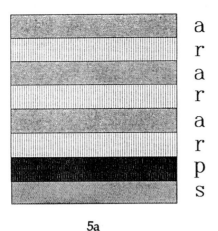

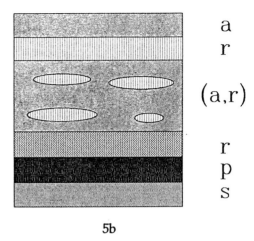

Figure 5. *Schematic representation of polyphased micro-structured occupation surfaces. (a) sub-type 1 : complex micro-layered sequence where distinct changes in human activities can be recognized. (b) sub-type 2 : homogeneous micro-structured unit where the repeated changes in human activities cannot be clearly defined except by the occurrence of residual micro-structured facies.*

accumulation of the overlying materials occurred rather rapidly after the formation of the occupation surface and did not generate strong mechanical disturbances. In microstratigraphic sequences showing regular alternation of structured micro-facies with sedimentary laminae of alluvial origin (e.g., Pincevent, Etiolles, Verberie; Upper Paleolithic sites of the Paris Basin, France) a better understanding of the duration of occupation phases can be gained by determining the time interval of flooding events (e.g., seasonal, decanal). This information would help to define the temporal framework of the occupation in addition to other archaeological data, such as lithic refitting, which are commonly used to argue that the phase of occupation was of short duration.

Complex microstratigraphic units can exhibit an alternation of micro-structured facies with layers deposited by natural processes. Micromorphological study of these polycyclic sequences (Figure 6), combined with other archaeological evidence, will yield some important information about human activities and environmental conditions.

Residual Structured Micro-Facies

The residual micro-facies differs from the structured micro-facies in the lack of lateral continuity at microcopic scales, because in this case, the typical sedimentary fabric of an occupation surface has been altered by postdepositional processes (Plate 11). Well defined units showing a structured micro-facies are juxtaposed with units characterized by a different microstructure, where the three distinct zones cannot be identified. The latter microstructure generally relates to bioturbation evidenced by a well developed

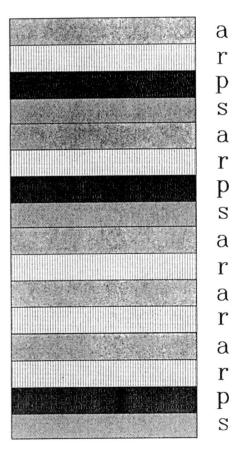

Figure 6. *Schematic representation of a polycyclic sequence formed by the alternation of phases of human occupation and of episodes of natural accumulation.*

channel microstructure and homogenized fabric. These features indicate that the structured fabric has suffered marked local disturbances induced by pedological processes which are not expected to have significantly modified the general organization of the archaeological unit. The pedological alteration may have been caused before burial due to a longer exposure of the occupation surface to natural agencies before its burial. They may have also been generated during the burial phase because the rate of sedimentation was slow while soil-forming factors were active. Observation of micromorphological features of the overlying layer generally enables a clear distinction between the two scenarios, which is important in defining the nature of environmental conditions that prevailed after the formation of the occupation surface. A particular situation was observed in Neolithic caves such as a site of Arene Candide (Early Neolithic cave, Italy) where the units juxtaposed to the human structured ones consist of loosely packed aggregates. The overlying layer is formed in this case of animal dung mixed with mineral residues produced by animal stabling (Wattez et al. 1989; Courty et al. 1991). These various features suggest that animal trampling caused the structural degradation of the occupation surface layer, attesting to a change in the use of the activity area.

Relictual Structured Micro-Facies

This is characterized by the occurrence of large aggregates with a fabric similar to the zones of the structured micro-facies. These are finely mixed with sedimentary materials, characterized by a microstructure differing from the one induced by human trampling (Plate 12). The different cases can be subdivided into two groups.

In one case, the latter microstructure relates to the effects of natural agencies, such as bioturbation, alluviation or colluviation (Plate 12). These processes have altered the original micro-facies either because of pedological disturbances or sedimentary reworking. The implications with respect to the preservation of the spatio-temporal context of human occupation differ in these various situations. When features produced by intense bioturbation or cryoturbation are observed, one can expect that the pedological disturbances occurred locally through homogenization processes, with minor alteration of the general organization of the archaeological layer. When evidence of sedimentary reworking are recognized, the original archaeological unit can be defined by studying the general geological context.

In the second case, the unit which contains fragments of occupation surfaces consists of loosely packed aggregates of various anthropogenic origins.

The heterogeneous composition and the microstructure suggest the unit results from human dumping. Fragments of occupation surfaces are thus in a tertiary position (as defined by Butzer 1982) and have consequently lost their original contextual significance.

Other Micro-Facies

This category groups a wide variety of micro-facies that can be of anthropogenic or of natural origin. No evidence of structural modifications induced by human trampling can be recognized at microscopic scales. Anthropogenic micro-facies relate to other kind of human activities which can be determined by their specific microstructure, such as loose packing of aggregates in human dumped layers. The discussion of other types of anthropogenic sedimentary microstructures is, however, beyond the scope of this paper and will require further study. When anthropogenic constituents of any size (artifacts or micro-artifacts) occur in a sedimentary matrix which shows only a microstructure created by natural processes, the former existence of a human structured micro-facies can be envisioned. Micromorphological study will then aim to determine if pedological or sedimentary transformations may have caused a total destruction of the original structure of human origin. The information gained from this study is essential in order to evaluate the degree of preservation of spatio-temporal relationships between the artifacts. The term virtual micro-facies with regard to human mechanical modifications can be used in this case. The term natural micro-facies has to be restricted to sedimentary materials which do not contain anthropogenic constituents and which have been deposited and transformed by natural agencies.

Conclusion

The micromorphological study of various archaeological contexts has helped to identify specific structural sedimentary signatures caused by human activities. These signatures can only be thoroughly visualized and understood by a careful examination at microscopic scales, examining the various sedimentary constituents and their arrangement. Some of these sedimentary features may be observed at macroscopic scales and can thus be grossly identified during excavation. However, archaeologists have not discussed the mechanisms of human induced modifications at sedimentary scales. This explains why occupation surfaces have not been identified in many archaeological contexts. The results presented in this chapter are a preliminary attempt to establish a system to interpret the meaning of archaeological sediments. This system requires the growth of a data bank of distinct types of anthropogenic sedimentary facies that are classified according to specific mechanisms produced by human activities. The microstructured facies discussed in this chapter are defined according to the various mechanisms (disaggregation, compaction, accumulation and redistribution) which permit description of the formation of occupation surfaces. The examples of anthropogenic sediments should be considerably enlarged and refined by future investigations.

The four defined types of sedimentary micro-facies were classified according to the degree of preservation of human induced structural modifications. Natural processes, and especially pedological transformations, have been shown to play a predominant role in the alteration of anthropogenic structural modifications. Only a few archaeological contexts offer optimal conditions for an accurate evaluation of the spatio-temporal framework of human occupations. The very common occurrence of relictual and residual structured micro-facies however attests to the fact that some important information about activity areas and environmental conditions can be gained through careful examination of the sedimentary context.

A better understanding of the effects of natural processes in short-term intervals, especially at seasonal scales, is required in order to determine more precisely the rhythms of human occupations. The sedimentary manifestations of human activities and their spatial organization also need to be more systematically investigated at all scales of organiza-tion. This goal should be efficiently achieved through an ethnoarchaeological approach (see Goldberg and Whitbread, this volume) because ethnological contexts provide well defined experimental situations in order to evaluate the interactions among cultural activities and sedimentary processes.

Acknowledgments

The authors of different archaeological teams are thanked for permission to work on their sites and to present preliminary results before extensive publication: N. Postgate (Abu Salabikh, Iraq), O. Bar Yosef (Netiv Hagdud, Jordan Valley), R.S. Bisht and the Archaeological Survey of India (Banawali, Kalibangan, Mitathal, India), Gatas project (dir. V. Lull, Gatas, Spain), D. Binder (Pendimoun, France), R. Maggi (Arene Candide, Italy), G. Aimé (Bavans, France), J. Courtin (Fontbrégoua, France), Y. Taborin, M. Olive and N. Pigeot (Etiolles, France), D. Baffier, P. Bodu, F. David, G. Gaucher, M. Julien, C. Karlin, M. Orliac and B. Valentin (Pincevent, France), F. Audouze (Verberie, France), A. Turcq (Roc Allan, France), J.-Ph. Rigaud and Y. Simek (Cave XVI and Vaufrey shelter, France), J.-M. Geneste (Combe Saunières, France), H. de Lumley (le Lazaret and Baume Bonne caves, France). The authors are grateful to Institut National Agronomique Paris-Grignon (laboratoire de Science des Sols et Hydrologie, directeur Professeur R. Calvet) for technical assistance with preparation of thin sections.

References Cited

Audouze, F., and C. Pèrlès.
In press. Structures naturelles, structures anthropiques et dynamique des sols d'habitat. *Actes du Colloque de Roanne-Villerest. Habitat du Paléolithique Supérieur.*

Bordes, F.
1975. Sur la notion de sol d'habitat en préhistoire paléolithique. *Bulletin de la Société Préhistorique Française* 72:139-144.

Bordes, F., J. P. Rigaud, and D. Sonneville-Bordes.
1972. Des buts, problèmes et limites de l'Archéologie Paléolithique. *Quaternaria* XVI:15-34.

Butzer, K. W.
1982. *Archaeology as Human Ecology.* Cambridge University Press, Cambridge.

Courtin, J., and P. Villa.
1982. Une expérience de piétinement. *Bulletin de la SociétéPréhistorique Française* 79 (4):117-123.

Courty, M. A., P. Goldberg, and R. I. Macphail.
1989. *Soils Micromorphology in Archaeology.* Cambridge University Press, Cambridge.

Courty, M. A., R. I. Macphail, and J. Wattez.
1991. Soils and Micromorphological Indicators of Pastoralism; with Special Reference to Arene Candide, Finale Ligure, Italy. *Rivista di studi Liguri*, A. LVII (1-4):127-150.

David, F., M. Julien, and C. Karlin.
1973. Approche d'un niveau archéologique en sédiment homogène, in Cujas (ed), *L'homme, hier et aujourd'hui*: 65-72. C.N.R.S., Paris

Leroi-Gourhan, A.
   1978. Plan au sol - parois - couverture, *Séminaire sur les structures d'habitat*:1-2: Unpublished report, Collége de France, Paris.
Leroi-Gourhan, A., and M. Brèzillon.
   1966. L'habitation magdalénienne n°1 de Pincevent, près Montereau (Seine-et-marne). *Gallia Préhistoire* 9 (2):263-385.
   1972. Fouilles de Pincevent. Essai d'analyse ethnographique d'un habitat magdalénien (la section 36), *7éme supplément à Gallia Préhistoire*. Paris: C.N.R.S.
Renfrew, C.
   1976. Archaeology and the Earth Sciences. In *Geoarchaeology*, edited by D. A. Davidson and M. L. Shackley, pp. 1-5. Duckworth, London.
Rigaud, J. Ph.
   1979. Contribution méthodologique à l'étude d'un sol d'occupation. *Revista do Museu Paulista* XXVI: 189-199. Sao Paulo.
   1982. Le Paléolithique en Périgord: Les données du sud-ouest Sarladais et leurs implications. Unpublished Thése de doctorat ès Sciences, University of Bordeaux I, France.
Schiffer, M. B.
   1976. *Behavioral Archeology*. Academic Press, London.
   1987. *Formation Processes of the Archaeological Record*. University of New Mexico Press, Albuquerque.
Stein, J. K., and W.R. Farrand.
   1985. *Archaeological Sediments in Context. Peopling of the Americas*. Center for the Study of Early Man, University of Maine, Orono.
Villa, P.
   1976. Sols et niveaux d'habitat au Paléolithique Inférieur en Europe et au Proche-Orient, *XIIIéme Congrès de l'U.I.S.P.P.*:139-155. Nice.
Wattez, J., M. A. Courty, and R. I. Macphail
   1989. Burnt Organo-Mineral Deposits Related to Animal and Human Activities in Prehistoric Caves. In *Soil Micromorphology: a Basic and Applied Science*. Edited by L. A. Douglas, pp. 431-439. Developments in Soil Sciences 19. Papers from the VIIIth International Working Meeting of Soil Micromorphology, San Antonio, Texas-July 1988. Elsevier Science Publishing Co., New York.

12

Micromorphological Study of a Bedouin Tent Floor

Paul Goldberg
Texas Archeological Research Laboratory

Ian Whitbread
British School at Athens

For over two decades archaeologists have exhibited an increased awareness and interest in the complexity of processes that are responsible for the formation of archaeological sites (Schiffer 1987). This is particularly true of the anthropogenic processes that are related to the activities that create sites. Our ability to infer distinct past human behavior is controlled, first by the resolution of the stratigraphic record, and second, by our ability to recognize individual stable surfaces that are commonly identified as 'living floors'. Living floors can be considered as the stratigraphic evidence for distinct events in the past. Once 'living floors' are recognized on a site, then a number of techniques can be used to recover and analyze the evidence of human activities.

Considerable attention has been paid to the archaeological implications of living floors as evidence for distinct events in the past (e.g., Leroi-Gourhan and Brézillon 1972; Yellen 1977; Binford 1978; Stevenson 1991), but the recognition of an actual 'living floor' or stable surface is often a difficult task. Even if they can be distinguished, it is not always clear what types and varieties of activities truly took place on their surfaces and which activities pre- or post-date the surface.

Most archaeologists are taught that a floor or a surface is identified by its packing density, color, the well patterned vertical and horizontal distribution of artifacts, or by features such as plaster lines. Joukowsky (1980: 180), for example, states that,

> floors are often hard-packed, and are generally associated with some sort of wall or ledge. A hard-packed floor created by trodden earth can be detected in the 'feel' of the excavation tool. In some cases, the debris collected over it will seem to almost peel off it.

Using these criteria alone, there are several problems associated with the identification of 'living floors' or stable surfaces in an archaeological context. For one, the different lines of evidence cited above often are poorly developed or only partly present in archaeological deposits because of postdepositional bioturbation. This makes recognizing living floors very difficult (Barker 1982:117). More importantly, the processes and the diversity of anthropogenic activities associated with the formation of stable surfaces in archaeological sites are rarely well documented. Trampling, treading, cleaning, flint knapping, cooking, and a variety of hearth focused activities are commonly linked to 'living floors' and inferred (Stevenson 1991), but clear, non-dubious criteria for reliable recognition of these varied and ephemeral features are just being developed in archaeology (Courty et al. 1989).

Past investigations have attempted to infer site activities and have used ethnoarchaeological studies, (e.g., Bienkowski 1985; Layne 1987; and Simms 1988 for the Bedouin tent context), geophysical strategies (e.g., Weymouth and Huggins 1985), and chemical analyses of sediments (e.g., generally phosphate, organic matter and nitrogen assays; Cook and Heizer 1965; Eidt 1984; Kolb et al. 1990). In addition, experiments have been conducted to examine the effects of artifact movement by trampling, or other biological disturbance (e.g., Stockton 1973; Moeyersons 1978; Villa and Courtin 1983; Gifford-Gonzalez et al. 1985).

Most research along these lines in soil science has previously employed traditional methods to examine soil modifications, and commonly using bulk samples in which the material has been homogenized. This is a problem because this homogenizes the sediments, thus mixing distinct strata, and destroying the original structure and geometry of the material.

Recently the technique of micromorphology (the study of undisturbed soils and soft sediments using petrographic thin sections), has played an increasingly prominent role in the evaluation of soil modifications. Micromorphological analysis looks at the composition, texture, and fabric (i.e., the identification and geometrical arrangement of solid elements and voids) of the intact sediments. Indeed, there is a considerable literature on the micromorphology of effects of soil disturbance (generally compaction) by machinery, humans and animals (e.g., Jongerius 1970, 1983; Murphy et al. 1977; Pawluk 1980). Most recently, micromorphology has been applied to several archaeological problems, and has demonstrated its value in uncovering anthropogenic impacts on sedimentation (Courty et al. 1989).

Archaeological materials attributable to human activities such as bone, ash, and organic matter are evident under the microscope and can be clearly interpreted. Consequently, we might expect to find in thin section a number of features that should be associated with anthropogenic activities, including:
- more organic matter, charcoal and ash near hearths;
- more organic matter, dung and hair in areas where animals are penned;
- greater compaction in trampled or transit areas, which might vary according to the specific activity;
- in areas that have been excavated in antiquity, there should be a looser fabric, with more voids;
- in filled areas (e.g., postholes for doors or for tripod supports for drinking liquids), porosity should be reduced (Courty et al. 1989);
- cleaning in sleeping or non-eating areas might be characterized by low organic matter and elongated voids;
- midden areas and privies should be richer in materials such as bone, phosphates, organic matter, diatoms, and shells;
- food storage areas should exhibit increased amounts of organic matter and seeds;
- areas of craft specialization should display traces of the specific craft undertaken, e.g. fibers, plaster, ceramic, glass, slags.

Most micromorphological research until the last decade has been qualitative and verbally descriptive. Recently, however, there has been an increased tendency to quantify thin section observations. This has enabled the quantitative measurement of a variety of parameters such as the size, shape, and orientation of grains and voids.

The objectives of this paper are:
1) to evaluate the feasibility of using thin sections to recognize living floors and their associated activities with lateral variations based on the micromorphological study of a recently abandoned Bedouin tent in the Negev Desert, Israel;
2) to describe the most diagnostic micromorphological features of thin sections of living floors: specifically composition, and the geometric arrangement of solids and voids (fabric). [Fabric is used here in the micromorphological sense to designate the arrangement of voids and solids within the thin section (Bullock et al. 1985).
3) to develop micromorphological criteria that can be used to recognize and characterize the composition and microfabrics associated with human modifications of Bedouin tent living floors, i.e., the substrate below which human activity has taken place, with the aim of linking micromorphological criteria with known activities that took place in the tent area.

The Tent And Its Characteristics

The Bedouin tent under study is situated in the area of Tell Be'er Sheva, ca. 5 km east of the city of Be'er Sheva (Israel Grid coord.: 135650/072700). It lies about 15-20 m above the current channel, on a south-sloping surface, about 3 m below the flattish, regional country surface formed by Upper Pleistocene sediments that flank the Nahal Be'er Sheva Valley.

This particular tent was selected for its relatively small size (area of about 80-100 m²), simple plan, and the access to information by the past inhabitant. The tent was comprised of one hemispherical "cell" and was inhabited by a Bedouin woman, aged 65-70, for a period of about 6 years. It was abandoned about 1.5 to 2 years prior to the time of sampling in August, 1989. A schematic rendering of the tent area and its components are shown in Figure 1.

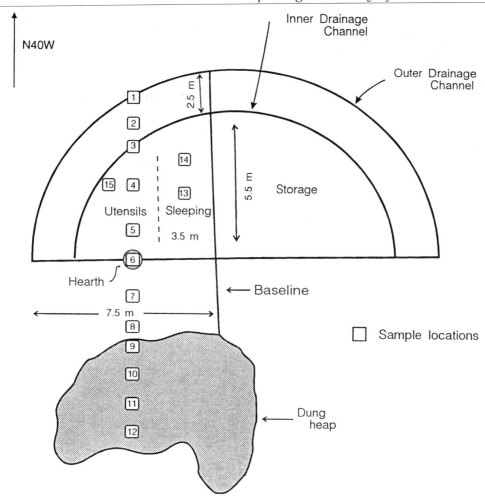

Figure 1. Generalized map of the Bedouin tent area used in this study, showing activity areas and sampling locales.

Sampling

Within the tent complex we endeavored to include in our samples the following features: a hearth used for cooking and warmth in winter, situated along the midline of the hemispherical tent area; a storage area used for utensils west of the hearth; the sleeping area situated in the eastern half of the tent; and an abandoned animal pen ~5 m south of the tent area that was used at the same time the tent was occupied. About 20 animals consisting of goats, sheep and cattle were kept in the pen at night. Remnants of the pen are characterized by concentrations of ash, charcoal, straw and fecal material; these accumulations begin roughly at the 9 m mark (Figure 1) and continue to the south (0 m mark), with the richest concentrations occurring at about the 2 m mark.

Additional observations indicate that in general, sediments are much softer outside the tent than inside. Moreover, at the time of occupation, the silty floor surface of the tent was purposefully compacted

and sprayed with water to keep dust down, a prevalent problem in this loessial terrain.

Samples were collected from the activity areas discussed above, at ~2 m intervals along a linear transect about 3.5 m west of the baseline (Figure 1). The transect started from the outer drainage channel that surrounds the tent, passed through the central hearth and continued to the dung concentration outside the tent area to the southeast. Additional samples were taken from other areas off the transect in order to ensure that all activity areas were sampled. All samples were collected intact, in their original context by a form of coring, using inverted aluminum soft-drink cans as corers, or by cutting out centimeter-size blocks that were wrapped in paper and masking tape to preserve their integrity.

A brief description of the samples follows:

TENT-1: From the outer drainage channel; soft, powdery, loose silt, noticeably darker than sterile loess deposits, and intimately mixed with fine rootlets and dung. Munsell color: 10YR6/3.

TENT-2: Sterile, hard, subangular-blocky silts from the area between the two drainage areas, still outside the confines of the tent. Munsell color: 10YR7/4.

TENT-3: From the inner drainage area; soft loose sediment, similar to that of TENT-1. Munsell color: 10YR6/3.

TENT-4: Angular blocky tan silt from undifferentiated activity area within the tent. Compact, with some very fine sand and possibly some fine charcoal integrated into the sample. Munsell color: 10YR6/4.

TENT-5: Compact, angular, blocky ashy silts resulting from ash being blown around by wind and then later compacted. Somewhat darker and greener color than sterile silts. Charcoal and ash are more abundant at surface. Munsell color: 10YR7/4.

TENT-6: From the central hearth, consisting of loose, powdery, ashy silt with charcoal dispersed throughout. Munsell color: 10YR7/4.

TENT-7: Taken from outside the confines of the tent, at edge of hearth area. The sediment is composed of compact tan silt with mottles of charcoal and organic matter in the upper part. Munsell color: 10YR5/4.

TENT-8: From outside the tent, between it and the dung accumulation area. Generally comprised of sterile, angular blocky silt, similar to that in sample TENT-2. At the top is a ~0.5 mm thick slaking crust. Munsell color: 10YR6/4.

TENT-9: At edge of dung accumulation area. Olive, soft powdery silt, with the upper 1 cm being slightly richer in organic matter, and consisting of a fluffy accumulation of stalks and stems of straw, and animal dung. Munsell color: 10YR6/4.

TENT-10: Within dung accumulation area. Dark brown, organic-rich silt, mixed with animal droppings and ash. Powdery and with little consistence. Munsell color: 10YR4/2.

TENT-11: Within dung accumulation area. Similar to TENT-10 but thicker and richer in organic matter; with ash, bone, and glass fragments. Munsell color: 10YR4/2.

TENT-12: Southern edge of dung accumulation area where organic-rich silt is much thinner (~5 cm) and sediments lighter in color; ash seems worked into matrix. Munsell color: 10YR4/3.

TENT-13: From sleeping area. Coarse, angular-blocky, dark brown silt, with organic matter/charcoal finely dispersed within matrix. Munsell color: 10YR6/4.

TENT-14: From sleeping area. Pale, tan, angular-blocky silt, with no traces of ash or organic matter. Munsell color: 10YR6/4.

TENT-15: From area where (cooking) utensils are kept. Sterile, angular-blocky tan silt, west of hearth.

Generally similar to sample TENT-2. Munsell color: 10YR7/3.

Sample Preparation, Treatment And Analysis

In the laboratory the samples were dried at 60⁰C for over 24 hours and impregnated under vacuum with polyester resin diluted with styrene. The hardened blocks were slabbed, and the slices were sent to the Laboratoire des Sols at the Institut National Agronomique (Grignon, France) where most were made into large (~14 x 7 cm) petrographic thin sections.

The thin sections were analyzed using two approaches. The first was qualitative, and involved micromorphological observation and description of the mineral and organic components of the samples at various scales, ranging in magnifications from 8x to 200x. Terminology and nomenclature follows that used by Bullock et al. (1986) and Courty et al. (1989), with semi-quantitative estimates based on visual charts presented in these works.

The second approach makes use of semi-automatic gray-scale image analysis in order to characterize the fabrics, and to quantify some of the constituents, particularly the size, shape, and orientation of voids (cf. Habesch 1990). Based on studies of soil compaction (e.g., Jongerius 1970, 1983; McSweeney et al. 1988; Murphy et al. 1977) we believed that voids would offer the best parameters for evaluating anthropogenic impacts on the living floor. Image analysis was performed at a magnification of 5x, using a Javelin CCD video camera, an Imaging Technology PCPlus frame grabber, and OPTIMAS (version 2.0) image analysis software (Bioscan, Inc.), running under Microsoft Windows (version 3.0).

Each thin section was sampled systematically upwards on a 1 cm grid, with a minimum of five frames per section. The images were captured under plane- and cross- polarised light. Each was filtered to enhance the mid-range of the gray scale. We subtracted the plane-polarised image from the cross-polarised image to isolate the voids and to remove opaque grains that otherwise would be mistaken as voids. A gray-scale threshold was then selected that included the void areas (light) and excluded the non-void material (dark). Finally, a binary filter converted the image to a simple black (non-void) and white (void) image.

For each sample we attempted to measure as many voids as possible, typically between 800 to 900 per image. Although we measured several parameters (e.g., void length, angle, center of gravity, circularity), for the purpose of the present paper we concentrated on breadth and area of the voids because these exhibited the most variation in our preliminary analyses. Measurements were imported into a spreadsheet for statistical analysis. The geometric means obtained using Statgraphics (version 4.0) were then displayed graphically using Surfer (version 4.0, Golden Software) (Figures 32 and 33). The significance of differences between void area and breadth populations within each sample was calculated using the Kolmogorov-Smirnov two-sample test (Siegel 1956) (Tables 1 and 2).

Micromorphological Descriptions

All of the samples examined possessed approximately the same constituents, although their proportions, geometrical arrangement (i.e., fabric) and porosity varied markedly. These components can best be considered in terms of inorganic and organic material and can be categorized as follows:

Inorganic Components

Quartz silt/fine sand: ~40-80 μm; angular to subrounded and rounded; traces of feldspar are included in this category. This material is ultimately derived from aeolian dust or the Pleistocene fluviatile silts that underlie the tent.

Calcareous silt : ~40-80 μm, composed of micrite (microcrystalline calcite), coarser crystalline calcite, foraminifera, aggregates of ash, and decomposed limestone. They are also derived from aeolian dust and local Pleistocene silts.

Quartz and chert sand: These are well rounded grains, ~250-600 μm in diameter that occur in low amounts (~1%).

Heavy minerals: These are confined to the silt fraction, and are similar to those found in the underlying sediments and those elsewhere in the Negev. The minerals include hornblende, zircon, rutile, glauconite, and augite.

Calcareous nodules: These are rounded sand and granule size aggregates consisting of grains of silt size quartz, feldspar and heavy minerals in a micritic matrix. They represent reworking of calcic soil nodules derived from Pleistocene sediments in the region.

Snail fragments: Sand size, tabular to arcuate grains composed of fibrous aragonite; occur as traces (<1%).

Organic Components

These are represented by various types of plant tissues and seeds. They are generally elongate, splintery shreds that vary in color from pale yellow and yellow brown, to brown and reddish brown; some charred pieces are found, occasionally with ash adhering to their surface. They are for the most part non- or weakly birefringent, and vary in size between silt and sand size remnants. Rounded wads and felt-like masses of vegetal matter are indicative of herbivore dung. Depending upon their relative proportion in the sediment, the organic components often provide a fluffy, open structure (cf. below results of image analysis).

In the following section we describe and characterize micromorphologically each of the samples. It should be noted that there were many similarities between samples and many of the samples exhibited complex fabrics (e.g., TENT-10, TENT-11 from the dung heap). Consequently, some of the samples are described together. In cases with complex fabrics, photographs help convey the essential aspects of each of the samples.

Drainage Channels

TENT-1 (outer drainage channel, Figures 1 and 3; Plates 1 and 2) and TENT-3 (inner drainage channel; Figures 6 and 7): These samples are characterized by an open, spongy microstructure with a total porosity of ~40-50%, and composed of calcitic and quartz silt intermixed with shredded organic (vegetal) matter. The coarse inorganic fraction is composed predominantly of silt-size quartz (~15-20%), and micritric and sparitic (some foraminifera) calcite (~5-10%). Also present are traces of sand size quartz and chert, snails, heavy minerals and sand to granule size grains of calcic nodules; solitary grains include one fragment each of bone and broken ceramic. Sand and silt size vegetal fragments (~20-25%), some burnt, are generally elongated and oriented parallel to the surface; locally, they are arranged in beds separated by more mineral-rich laminae. Several are remains of dung pellets.

Silt size calcite of the fine fraction forms a relatively minor component (~2%). Traces of fine silt size calcareous ash are also present, and are most clearly displayed in association with charred vegetal matter.

Several fragments of broken slaking crusts are prominent just below the present-day surface (Plate 2). These fragments are characterized by thinly laminated and commonly graded fine calcareous silt and coarser quartz silt, and are oriented obliquely to the surface.

TENT-3 is overall similar to Tent-1 but has a greater number of seeds and an overall greater proportion of quartz and calcareous silt in which shredded vegetal

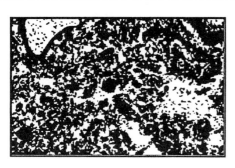

Figure 2. Binary image (1f6) from upper part of sample TENT-1 (outer drainage channel). Note general openness of the sample. See text for details relating to methods used to obtain images.

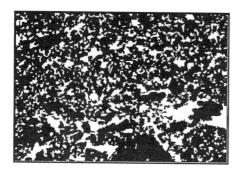

Figure 3. Binary image (1f5) from lower part of sample TENT-1 (outer drainage channel).

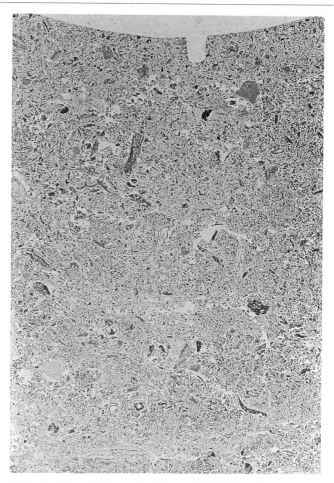

Plate 1. Macrophotograph of sample TENT-1 showing open, sponge-like microstructure and high content of vegetal matter. Plane polarized light (PPL). Length of field is 6 cm.

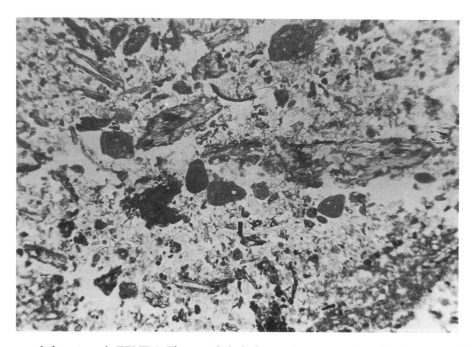

Plate 2. Photomicrograph from sample TENT-1. The rounded, darker grains are remains of carbonate nodules. Note the fragment of slaking crust in the lower right corner that exhibits faint but distinct bedding. Horizontal field of view is 1.7 mm.

matter is imbedded. In addition, there are a number of larger chamber-like channels between horizontal, elliptical peds.

Inter-channel Area

The inter-channel area, represented by TENT-2 (Figures 4 and 5), consists of compact calcareous quartz silt with inclusions of vegetal matter. The microstructure (porosity of ~10-20%), is a fine crack with numerous vesicles and voids occupied by modern root fragments. The upper 1 cm is locally richer in vegetal fragments and is more porous.

Other quantitatively minor constituents consist of snail fragments, traces of quartz and chert sand, solitary grains of bright terra rossa clay (probably burned) and bone, and reworked calcic nodules. Some of these nodules are coated with a ~150 μm thick mixture of quartz silt and fine, dusty calcareous silt. Vegetal matter is dispersed throughout the sample (~1%), but is concentrated in the upper left hand portion. The fine fraction consists of calcareous silt and locally shows signs of being washed, resulting in

areas that are depleted in fine calcareous silt but richer in quartz silt. Associated with these are prominent traces of broken remnants of slaking crusts, particularly in the upper 10 mm of the thin section.

General Activity Area

TENT-4 (Figures 8 and 9; Plates 3a and 3b): Compact quartzitic and calcareous silt with ~5-10% porosity resulting from a vertical system of elongate, elliptical to circular pores produced by roots. The fine silty calcareous fine fraction is more prominent in this sample (~25-30%). Quartz sand, snails, silt size bone, and fragments of limestone appear in trace amounts, whereas calcareous nodules reach ~2-5%. Numerous slaking crusts (~ 0.8 mm thick up to ~1.2 mm wide) occur, especially in the upper part of the sample. As in TENT-2, washed zones are developed with better sorting expressed by the presence of quartz silt and the lack of finer calcareous silt. Organic matter is relatively rare (<1%), being finely comminuted (fine sand size) and well incorporated into the matrix.

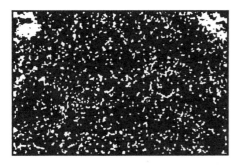

Figure 4. Binary image (2f3) from upper part of sample TENT-2 (inter drainage area). Note the uniformity of the voids, which are generally fine.

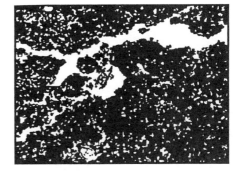

Figure 5. Binary image (2f1) from lower part of sample TENT-2 (inter drainage area).

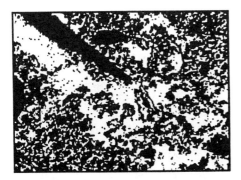

Figure 6. Binary image (3f5) from upper part of sample TENT-3 (inner drainage channel). Note similarity to upper sample from outer drainage channel.

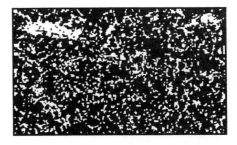

Figure 7. Binary image (3f1) from lower part of sample TENT-3 (inner drainage channel). Compare to lower sample from outer drainage channel.

Hearth and Surroundings

TENT-5 (Figures 10 and 11) is troublesome to characterize due to its complexity. It is comprised of compact, massive silt and is overall similar to TENT-4 but contains many more rounded sand and granule size reworked calcic nodules and little void space, with traces of pottery fragments. There is also a high incidence of rounding in general, including aggregates of organic matter and dung, and aggregates of coarse and fine silt. Many of these are coated with ~100 μm thick mantles of fine and coarse silt.

Local domains of fine calcareous silt and ash, mixed in with areas of quartz silt devoid of fine fraction, that probably result from washing or biological activity, which is represented by abundant micropassage features. Numerous fragments of slaking crusts are also present, and tend to be well rounded.

TENT-6 (Figures 12 and 13; Plate 4) is difficult to describe due to its complexity. The thin section is characterized by a very heterogeneous composition, and loose, aggregated appearance with an abundance of linear vegetal shreds in the top 20 mm. Snail shells, seeds, charcoal, fragmented vegetal remains, and whole sheep/goat droppings are relatively abundant.

The fine fraction is ashy and composed of fine calcareous silt, locally in the form of disrupted bands interbedded with charcoal and pieces of vegetal matter.

TENT-7 (Figures 14 and 15) is characterized by finely laminated, compact ashy silt with washed areas, and numerous slaking crusts that parallel the present-day surface; there are also some reworked, rounded fragments of slaking crusts in the lower part of the sample. These are interbedded with fine, elongated scraps of fresh vegetal matter. The upper part is particularly dense and is rich in finely disseminated to amorphous organic matter that is locally well incorporated into the matrix.

Area Between Tent and Dung Heap

TENT-8 (Figures 16 and 17) overall is quite similar to sample TENT-2, being a compact, heterogeneous mixture of quartz and calcareous silt in a fine calcareous silty matrix with relatively low amounts of vegetal debris and only traces of charcoal. Porosity (~5-10%) is mostly in the form of fine joints and large vughs associated with roots. Material is commonly

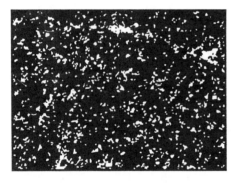

Figure 8. Binary image (4f4) from upper part of sample TENT-4 (general activity area). Note similarity with TENT-2 sample.

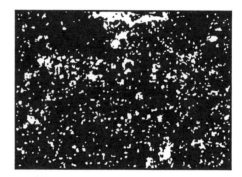

Figure 9. Binary image (4f3) from lower part of sample TENT-4.

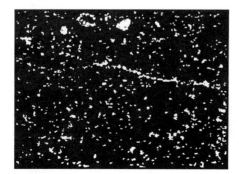

Figure 10. Binary image (5f3) from upper part of TENT-5 (near hearth).

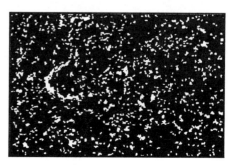

Figure 11. Binary image (5f1) from lower part of TENT-5.

aggregated into rounded, sand- to granule-size pieces, with numerous disrupted and intact slaking crusts, particularly at present-day surface; some are oriented vertically to the modern surface. The matrix is locally washed and several micropassage features can be observed. Traces of snail shells and one bone fragment occur.

Dung Heap and Surroundings

TENT- 9 (Figures 18 and 19; Plate 5) is comprised essentially of two parts. The lower 6.5 cm consists of the same material as that found in samples TENT-2, TENT-8, etc., including washed and bioturbated material, disrupted slaking crusts and vertically elongated pores due to modern roots. Vegetal remains are relatively rare, although some decomposed fecal pellets of goats/sheep are incorporated into the matrix.

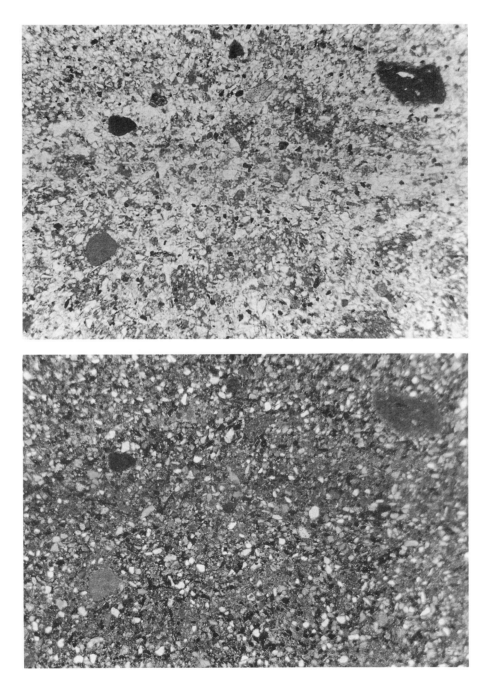

Plate 3. Photomicrographs of sample TENT-4; a) is in PPL and b) in cross polarized light (XPL). Visible here is the silty calcareous and quartzitic matrix with rounded sand size grains composed mostly of reworked carbonate nodules.

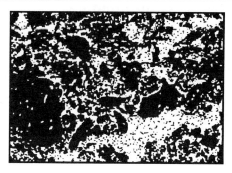

Figure 12. Binary image (6f5) from upper part of TENT-6 (hearth). Note the amount of large voids.

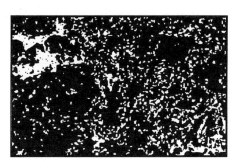

Figure 13. Binary image (6f1) from lower part of TENT-6.

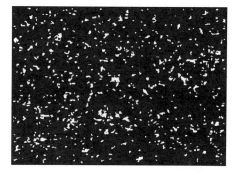

Figure 14. Binary image (7f3) from upper part of TENT-7 (south of hearth area).

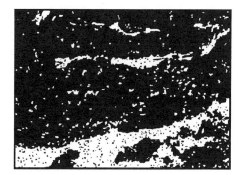

Figure 15. Binary image of (7f1) from lower part of TENT-7.

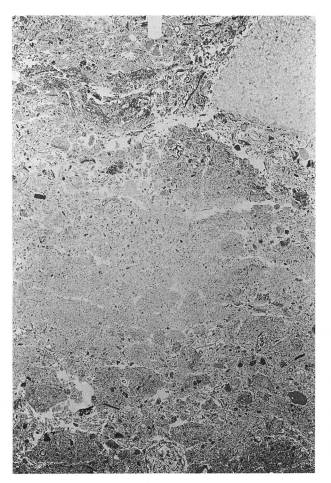

Plate 4. Macrophotograph of sample TENT-6 (hearth). Note the heterogeneous composition and the rounded aggregates of the ashy calcareous silty matrix; a goat dropping is illustrated at the bottom of the photograph. Long, vertical field of view is 7.5 cm.

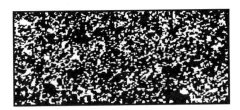

Figure 16.Binary image of (8f4) from upper part of TENT-8 (north of dung heap).

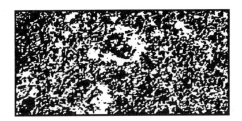

Figure 17. Binary image of (8f1) from lower part of TENT-8.

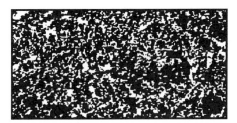

Figure 18. Binary image of (9f6) from upper part of TENT-9 (north end of dung heap). Note subdued spongy nature of sample.

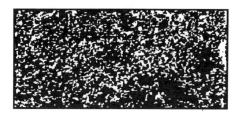

Figure 19. Binary image of (9f1) from lower part of TENT-9.

The upper 1.5 cm is markedly different and the contact with the underlying material is sharp (Plate 5). It is characterized by a loose (~30% porosity), spongy framework of quartz and calcareous silt, and silty aggregates (~30%), as well as vegetal fragments, rounded, sand size remnants of goat/sheep dung and seeds (~40%). The fine calcareous silty matrix/fine fraction is locally washed and absent from this upper part.

TENT-10 (Figures 20 and 21; Plate 6) displays a similar zonation as that in sample TENT-9, although the upper cultural part is thicker (~4-5 cm thick), and is much richer in charcoal (locally up to ~5%) and ash. The uppermost 1 cm is composed solely of elongated shreds of vegetal fragments that produce a spongy structure (Plate 6). The lower part has a coarse subrounded structure and is composed of aggregates of ashy quartz and calcareous silt. Vegetal material and charcoal are rare and well incorporated into the matrix which is extensively bioturbated and washed; slaking crusts are highly disrupted. A few bone fragments were observed.

Between these two zones there is a ~1.5 cm thick transitional band composed of relatively compact ashy silt with finely disseminated charcoal and reddened (burned) dung and vegetal fragments.

TENT-11 (Figures 22 and 23) represents a continuation of the trend found in sample TENT-9. It is comprised predominantly (~8.5 cm thick) of 'cultural material' and ~1 cm thick of more sterile silty deposits. The character of the upper part of the

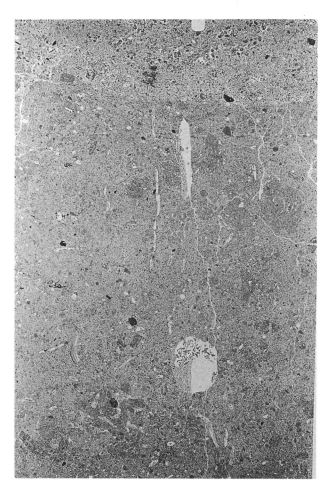

Plate 5. Macrophotograph of sample TENT-9, from edge of dung area. Note the spongy porosity and the lack of finer silts in the upper 1.5 cm. The lower part is more compact and contains several aggregates and fragments of slaking crusts. Long, vertical field of view is 7.5 cm.

sample is also somewhat different from those described previously.

There is a great deal of heterogeneity and an abundance of aggregated fragments; the fabric is quite fluffy and loose. Charcoal is widely distributed throughout the thin section (~10%) and occurs both as finely comminuted and coarser granule-size grains. There is a greater incidence of reddening (burning) of fragments of organic matter, grains of silt, calcic nodules and pottery.

TENT-12 (Figures 24 and 25; Plates 7 and 8) is similar to others from the dung heap area, although the 'cultural layer' is ~3.5 cm thick. Notable features include a platy structure, a rounded grain of *kurkar* (Pleistocene calcareous sandstone), ~1 cm diameter, a surface layer typified by loose, mm size vegetal fragments. These become successively more fine grained below the surface. The lower, 'sterile' part is partially aggregated and exhibits a few micropassage features. Vegetal fragments and dung are relatively rare, but when present are well integrated into the matrix.

Sleeping Area

TENT-13 (Figures 35 and 36) consists of compact, massive quartz and calcareous silt with a well defined slaking crust at the surface and broken crusts within the matrix. Void space is provided principally by modern roots that produce round to elliptical, vertically oriented voids and channels. Additional components are snail fragments (~2%) and rounded calcic nodules (~2%); vegetal fragments and dung are quite rare (<1%) and are typically sand size. They are well integrated into the matrix along with angular, sand size fragments of charcoal that are distributed throughout the slide. Several bone fragments were observed. The matrix is locally washed, with partial removal of the fine fraction.

TENT-14 (Figures 26 and 27) is virtually identical to TENT-13, with numerous washed domains and broken slaking crusts, and several bone fragments.

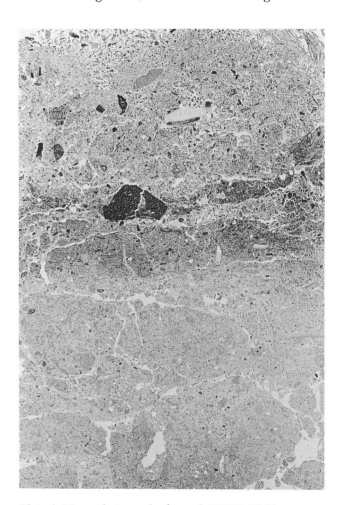

Plate 6. Macrophotograph of sample TENT-10 (dung area). Note the spongy upper cm composed of loose vegetal fragments. This overlies a denser and darker band composed of ashy silt with charcoal. The lower part is characterized by rounded aggregates of ashy quartz and calcareous silt. Long, vertical field of view is 7.5 cm.

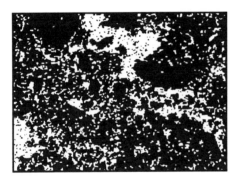

Figure 20. Binary image of (10f7) from upper part of TENT-10 (dung area). Note openness of sample; cf. Plate 6.

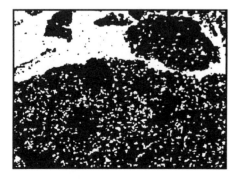

Figure 21. Binary image of (10f1) from lower part of TENT-10. Although a binomial image, the aggregate form of the sediments from this lower part are clearly visible (cf. Plate 6).

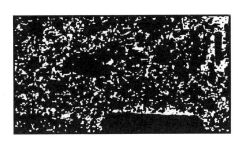

Figure 22. Binary image of (11f5) from upper part of TENT-11 (dung area).

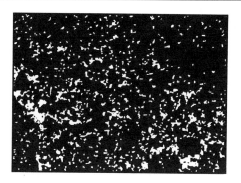

Figure 23. Binary image of (11f1) from lower part of TENT-11.

Figure 24. Binary image of (12f4) from upper part of TENT-12 (dung area); cf. Plate 7. Note the abundance of vegetal fragments and the spongy structure.

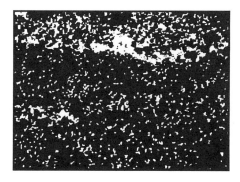

Figure 25. Binary image of (12f1) from lower part of TENT-12; cf. Plate 7. The compactness of the more sterile silts is evident in the lower part of this image.

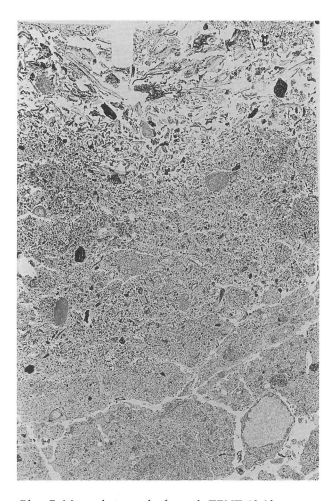

Plate 7. Macrophotograph of sample TENT-12 (dung area). Note the similar zonation to that in photo 5, and the coarse blocky structure of the lower, 'sterile' part of the slide. The light coated grain in the lower right is composed of kurkar (Pleistocene calcareous sandstone). Long, vertical field of view is 4.8 cm.

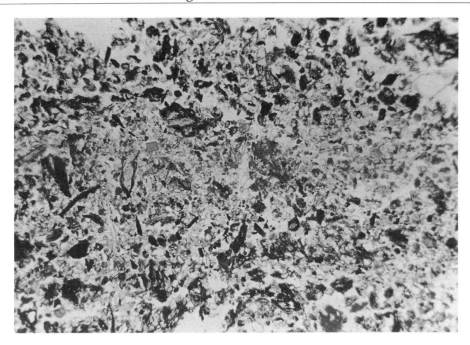

Plate 8. Photomicrograph from upper part sample TENT-12 (dung area) showing intermixing of shreds of charcoal with calcareous and quartzitic silt. Horizontal, field of view is ~1.4 mm.

Kitchen Area

TENT-15 (Figures 30 and 31; Plate 9) is similar to TENT-13 and TENT-14, but more massive and compact, with little pore space. It is lacking in slaking crusts, either at the surface or as fragments at depth. Traces of charcoal occur as well as vegetal and dung fragments that are ~1 mm in diameter.

Discussion Of Micromorphological Observations

Although the above descriptions suggest a high degree of variability between samples, there are certain characteristics that typify specific groups of samples or kinds of materials. First, there are samples that are comprised essentially of the loessial substrate, not in association with the hearth or the dung heap or from the drainage channels. These samples TENT-2, TENT-4, TENT-13, TENT-14 and TENT-15, are characterized by compact, massive quartzitic and calcareous silts and calcic nodules and numerous whole or disrupted slaking crusts. Whole crusts are particularly well developed at the upper surface of the samples, though fragments are scattered throughout the profiles.

Remains of these crusts can be interpreted in two ways. One is that they represent a series of formerly exposed surfaces that were buried in the past and have been subsequently disrupted by a variety of means (cracking, desiccation, trodding by animals, human treading, soil bioturbation) not necessarily related to the present occupation of the tent. Another interpretation is that they are more or less coeval with the tent occupation and depict a permanent and stable surface cover in the absence of sedimentation, on which repeated turbation (expressed by micropassage features) of the substrate disrupted the slaking crusts that periodically formed.

Porosity is generally low, and results from roots, presumably of grassy vegetation; additional porosity is tied to planar voids (e.g., crack structure) probably due to wetting/drying, and similar to those found in the underlying Pleistocene silts.

'Occupation deposits' can be divided into two types: directly 'anthropogenic' (e.g., hearth), and faunally related (e.g., dung heap). Anthropogenic deposits are essentially those associated with the structural elements of the site, such as the hearth area and the channels. In the former case, the composition and structure of the material is a direct result of human activity. Here the sediments are richer in calcareous ash, charcoal and vegetative matter. More strikingly, they exhibit a high proportion of aggregation of the silty matrix, presumably by bioturbation; in certain cases (e.g., sample TENT-5), there is also a high degree of compaction.

The channel samples (TENT-1 and TENT-3) have a very distinctive composition and structure. They are characterized by an abundance of fresh vegetal frag-

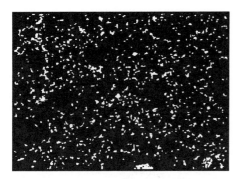

Figure 26. Binary image of (13f4) from upper part of TENT-13 (sleeping area). Note overall uniformity of voids.

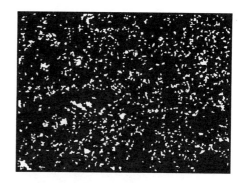

Figure 27. Binary image of (13f2) from lower part of TENT-13.

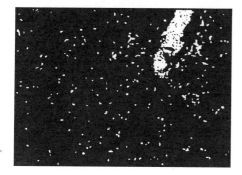

Figure 28. Binary image of (14f2) from lower part of TENT-14 (sleeping area). Note similarity with TENT-13.

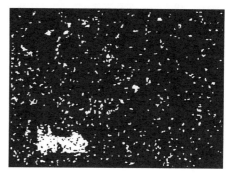

Figure 29. Binary image of (14f1) from lower part of TENT-14.

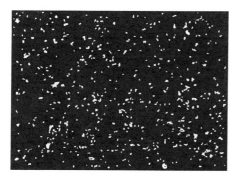

Figure 30. Binary image of (15f2) from lower part of TENT-15 (kitchen area). Compare with compactness exhibited in macrophotograph (Plate 9).

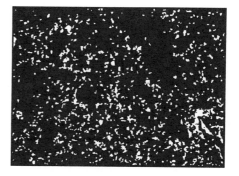

Figure 31. Binary image of (15f4) from lower part of TENT-15. Note uniformity of void size and distribution.

ments that are evenly distributed throughout the sample. Moreover, the structure is open and homogeneous throughout. Of note is the absence of layering, which one might expect if the channel was periodically filled with water and eventually filled-in through natural sedimentation. Instead, the homogeneity of the channel fill implies that it was deposited relatively rapidly, perhaps under dry conditions, by airborne mobilization of material, particularly the vegetal fragments.

Faunally-related accumulations are essentially confined to the area of the dung heap (samples TENT-9, TENT-10, TENT-11, TENT-12). They are typified by aggregated structures and sub-horizontal planar voids that conform to crude layering. The lower layers tend to be more compact and generally contain coarser particles. Upwards, the material is gradually more finely comminuted. The top centimeter is composed of loose, coarse, well-sorted vegetal fragments, reminiscent of the channel deposits. The

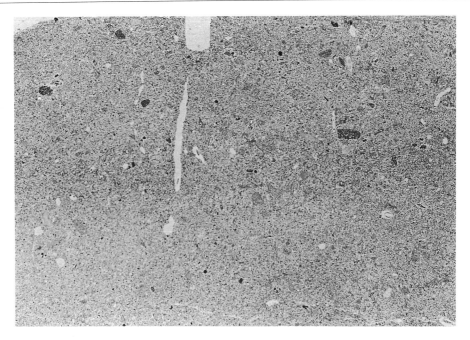

Plate 9. Macrophotograph of TENT-15 (kitchen area). Note massiveness and compactness of sample, and overall fine grain, with only traces of charcoal or vegetal matter. Vertical field of view is 5.5 cm.

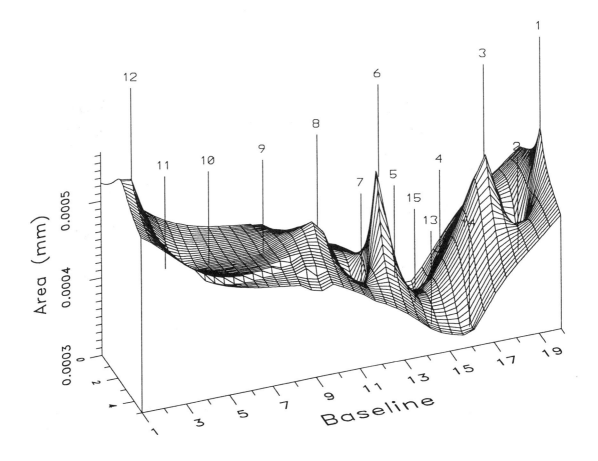

Figure 32. Net diagram showing the distribution of void areas of upper (surface) samples across the site.

composition of the faunal layers is characterized by an abundance of charcoal and organic matter (some burned), ash, coarse lithic elements (e.g., calcic nodules and kurkar) and pottery.

The lower boundaries, between the dark faunal layers and the lighter sterile substrates are generally sharp and smooth, and less frequently, abrupt and wavy (Courty et al. 1989:33).

Image Analysis Results

We selected the uppermost and lowermost images (Figures 2 through 31) from each thin section profile in order to determine whether the inter thin section variation (i.e., from one sample to another across the tent site) is likely to be significant in terms of activity associated with the tent occupation. Although images intermediate between the upper and lower parts of each profile were captured, and their statistical attributes examined, they have not been included in the final analysis. In taking only the uppermost and lowermost images, we aimed to examine broad trends in the structure of the substrate by comparing the least disrupted part of each profile (lowermost) with the part of the profile that is most recently affected by human occupation (uppermost). We charted the spatial distribution of void area for both the surface and basal samples across the tent area, in which void area is used to represent void size regardless of shape (Figures 32 and 33); plots of void breadth were similar. For the most part, the maximum lengths of the voids lie more or less horizontal, so void breadth is used as an indication of compaction in the vertical direction. We also graphed the surface across the tent site represented by differences between the upper and the lower void area values (Figure 34). The results show that the differences are greatest in profiles from the northern part of the animal pen, the hearth, and the inner and outer drainage channels. They are least for the inter-channel area, the general utility area, and moderate for the sleeping areas.

For each image we calculated the mean and standard deviations of the void areas (see chapter Appendix) and breadths, and determined the likelihood that the populations are statistically different for each sample. Tables 1 and 2 show that the differences between the void populations of the upper and lower samples are statistically significant for the areas in TENT-TENT-3, TENT-4, TENT-6, TENT-7, TENT-10, TENT-12 and TENT-15; and for the breadths in TENT-3, TENT-4, TENT-6, TENT-7, TENT-9, TENT-10, TENT-11, TENT-12 and TENT-15. It should be noted, however, that for some of the samples (e.g., TENT-3), the difference is close to the critical value. These data include all of the voids measured in the image. For

comparison, we also calculated the significance for voids greater than 30 µm, since we believed that this marked the cutoff between the smaller, packing pores and voids produced by roots, and the larger voids associated with depositional or anthropogenic activities associated with the dung heap or hearth, for example. These are significantly different for areas in TENT-3, -6 and -12; and for breadths in TENT-2, -6, -10, -12 and -15. The greater significance when all voids are taken into account reflects, in part, the increased sample size. However, small voids may be more susceptible to pressure (e.g., closed) from surface activity or infilling through water spraying than larger voids. In other words, a given amount of compression will have a greater net effect on a small void than on a large one. This has to be offset against the fact that packing voids in a framework supported by grains of inorganic material will have to be infilled through translocation since the framework material will not allow them to be collapsed into smaller, disconnected voids. Furthermore, if the section is dominated by large voids, their collapse may preclude any change in the sizes of smaller voids.

We charted the deviations between the maximum observed difference and the critical difference values for both areas and breadths (Tables 1 and 2) in order to visualize the degree of discrimination between the upper and lower void populations across the site (Figures 35 and 36). Thus a negative number indicates that the upper and lower pairs are not significantly different. The surface chart of void areas over the tent site, shows that the upper part of the inner drainage channel is relatively open, but that there is a slight decrease in surface void area in the sterile area between the channels and in voids in the upper part of the outer drainage channel. Voids in the upper part of the profile are smaller in size in the kitchen, and to a lesser extent in the sleeping area, compared with the adjacent general activity area. The upper profile voids are much smaller than lower profile voids either side of the hearth, while upper profile voids are larger than lower profile voids within the hearth. Upper profile void sizes increase over their lower profile counterparts as one moves into the animal pen. This pattern implies that smaller voids occur in the upper part of the profiles, compared to the lower parts of the same profiles, in areas that encountered maximum activity around the hearth and in the kitchen and sleeping area. The size reduction may have resulted from the water spraying of the ground such as by filling the voids with finer material, or through compaction of the voids by trampling; the lack of observed void coatings or infillings supports the latter hypothesis. Upper profile voids are larger than lower profile voids where the presence of ash or organic

Table 1. Tent Final Kolmogorov-Smirnov Two-Sample Test Results.

Full set of samples (i.e. maximum n)		n	Max Diff.	Critical Diff. 95%	Diff. Populations	Description
Tent 1	Area	972	0.014403	0.061690853	NO	Outer drainage channel
	Breadth	972	0.026721	0.061690853	NO	Outer drainage channel
Tent 2	Area	828	0.065217	0.066840353	NO	Sterile
	Breadth	828	0.038647	0.066840353	NO	Sterile
Tent 3	Area	988	0.065789	0.061189293	YES	Inner drainage channel
	Breadth	989	0.07179	0.06115835	YES	Inner drainage channel
Tent 4	Area	793	0.103405	0.068299467	YES	Undifferentiated activity area
	Breadth	793	0.069357	0.068299467	YES	Undifferentiated activity area
Tent 5	Area	679	0.022091	0.073810648	NO	Edge of hearth
	Breadth	697	0.025037	0.072851335	NO	Edge of hearth
Tent 6	Area	914	0.112691	0.063618117	YES	Center of hearth
	Breadth	914	0.125821	0.063618117	YES	Center of hearth
Tent 7	Area	585	0.095726	0.079519927	YES	Outside tent edge of hearth
	Breadth	585	0.119658	0.079519927	YES	Outside tent edge of hearth
Tent 8	Area	962	0.04158	0.062010662	NO	Sterile between tent and dung
	Breadth	962	0.046778	0.062010662	NO	Sterile between tent and dung
Tent 9	Area	983	0.0539166	0.061344714	NO	Edge of dung heap
	Breadth	983	0.0813835	0.061344714	YES	Edge of dung heap
Tent 10	Area	898	0.079065	0.064182368	YES	Dung heap
	Breadth	898	0.066815	0.064182368	YES	Dung heap
Tent 11	Area	786	0.064885	0.068602925	NO	Dung heap
	Breadth	786	0.085242	0.068602925	YES	Dung heap
Tent 12	Area	602	0.290698	0.078389097	YES	Southern edge of dung heap
	Breadth	602	0.297342	0.078389097	YES	Southern edge of dung heap
Tent 13	Area	848	0.035377	0.066047439	NO	Sleeping area
	Breadth	848	0.03066	0.066047439	NO	Sleeping area
Tent 14	Area	309	0.071197	0.109414446	NO	Sleeping area
	Breadth	309	0.058252	0.109414446	NO	Sleeping area
Tent 15	Area	559	0.184258	0.08134821	YES	Cooking utensils
	Breadth	559	0.146691	0.08134821	YES	Cooking utensils

Table 2. Tent Final Kolmogorov-Smirnov Two-Sample Test Results.

Large voids samples (i.e. >0.03mm dia.)		n	Max Diff.	Critical Diff. 95%	Diff. Populations	Description
Tent 1	Area	282	0.049645	0.1145327	NO	Outer drainage channel
	Breadth	374	0.069519	0.099453	NO	Outer drainage channel
Tent 2	Area	110	0.090909	0.1833824	NO	Sterile
	Breadth	206	0.135922	0.1340048	YES	Sterile
Tent 3	Area	236	0.127119	0.1251981	YES	Inner drainage channel
	Breadth	328	0.10061	0.1061982	NO	Inner drainage channel
Tent 4	Area	131	0.152672	0.1680422	NO	Undifferentiated activity area
	Breadth	178	0.08427	0.1441597	NO	Undifferentiated activity area
Tent 5	Area	92	0.076087	0.2005211	NO	Edge of hearth
	Breadth	142	0.042254	0.1614023	NO	Edge of hearth
Tent 6	Area	173	0.236994	0.1462281	YES	Center of hearth
	Breadth	250	0.164	0.1216421	YES	Center of hearth
Tent 7	Area	89	0.101124	0.2038726	NO	Outside tent edge of hearth
	Breadth	138	0.108696	0.1637248	NO	Outside tent edge of hearth
Tent 8	Area	254	0.114173	0.1206805	NO	Sterile between tent and dung
	Breadth	333	0.081081	0.1053979	NO	Sterile between tent and dung
Tent 9	Area	251	0.0996016	0.121399541	NO	Edge of dung heap
	Breadth	340	0.0823529	0.104307238	NO	Edge of dung heap
Tent 10	Area	137	0.145985	0.1643212	NO	Dung heap
	Breadth	202	0.163366	0.1353251	YES	Dung heap
Tent 11	Area	139	0.057554	0.1631348	NO	Dung heap
	Breadth	198	0.090909	0.1366851	NO	Dung heap
Tent 12	Area	54	0.296296	0.2617321	YES	Southern edge of dung heap
	Breadth	96	0.197917	0.1962991	YES	Southern edge of dung heap
Tent 13	Area	95	0.084211	0.1973295	NO	Sleeping area
	Breadth	159	0.069182	0.15253	NO	Sleeping area
Tent 14	Area	28	0.178571	0.3634753	NO	Sleeping area
	Breadth	35	0.142857	0.3251022	NO	Sleeping area
Tent 15	Area	42	0.166667	0.2967763	NO	Cooking utensils
	Breadth	68	0.25	0.2332381	YES	Cooking utensils

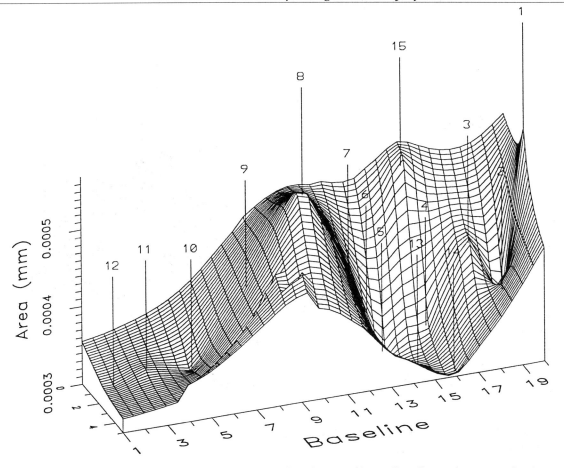

Figure 33. Net diagram showing the distribution of void areas of lower (basal) samples across the site.

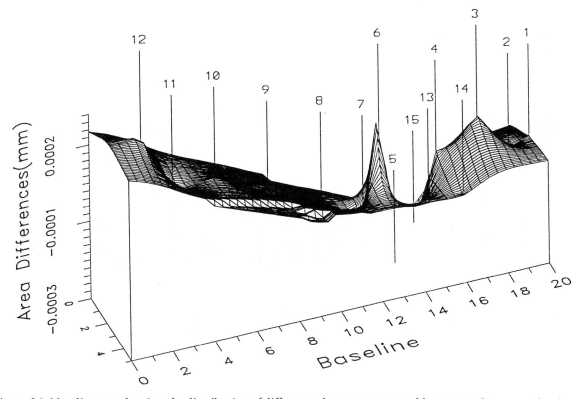

Figure 34. Net diagram showing the distribution of differences between upper and lower samples across the site.

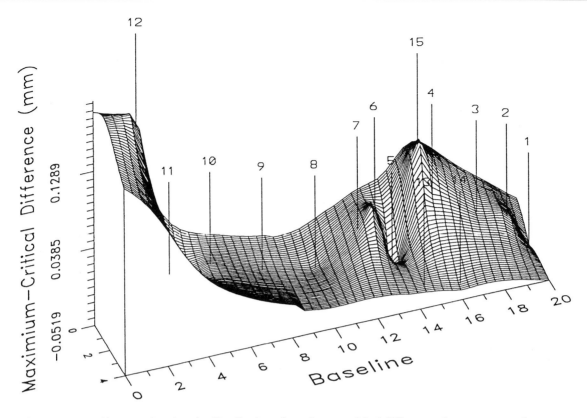

Figure 35. Net diagram showing the distribution of maximum-critical differences between upper-lower mean areas for each sample locality.

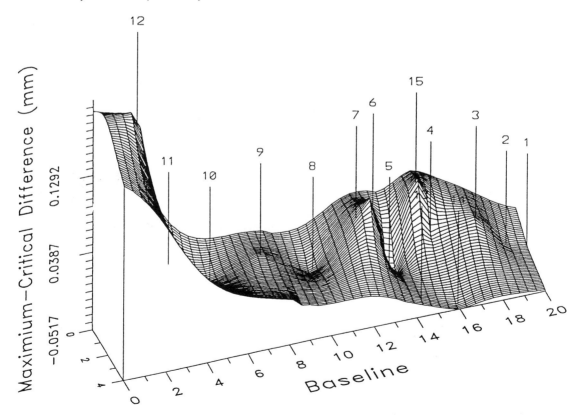

Figure 36. Net diagram showing the distribution of maximum-critical differences between upper-lower mean breadths for each sample locality.

matter have formed an open structure in the upper part of the profile.

The areal distribution of differences in the breadth of voids within the profile of each thin section (not shown) is similar to that for void area, but compaction of upper profile voids compared to lower profile voids is more sharply defined. Here, the open microstructure in the upper part of the profile of the animal pen and the hearth, and indeed the inner channel, is clearly distinguished. In contrast, upper profile voids are more compacted than lower profile voids between the two drainage channels, around the hearth, and between the tent and the animal pen, that is, at the entrance to the tent. This pattern indicates that compaction can be detected in the microstructure of floor deposits and, if adequately mapped, the pattern can be used to identify areas of relatively high activity. This assumes that the voids reflect mostly the activity of humans/animals at the site rather than postdepositional processes such as bioturbation.

Discussion

The micromorphological analyses (both the qualitative observations and quantitative image analyses) show that there are clear differences both within and between the soil thin sections. This is reflected in both the composition and texture of the samples. In layers where 'cultural effects' appear to be limited (sleeping areas, general activity areas, the kitchen, or the from the silty base of most samples) the samples are generally compact quartzitic and calcareous silts, with relatively low proportions of vegetal fragments and charcoal; the materials are generally compact with microstructures generally typified by fine fracture planes, and biopores produced by grassy roots. Measurements demonstrated that overall, these samples had uniformly relatively small void sizes from top to bottom.

In the more visible cultural units on the other hand (hearth and dung heap samples), the sediments were much more open, a feature related to the increased amount of vegetal matter, charcoal and ash; they also display a greater degree of aggregation, presumably as a result of turbation. Quantitative analyses bear this out, and in these cultural units the upper organic rich samples have larger and broader voids than the generally 'sterile' substrates.

These results appear to come out in spite of a number of methodological problems that were encountered in this study and that no doubt contributed a certain amount of 'noise' to the data. This includes problems of scale, both in terms of field sampling, but more critically, in terms of the captured images: a typical thin section encompasses between 20

to 40 cm2, of which each image is ~10-6 mm^2. This issue was addressed by the large number of voids that were measured. Since the thin sections are approximately 30μm thick no voids <30 μm in diameter were considered due to the risk of statistical error. Table 2 shows that when considering only voids larger than 30μm there are significant differences between upper and lower void populations in the inter-channel sterile (TENT-2), the inner drainage channel, the hearth, the dung heap and the kitchen area. Most of these differences reflect the open character of the organically rich deposits (the hearth and the dung heap) rather than the presence of compaction in areas that are liable to have been trampled. The additional information supplied by including voids smaller than 30μm does approximately follow the expected trend for predicted compaction and, thus, the smaller voids appear to be more sensitive indicators of compaction than larger voids. Although more significant differences in void populations greater than 30μm in size would have been desirable, the presented data suggest that the magnitude of living-floor compaction, on this type of lithological substrate, is such that it can only be studied morphologically at the microscopic scale, even though it may be sensed by 'feel' during excavation.

Genuine depositional processes (i.e., vertical accumulation of material and not *in situ* reworking) are exhibited mostly in the dung heap and channel areas. In the dung heap area different materials accumulated by a variety of processes: goat dung built up as a result of penning of animals. Although much of this has decayed, distinct, intact pellets are common in thin section; bone, charcoal, ash, glass and pottery accumulated through dumping, producing a midden deposit; and the mineralic components (silt, sand, calcic nodules, snail shells) are ubiquitous in the area and could have easily been blown around or included with the dumped material.

In the channel areas we see the deposition of a fluffy mixture of vegetal matter and mineral silt. These materials probably accumulated by a combination of runoff from the tent and aeolian deposition. The latter process would seem to be more prominent since these sediments are quite open and do not display any signs or remnants of bedding. At present, one can observe straw and remains of dung being blown around the tent and Tell Sheva areas during the afternoon sea breeze.

Postdepositional processes are represented primarily by bioturbation resulting in the well pronounced aggregation of the sediments, primarily in the hearth and dung area. Bioturbation and aggregation of grains are greatest within TENT-10 in the dung heap area, but begins already with TENT-5 adjacent to the hearth and increases in the direction of the dung heap. The agents of bioturbation were not observed.

Another important postdepositional feature is the slaking crusts that are well-expressed in many of the samples (Courty et al. 1989). These formed by wetting of the loessial substrate, either by rainfall or by purposeful spraying in order to reduce the amount of blowing dust. Related to these crusts and the puddling of water is the washed appearance of many of the samples, where the calcareous fine fraction has been locally removed resulting in local domains of coarse quartzitic and calcareous silt.

Concluding Comments

These results clearly illustrate the potential that thin section analysis has in evaluating site formation processes and inferring former human activities at archaeological sites. However, the degree to which the technique can be applied to the archaeological situation depends upon a number of considerations: the types of sites to be investigated, (i.e., climate, age, type of substrate, types of activities); comparable ethnoarchaeological studies yet to be performed; experiments that would simulate a variety of human and biological activities, such as trampling, sweeping, flint knapping, spraying of substrate, and bioturbation. On the basis of our results we are not able to infer specific activities that took place at the site, such as sweeping, cooking, or craft specialization.

Future work should also include sampling from other tents or in other, comparable ethnoarchaeological situations. This would provide information about the variability of the features observed in this study. This study is meant to demonstrate that micromorphological analysis (both qualitative observations and quantitative results generated by image analysis) has potential in gaining inroads to inferring past activities at a modern tent encampment and to understanding site formation processes. It does not pretend to represent all cases of Bedouin tents in Israel or elsewhere, nor tents from other locations in the world. Rather, it attempts to show what the method can potentially achieve.

Finally, it should be pointed out that we did not exhaust all the possibilities of the quantitative analyses. In the future it would be fruitful to concentrate on the solid fraction, including the size, shape and orientation of the grains rather than voids. For example, much of the solid fraction is composed of vegetal fragments and one would expect them to be quite sensitive to compaction by trampling. Similarly, the amount of aggregation of the mineral fraction, is presumably produced by bioturbation, and could be easily verified and quantified using the procedures outlined above.

Our results show that some sense of relative compaction and openness can be detected by quantitative micromorphology. However, further work is needed to determine satisfactory sampling strategies and achieve better statistical results.

In both qualitative and quantitative terms, it is clear that the micromorphological results and approach demonstrate the feasibility of applying the technique to characterize living floors. Separate broadly defined activity areas do in fact, show significant differences under the microscope.

Acknowledgments

This project was carried out with the financial support of the Care Foundation, London. We gratefully acknowledge the aid of Dr. Thomas E. Levy (formerly of Hebrew Union College, Jerusalem and currently at the University of California, San Diego), and his assistant Mr. Ibrahim Al-Assam for helping us locate the tent used in this study. Dr. Yuval Goren, (then a doctoral candidate at the Institute of Archaeology, Hebrew University) assisted in several aspects of the field work. Much of the analysis and research reported here was performed at Harvard University and at the Massachusetts Institute of Technology. Comments by Drs. M. Schiffer, M. Petraglia and B. Bousman helped clarify certain fluffy points in the text. Additional editorial notes by Ms. S. Sherwood are appreciated.

References Cited

Barker, P.
 1982 *Techniques of Archaeological Excavation,* 2nd edition. Universe Books, New York.
Bienkowski, P.
 1985 New Caves for Old: Beduin Architecture in Petra. *World Archaeology* 17(2): 149-160.
Binford, L.R.
 1978 Dimensional Analysis of Behavior and Site Structure: Learning from an Eskimo Hunting Stand. *American Antiquity* 43: 330-361.
Bullock, P., N. Fedoroff, A. Jongerius, G. Stoops, and T. Tursina
 1986 *Handbook for Soil Thin Section Description.* Waine Research Publications, Wolverhampton.
Cook, S.F., and R. Heizer
 1965 *Studies on the Chemical Analysis of Archaeological Sites.* University of California, Publications in Anthropology, no. 2.
Courty, M.A., P. Goldberg, and R.I. Macphail
 1989 *Soils and Micromorphology in Archaeology.* Cambridge University Press, Cambridge.
Eidt, R.C.
 1984 *Advances in Abandoned Settlement Analysis: Applications to Prehistoric Anthrosols in Colombia, South America.* The Center for Latin American Studies, University of Wisconsin-Milwaukee.
Gifford-Gonzalez, D.P., D.B. Damrosch, D.R. Damrosch, J. Pryor, and R.L. Thunen
 1985 The Third Dimension of In Site Structure: An Experiment in Trampling and Vertical Dispersal. *American Antiquity* 50: 803-838.
Habesch, S.M.
 1990 The Evaluation of Pore-Geometry Networks in Clastic Reservoir Lithologies using Microcomputer Technology. *Computers & Geology* 6:91-110.
Joukowsky, M.
 1980 *A Complete Manual of Field Archaeology.* Prentice-Hall, Englewood Cliffs.
Jongerius, A.
 1970 Some Morphological Aspects of Regrouping Phenomena in Dutch soils. *Geoderma* 4:311-331.
 1983 The Role of Micromorphological Research in Agricultural Research. In *Soil Micromorphology,* edited by P. Bullock and C.P. Murphy, pp. 111-138. A B Academic Publishers, Berkhamsted.
Kolb, M. F., N. P. Lasca, and L. G. Goldstein
 1990 A Soil-Geomorphic Analysis of the Midden Deposits of the Aztalan site, Wisconsin. In *Archaeological Geology of North America,* edited by N.P. Lasca, and J. Donahue, pp. 199-218. Geological Society of America, Centennial Special Volume 4. Boulder, Colorado.
Layne, L.
 1987 Village-Bedouin: Patterns of Change from Mobility to Sedentism in Jordan. In *Method and Theory for Activity Area Research: An Ethnoarchaeological Approach,* edited by S. Kent, pp. 345-373. Columbia University Press, New York.
Leroi-Gourhan, A., and Michel Brézillon
 1972 Fouilles de Pincevent. *Gallia Préhistoire,* Supplement 7.
McSweeney, K., Heshaam, A.A., Le Masters, G., and L.D. Norton
 1988 Micromorphological and Selected Physical Properties of a Moldboard-Plowed Soil With and Without Residue Cover. *Soil and Tillage Research* 12:301-322.
Moeyersons, J.
 1978 The Behaviour of Stones and Stone Implements, Buried in Consolidating and Creeping Kalahari Sands. *Earth Surface Processes* 3:115-128.
Murphy, C.P., P. Bullock and K.J. Biswell
 1977 The Measurement and Characterisation of Voids in Soil Thin Sections by Image Analysis. Part II: Applications. *Journal of Soil Science* 28:509-518.
Pawluk, S.
 1980 Micromorphological Investigations of Cultivated Gray Luvisols under Different Management Practices. *Canadian Journal of Soil Science* 60:731-745.
Schiffer, M.B.
 1987 *Formation Process of the Archaeological Record.* University of New Mexico Press, Albuquerque.

Siegel, S.
  1956 *Non-Parametric Statistics for the Behavioral Sciences.* McGraw-Hill-Kogakusha, Ltd, Tokyo.
Simms, S.R.
  1988 The Archaeological Structure of a Bedouin Camp. *Journal of Archaeological Science* 15:197-211.
Stevenson, M.G.
  1991 Beyond the Formation of Hearth-Associated Artifact Assemblages. In *The Interpretation of Archaeological Spatial Patterning,* edited by E.M. Kroll and T.D. Price, pp. 269-299. Plenum Press, New York.
Stockton, E.D.
  1973 Shaw's Creek Shelter: Human Displacement of Artifacts and its Significance. *Mankind* 9:112-117.
Villa, P., and J. Courtin
  1983 The Interpretation of Stratified Sites: a View from Underground. *Journal of Archaeological Science* 10: 267-281.
Weymouth, J.W., and R. Huggins
  1985 Geophysical Surveying of Archaeological Sites. In *Archaeological Geology,* edited by G. Rapp, Jr., and J. A. Gifford, pp. 191-235. Yale University Press, New Haven.
Yellen, J.
  1977 *Archaeological Approaches to the Present: Models for Reconstructing the Past.* Academic Press, New York.

APPENDIX - Geometric Means and Standard Deviations of Void Areas and Breadths for Samples used in this Study.

Sample	No.	Area Geom. Mean	Std. Dev	Breadth Geom. Mean	Std. Dev
1f5	973	5.42E-04	0.0116014	0.0271044	0.0613084
1f6	982	5.49E-04	0.030009	0.0271	0.0700424
2f1	828	3.61E-04	0.0359535	0.0216519	0.0557153
2f3	968	3.32E-04	5.12E-03	0.0206447	0.0243803
3f1	1011	4.34E-04	6.99E-03	0.024112	0.0300956
3f5	989	5.22E-04	0.0502794	0.0271797	0.0746275
4f4	906	3.39E-04	2.13E-03	0.0212598	0.0223961
4f5	441	3.02E-04	0.0102652	0.0183157	0.0312984
5f1	941	3.15E-04	1.28E-03	0.0196754	0.0178918
5f3	679	3.14E-04	1.58E-03	0.0198209	0.0189744
6f1	914	3.66E-04	8.58E-03	0.0224558	0.0384678
6f5	929	5.62E-04	0.032027	0.0271493	0.058016
7f1	585	4.23E-04	0.0566453	0.0222538	0.0555017
7f3	642	2.80E-04	7.35E-04	0.0202626	0.0157858
8f1	1004	5.24E-04	9.83E-03	0.0259709	0.0466743
8f4	962	4.60E-04	2.72E-03	0.0246735	0.0318815
9f1	992	4.22E-04	2.11E-03	0.0233389	0.0246157
9f6	983	5.17E-04	2.96E-03	0.0264054	0.0343713
10f1	898	3.41E-04	0.0588444	0.0207937	0.0726022
10f7	1009	4.22E-04	0.0200658	0.0233564	0.0494676
11f1	786	3.51E-04	2.61E-03	0.0214911	0.027452
11f5	873	4.21E-04	2.45E-03	0.0231828	0.0249402
12f1	944	3.38E-04	8.34E-03	0.020886	0.0303038
12f4	602	5.88E-04	0.0576928	0.026071	0.0903916
13f1	517	3.33E-04	7.03E-03	0.0196804	0.0318155
13f4	848	2.94E-04	2.94E-04	0.0191288	0.0144275
14f1	591	3.13E-04	9.50E-03	0.0191237	0.0264662
14f2	309	2.73E-04	0.0117252	0.0186484	0.029018
15f2	559	2.45E-04	4.33E-04	0.0170339	0.0107244
15f4	840	3.58E-04	1.66E-03	0.0211398	0.0193231